A is for Ambler. It is also for Authoritative, Amusing, Accurate, Accessible, and Altogether Admirable – all words that perfectly describe Tim Ambler's masterful and pithy A to Z of marketing.
Winston Fletcher, Chairman of the Advertising Association & Chairman of Delaney Fletcher, Bozell

A unique blend of expertise, wisdom and humour. A must for marketers.
James Hulbert, RC Kopf Professor of International Marketing, Graduate School of Business, Columbia University

An outstanding practical approach towards real world marketing.
Paul Clayton, Senior Vice President, Worldwide Marketing, Burger King

Enjoyable and dangerously candid.
Tom Robertson, Sainsbury, Professor of Marketing & Deputy Principal, Programs & Marketing, London Business School

Well written and highly readable, it demystifies the marketing process.
Nicholas Turnbull, Director General, The Marketing Society

THE FINANCIAL TIMES GUIDE TO

MARKETING

From Advertising to Zen

Tim Ambler

London · Hong Kong · Johannesburg · Melbourne
Singapore · Washington DC

PITMAN PUBLISHING
128 Long Acre, London WC2E 9AN

A Division of Pearson Professional Limited

The first edition of this book was published as
Need to Know Marketing by Century Business.

British Library Cataloguing in Publication Data
A CIP catalogue record for this book can be obtained
from the British Library.

ISBN 0 273 62032 0

3 5 7 9 10 8 6 4

Typeset by Northern Phototypesetting Co Ltd, Bolton
Printed and bound in Great Britain by
Redwood Books Ltd, Trowbridge, Wiltshire

*The Publishers' policy is to use paper manufactured
from sustainable forests.*

About the Author

Tim Ambler is currently Grand Metropolitan Senior Research Fellow at London Business School where he teaches Global Marketing and Doing Business in Greater China. His research interests include brand equity, how advertising works, marketing in China and other international markets and relationship marketing. He holds an MA (mathematics) from Oxford an SM (majoring in marketing) from the Sloan School, Massachusetts Institute of Technology and is a Fellow of the Institute of Chartered Accountants. Before becoming an academic, Tim Ambler spent some 30 years in business, initially as an accountant, switching to marketing in 1969. As Marketing Director for International Distillers and Vintners (IDV) for the UK during the 1970s, he was associated with the launch of Bailey's Irish Cream, Le Piat d'Or and the rise to leadership positions of Smirnoff Vodka and Croft Original Cream Sherry. More recently he held overall international marketing responsibility for IDV and worked extensively in the USA, Canada, Africa and emerging markets. IDV's development during the 1980s was a combination of new brand development, brand acquisitions which then needed to be integrated with the IDV network, new market entries, and organic brand development. He now believes in pragmatic approaches to marketing on the one hand and the need for people based, relational, theories of international marketing on the other. His experience and research combine to underscore the importance of brands and the marketplace as the place to understand them.

CONTENTS

ACKNOWLEDGEMENTS

Many current and previous colleagues and friends have participated in the production of this book. Some knowingly and some just in the marketing they taught me. To mention a few risks the appearance of ingratitude to the others and I must apologize for that. I am particularly glad of the improvements suggested by those who took part in the "Building Brand Equity" courses arranged by Grand Metropolitan, Chip Perry and Paul Davey being especially kind.

At the same time I must stress that none of these views are necessarily shared by them or other, colleagues old or new. Inaccuracies, errors and omissions are mine alone.

I am most grateful to George Bull, Paul Curtis, Clive Holland, Keith Holloway, Don Knight, Peter Lane, Andy Melmoth, Steve Messenger, Adrian Sauter, Tony Scouller and Lance Wilson for reading and commenting. Also, at (or previously at) London Business School: Laura Cousins, John Cripps, Tom Robertson, Phil White and Morgen Witzel. And, of course, to those generous spirits who provided endorsements for the cover.

At Pitman Publishing, my thanks to to Richard Stagg who has been uniformly enthusiastic, Amelia Lakin and the editors, Sally Green and Phebe Kynaston, who improved the manuscript with great efficiency and charm. At Random Century, my thanks go to Elizabeth Hennessy for her kindness, and generosity in her support. My thanks most of all go to Paddy Barwise, also at LBS, who has been a great supporter of this project and encouraged me to press on regardless.

To all those, and many more, I really am most grateful.

Dear Val,

Congratulations on your appointment as the General Manager of your business. You have done tremendously well. I do not know what happened to your predecessor but if you have to take over on Monday, you have little time to get ready.

You were telling me the other day that you had no idea what your colleagues in marketing do. Clearly they enjoy spending the company's money but is it all worthwhile? On Monday they will be spending your money. You might like to read this book over the weekend to discover where the money is going and what it should be doing for you. This is all you need to know about marketing.

Can you be up to speed by Monday? In this wonderful world where reality is image and tangible products are but a bundle of perceptions, marketing people pass through the looking glass several times a day. The weekend gives us plenty of time. Anyway, you can keep a copy in your new executive washroom. Nip out of the meeting; the book is arranged alphabetically for rapid reference.

You would rather be playing golf but give it a miss this time. We are talking serious money. Your success in your new role depends very largely on how well you market your products. Your job is not to be the expert marketer but to provide the right environment for marketing talent to flourish. That requires understanding.

Marketing is not for those who expect neat and tidy answers. Here the conventional mixes with challenges and novelties. Dip into the bran tub anywhere and question what you bring out. The book is a marketplace of its own: chapters and ideas compete with one another for your attention. Are they consistent? Is marketing?

As you know, I have a bias to branded consumer goods, and the drinks business within that, since that is my background, but the lessons apply equally to your business. Every chapter ends with action points expressed as a memo to file.

Enjoy the weekend. This is a book to relax to. Filter it through that mental twilight where the impossible becomes likely. Suspend disbelief and allow the subconscious to retain only what it needs. You have been under stress; take it easy now.

The best marketing in the world can only give luck a chance.

Yours affectionately,

Tim

INTRODUCTION

PATHWAYS IN MARKETING

Competent guides can offer many different rambles through the terrain they love: well-trodden paths for the nervous, highs and lows for the intrepid.

The A–Z format of this guide should encourage you to choose your own path, to dip into it occasionally or for easy reference. Surprisingly, the progress from Advertising to Zen turns out to have a manic logic of its own. Advertising gave birth to modern marketing at the beginning of this century. Brand Equity defines what a brand is and measures the main objectives for marketers. As a new century dawns, we witness the success of Asia Pacific businesses with quite different traditional philosophies. Foresight indicates that in 2020 China will be the world's largest economy and world trader. None of us will be untouched by Chinese business thinking. Do they know something the West does not? The short answer is yes; Zen and some of the other chapters review why.

The chapters A–D cover the fundamental issues. The practical tools of the marketing craftsperson mostly begin with the letter P. Together they are known as the "marketing mix," that combination of activities which should bring the best result. A – D and the P chapters alone would provide a similar grounding in marketing to most textbooks, though more idiosyncratically. There are very few rules in marketing and you are welcome to disagree.

Measurement and control of marketing should be as professional as for any other business area, perhaps more so. The life of the business is at stake. The challenge here is to stay real. Appendix 1 supplements these chapters with a light-hearted glossary of technical terms. Space does not allow it to be comprehensive. Appendix 2 lists a few recommended readings to follow up particular interests.

The people chapters represent a greater emphasis on the internal human factors than you will find elsewhere. Quite simply, all professional marketers know the principles and money is plentiful for those who can justify it. That justification and subsequent delivery of the objectives separates the winners from the losers. The people, and how they work together in the marketing context, do all that. Do they innovate? Do they accept each others' ideas?

Read then from A to Z or Z to A. For those who prefer a more prosaic path through this book, here is one of many alternatives (the chapter number is shown after each title):

Principles

1. **Marketing today and tomorrow** (13) What "marketing" is and where it is going in the future. Why marketers and economists are at loggerheads. The ideal economic world is rational, has perfect information and perfect competition, i.e. similar products are interchangeable. Marketers recognize, indeed pander to, both sides of the human mind, partial information and seek to differentiate their products. Economic texts thus mislead marketers. How different forms of marketing evolved and what the differences are: business to business/industrial, services, retail, direct. There are three ways of thinking about marketing: the traditional or "neo-classical" based on economics, "conflict," and "relationships."

Marketing can be seen as conflict between companies seeking the same business or as cooperation between suppliers and customers. Both are valid but the cooperative approach recognizes that marketing is a win-win, not a zero sum, game.

2. **Kamikaze and guerrilla marketing** (11) Two varieties of conflictual marketing should form part of the marketer's armory. Kamikaze marketing refers to the situation where your own brand commits suicide, e.g. with a price cut, in order to disable a larger competitor. No one would intentionally annihilate their own major brand in this way but flanker brands may be expendable. Guerrilla marketing is, roughly, the opposite. Here you seek to wear down a larger opponent through improvisation, surprise and the avoidance of direct competition.

3. **Relationship marketing** (25) Only in the 1990s has the importance of relationships come to the fore though building networks of value added relationships have been practised since the dawn of marketing. Avon ladies and Tupperware parties were what is now called network marketing. Part of the recent emergence is technological: computers now store so much information on us all that the brand offering and communications can be personalized. This chapter represents the third, and arguably the most important, view of marketing.

4. **Brand equity** (2) The "brand" is what distinguishes one product or service from another and thus branding is what marketing is about. "Brand equity" is the asset the marketer is building. It should be measured alongside profit when deciding choices and reviewing results.

5. **Extensions and brand families** (5) Advantages and pitfalls in extending the brand to cover new products. Stretching expertise and credibility versus better value from advertising. Measures to determine extension. Families of brand names.

6. **Category management and other heresies** (3) Any marketer with a portfolio of brands has to manage the combination to maximize the company as a whole. Where the different brands are in the same category, e.g. laundry detergents, this may mean hard decisions. The other root of category management is in the retail store where the shopkeeper wants to maximize the returns from the category as a whole and is indifferent to individual brands. We trace where these necessary disciplines descend into profit losers from the brand owner's point of view. The pitfalls of supplying your brand under a private, i.e. retailer's, label. Failure to acknowledge brand primacy in marketing is "heresy" but the disorder is no longer life threatening. Maybe it should be.

7. **Quantity ergo Sumo** (24) Size is not everything, however important it may be to Japanese wrestlers. Yet marketers are preoccupied by it. Sales volume and market share are key success indicators. Chasing volume with inadequate brand equity is a formula for disaster. Explain to the people upstairs that optimize beats maximize. Then agree the measures that really matter.

8. **Global marketing** (7) The business world is going global, barriers are reducing, even the smallest businesses are trading beyond their national borders. Marketing in many markets is different, and requires different skills, to the domestic variety. This needs a book of its own but key differences are headlined.

9. **Zen and now** (34) The final chapter brings together two thoughts which are really one: paradox and oriental thinking. Partly because marketing is the business of innovation there are no rules for success. Every truth is also an untruth; what worked yesterday will not work tomorrow; today's disaster may be next week's lifesaver.

The marketing mix

As noted above, alliteration groups most of the practical tools together. The marketing mix is traditionally seen as comprising the Four Ps: product, pricing, place (distribution), and promotion. Some non-marketers believe marketing is just the promotion of whatever goods the business has for sale and in so doing forget that it all starts with the product and service, which, usually together, form the offering.

1. **Positioning – marketing's martial art** (16) The foundation of all marketing is the positioning statement: if you receive a brand plan without one, chuck it in the bin. Of course, it may exist under other guises, but the marketer needs to make clear for whom the brand is intended, why they should buy it, and what the competition is. This is the raison d'être for the brand's existence. The strength of its DNA coding will determine its success in life. A brand also "positions" itself in the consumer's mental battleground of competing brands. If your brand cannot kill the others, and mostly it cannot, then use the basic tools of survival.

Product

2. **Product satisfaction** (17) If the product, be it tangible or ephemeral, does not meet the consumer's need, forget the rest of the marketing mix. If it does, but no better than any other product, you may get by. Relentless focus on quality differentiates great marketing. Relative perceived, by the end user, quality is the single best guide to future profitability. To be better, you first have to be different. Coming to terms with the product life cycle.

3. **Packaging for the party** (18) Every time we get out of bed, or go out to meet new people, we repackage ourselves. Repackaging does not change what is inside – indeed it should preserve it – but it does make the product socially acceptable.

4. **Novation** (14) Marketing can also be seen as continuous managed innovation. An organization of people creating great ideas will get nowhere.

5. **Heritage matters** (8) One of the many paradoxes of marketing is the simultaneous search for novelty and retention of the familiar. Gnomic advice, such as "be bold but careful," is passed around. Factoring heritage

into new brands is even more difficult than dissuading exuberant brand managers from dumping the existing baggage.

Price

6. **Value marketing** (30) Every decade needs new maps of what the consumer considers value for money and, more fundamentally, what is important. Whale meat would be a difficult sell in North America today. Yet what the marketer usually means by value is lower price. Each generation convinces itself that the market has never been so competitive. In Tyre and Sidon they talked of little else. Value is perceived quality divided by price; both should be considered together.

7. **Pricing in grandmother's footsteps** (19) A traditional children's game provides the framework for classic pricing strategy: small unobtrusive steps upward but, when caught out of position, a conspicuous large step down. Managing price is not, of course, this simple. Myths and mysteries of price elasticity.

Place

8. **Distribution channels** (4) Modern logistics and information systems are bringing producers and consumers closer together and yet the connections are becoming more varied and complex. Quick Response and Efficient Consumer Response systems are recent manifestations of the trend and require management to rethink their relationships with retailers, intermediaries, and competitors.

Promotion

10. **Advertising kite high** (1) After a century or so of formal study, we do not know how advertising works. It is a craft, not a science. Advertising is the most conspicuous aspect of marketing and attracts more than its fair share of critics, in and outside the business. If you are only wasting half your money, you are beating the odds. The chapter provides guidelines on how to improve them further. While advertising is the theme, much applies to any creative marketing service agency.

11. **Which agency?** (31) The plethora of different types of agencies, and the specialisms within them, requires more than passing thought for

what meets your needs. "Above the line" is traditional advertising, the "line" separating commission from the media from payment by the client. Below the line and through the line, direct and integrated, separate media and creative hot shops are just some of the choices.

12. **Public relations** are private affairs (20) "Free" advertising in media's editorial columns may look more attractive than advertising and, for some brands, it is. PR can also appeal dangerously to the vanity of the marketer. Check the mirror on the way out.

13. **Promotions, coupons and giveaways** (21) The wastage inherent in advertising pales into insignificance beside price-offs. Many have likened it to heroin: it gives sales a great buzz at the beginning. The habit is hard to kick especially if the peer group is similarly afflicted, but if the habit persists, the brand dies prematurely. Other "below the line" promotions are more health giving, notably sampling. We range across the alternatives.

14. **Personal selling** (22) The most traditional, and perhaps most underestimated, marketing tool. Mass techniques are cheaper, per message delivered. Modern technology is filling in the gap with telemarketing (phones) and interactive networks. The sales persons' eyes and ears are more important than their mouths, provided, of course, the home office listens to them. Can the brand manager sell the brand in real life? Idolize sales people.

Measurement and control

Marketing cannot be done by numbers; and it cannot be done without. The profession includes all shades of this opinion. Quantification and control may well shackle creativity and innovation. On the other hand, it is hard to know how much money has been made if it is not counted. A modern solution to this dilemma is to assign specific marketing-friendly accountants as scorers, thus releasing us marketers to be the true artists we yearn to be. Maybe.

1. **Pragmatic planning** (23) Honest marketers do not divorce themselves from the consequences of their actions, though the temptations of job hopping are real enough. Probably only 50 percent of all junior marketers, in North America and the UK, are in the same jobs when the results of their plans become known. Companies that accept that must also

accept the consequences: close involvement by senior management and/or a lack of corporate learning. Planning is learning and learning, to be effective, should be enjoyable, or at least tolerable, to the learners. Control numbers, therefore, need to be a by-product of the process, not its rationale.

2. **Surgical segmentation** (27) A sophistication of the target market concept is to identify multiple targets each of which receives marketing treatment appropriate to itself. For example, the marketing of airline seats to the packaged holiday market will differ from that to business travellers. The upside of this complication is increased profits from better use of marketing resources.

3. **Research is always incomplete** (26) Mark Pattison knew about analysis paralysis in 1875. If you never heard of him, your research is ... Fortunately we do not have to worry about it: marketing is more subjective than scientists would have us believe. The strengths and dangers of external research are reviewed.

4. **Information systems survival kit** (9) Marketing has long been the Cinderella of information systems. Suddenly, the data drought has become a deluge. The marketer is more likely to be knocked over than be refreshed by it. Some practical solutions bring order to the excess.

5. **Rule of Chi** (32) A lighter look at life's natural balancing act. Look for the downside of the upside or the upside of the down.

6. **Beyond the J Curve** (10) Trends and forecasts preoccupy marketers, and rightly so. The difference between what they achieve and what would have happened anyway is what they are about. In prizing resources out of the system, marketers do employ a little optimism from time to time. They make regular use of the J Curve, otherwise known as the hockey stick, in forecasting a bright future from a bleak past. The trend reversal may be based on a realistic estimate, or a recognition that they will not get a budget with anything less. Distinguishing realism from blind optimism.

People

These chapters bring together some issues in managing marketers or, more accurately, marketers managing themselves. Ultimately, management's skill in recognizing and developing good marketing concepts determines whether the business will thrive, or just survive, or die. A bit heavy that? Do not drop the coffin on your foot.

1. **Organization structure and entropy** (15) The second law of thermo-dynamics states that entropy, the natural state of disorder, always increases and when two systems are brought together, the entropy of the combination is greater than the sum of the two previous entropies. You knew that. The consequence for management is to keep the size of busi-ness units as small as economically feasible. It explains why fewer people, up to a point, get more done. Entropy has much to teach us about the size of product portfolios and the teams that market them. Some mar-keting functions should be kept in house and others are better outsourced.

2. **Training the professionals** (28) There are now huge financial pressures to keep brands in trim, but not so their managers. Yet who else will keep the brands in trim but their managers. Creative excuses, and I have used them all, abound: people shortages since we downsized, courses are out of date or theoretical or otherwise useless, or I have to use any spare time to train my people. The training we give is, of course, much better than the training we receive. Therein lies the solution. Persuade your mar-keters to teach and they will have to blow off the cobwebs.

3. **Failures bring success** (6) Toddlers do not learn to stay on chairs by reading a book; they learn by falling off. A firm that wants large successes should encourage small failures. Otherwise they will get neither. Encour-aging failure in some cultures, such as the USA which despises it, is far from easy. Some practical steps.

4. **The educated lunch** (12) Getting away from roles and rituals for free format focus on improvement. Lunch is playtime and more adventurous ideas are tolerated.

5. **Ugly duckling** (29) Truly major breakthroughs are usually unrecognized until they become swans. Then, it turns out, everyone knew them as swans all along. Management needs practical systems that make allowances for nature. The champion system, as formulated originally by 3M, is developed here as a process for new product and brand develop-ment. By contrast, the conventional hopper system where many ideas elicited by brainstorming are progressively reduced to one winner can be

discarded. It may work (there are no rules in marketing) but mostly it will not. We review why.

6. **"Yes" is no decision** (33) Late in the book is time to recap on decision making in marketing organizations. Having your plan approved is a warm feeling but too often it signifies inattention. The post prandial grunt that accepts "May I go out to play, Daddy?" is all too often followed by "Where the hell are you?" However disagreeable it may seem to both parties at the time, the planners and approvers need to hassle each other long enough to ensure that both sides believe in the plan and are committed to it enough to withstand the vicissitudes that will follow.

These chapters address issues with a mixture of philosophy and pragmatism, radicalism and recognition that business practices got that way because they work. New reflections on old problems, these images are intended to remind us that marketing should be fun. Otherwise it would just be money.

1

ADVERTISING KITE HIGH

Getting great advertising from your agency

Key issues
● **The importance of advertising to the marketer** ● **How does advertising work?** ● **Advertising agency–client relationships** ● **Briefing the agency** ● **How much to spend** ● **Decision making: does research help?** ● **Accepting the campaign, or not**

Whenever you book a table at the very latest restaurant, you can be sure your advertising agency was there the week before. Whether or not advertising should be the genesis of marketing, its initial letter gets it ahead. What else happened before the apple was advertised to Eve?

THE IMPORTANCE OF ADVERTISING

Mass marketing began with advertising. Newspapers and magazines had space to fill; advertising agents sold it. While, as indicated above, advertising goes back to the dawn of time, it had become, by 1797, a sufficiently important business in the UK to be worth taxing. That idea has occurred to many governments since. The number of recorded advertisements in the UK rose from about 0.5 million in 1800 to 1.9 million in 1848. Naturally many more evaded duty. The tax was abolished in 1853. The first recorded advertising agency seems to have been William Tayler in 1786. Numbers grew to about 300 in 1886. Media commissions varied widely from the norm of 10 percent. There was already a split between space only agencies, today's media shops, who might keep as little as 2.5 percent and rebate the rest, to full service agencies – Charles Barker, Mather and Crowther, and E H Benson were some of the first – who regarded any rebates as sinful.

In the USA, F W Ayer is credited with first recognizing, in the 1880s, the potential of providing advertisers with copy, artwork, and media advice and he founded the first US advertising agency in the modern sense. There were of course many other agencies of all types. He called it N W Ayer and Son because he thought his father's image was better. A few years later, he established the 15 percent commission rate on openly disclosed space charges. This eventually became the standard both in the UK and the USA, and survived until recently. We will review alternatives later.

That the agent is paid by the media, not the advertiser, is still important today. That is not to suggest that the agent is the *representative* of one or more media; their raison d'être is to be independent of both media and advertiser. Nevertheless the cash cycle has a bearing on relationships. The expression "above the line" used for advertising refers to the line drawn between work remunerated by the media and that paid by the client. Conversely, "below the line" means anything commissioned by the client be it creative work or promotions. If the agency is on 15 percent media commission, expect a charge of 17.65 percent on anything else (agencies long since worked out that 15 percent of the net, 85 percent, cost of media = 17.65 percent. You wouldn't want to lunch with anyone stupid would you? Just be sure to pick up the tab or it will cost you 17.65 percent more.)

The role of the advertising agent was to design messages to fit both the consumer's and the product's needs. The agent's independence from the manufacturer promoted objectivity: the consumer's view of the product and the producer's view of the consumer. In the 1930s, Rosser Reeves, later a co-founder of the Ted Bates agency, first described the importance of the "Unique Selling Proposition" as a communication bridge between product and consumer. The consumer wanted to know, concisely, what the brand offered; the marketer needed to know where the brand's strength or opportunity lay. Vocabulary has changed but USP still sits at the heart of differentiating or positioning a brand.

> **The role of the advertising agent was to design messages to fit both the consumer's and the product's needs.**

Just as advertising was a progenitor of consumer brand marketing, so that in turn begat the myriad forms of marketing that exist today: industrial, retail, business to business, network, services, direct, database, internal, and so on. This chapter concentrates on display advertising for known consumer brands because that is where the vast majority of advertising expenditure lies. Thus we exclude small ads (classified), business to business, and the introduction of new brands, all of which need separate consideration. Consumer "brands," (see chapter 2, "Brand Equity") covers almost everything else which is advertised, be it retail stores (e.g. Safeway), the Salvation Army, durables, or fast moving consumer goods ("fmcg"), the traditionally dominant advertising sector whose share of advertising is now in decline.

Today, advertising and marketing are frequently confused. To the general public, advertising is the most conspicuous sign of marketing. In the 1950s and 60s, many companies had their marketing function handled by their advertising agency. Some still do. But since the last century, the scales have progressively tipped to the point where advertising has become just one element in the communications sector of a marketing program alongside public relations, promotions, direct methods using electronic databases, and personal selling.

> **To the general public, advertising is the most conspicuous sign of marketing.**

This division into many media has been seen by some as dissipation or, at least, confusion. All marketing activities should be anchored in the positioning of the brand. The term "integrated marketing communications" indicates the intention to ensure consistency of messages to all customers. Effective communication requires the marketer to simplify the brand proposition and select perhaps only one of its many appeals. To reinforce the advertising, other marketing activities will be similarly focussed.

Television created the golden age of advertising. This friendly intruder into almost every home achieved more attention to fewer channels than any medium in history. Television was the vehicle to persuade the mass millions. Through the 1950s and into the 1970s, fmcg brand owners rushed to exploit television's potential.

New technology brought alternative channels, cable, satellites, video, Walkmans, and CDs. Print media choice multiplied. Consumers tired of the four TV channels and efficiencies for advertisers deteriorated. The growing strength of retailers diverted budgets to "promotions," a word that has gradually shifted its meaning to embrace many different marketing activities, often just trade discounts. The economic troughs of 1974, 1981, and 1990 pressurized the advertiser to cut fat and the agency to provide the fat to be cut.

Some advertisers claim that the changes have been refreshing: agencies are more attentive to client demands, and have streamlined their three key functions of creative content, media buying and client service. If the client doubts the value of any of these three, they can be bought separately.

For fmcg, advertising is not the force it was. Its share of budget declined from about 50 percent in the early '70s to 20 percent twenty years on. The size, or share, of budget is, nevertheless, not the issue even though marketers tend to define the importance of their job in expenditure terms. Spending a large media budget provides great satisfaction but does not necessarily indicate the importance of the brand. Many valuable brands in industrial markets have minimal advertising expenditures. Moët et Chandon champagne climbed to leadership with no advertising at all.

The importance of advertising lies not in the size of budget but what it can do. In a word, it is "charm." PR can do this too. They both communicate the nicest things about the brand in the nicest possible way. Usually. Some ads hector successfully. Others gain awareness and attention in disagreeable ways but even the most virulent forms intend to leave the (potential) customer better disposed to purchase and/or prepared to pay more. The importance of advertising is that it speaks directly to the customer about whatever aspect of the brand matters most to the customer. Thus advertising and PR communications directly build, and should be measured by, brand equity.

HOW THEN DO THESE DIFFERENT APPROACHES WORK?

Models of consumer response to advertising have historically been based on four main approaches:[1]

1. Black box, i.e. whatever is going on in the customer's mind is too hard to unravel. The researcher seeks to know what prompts cause what consumer behavior ("conation" in academic speak, or "do" to you and me) but cares not, or knows not, why. Econometric modeling classically fits lines to the sales and spending data to estimate optimal expenditure. After 30 years of development, these techniques convince some of their sophistication. Others believe a ruler would be as reliable.

2. Economists believe that consumers are no more than rational information processors. Advertising cannot bend consumer preferences because they assume that away. Therefore advertising is effective only to the extent it feeds the intellect with new information. Thus the consumer's mind

---

[1] This summarises a rather laborious review of 200 academic writings on the subject: Demetrios Vakratsas & Tim Ambler "Advertising Effects: A Taxonomy and Review of the Literature," Working Paper, London Business School, 1995.

sequence is information → think → do. When an expert is buying a PC for home use, for example, that expert may be strictly concerned with factual matters of size, speed, and durability. Workhorse PCs, as distinct from Macintosh or Toshiba, provide this data to appeal to this limited market.

3. Everyone else believes that our emotions ("feel" or "affect" in academic speak) influence many of our buying decisions but there is dispute over the sequence of events. The classic model was AIDA (Awareness, Interest, Desire, and Action) which has since been overtaken by "hierarchy of effects" terminology. Both assert that, after cognition has clicked in, i.e. awareness, affect is also stimulated and purchase results. This is the "strong" theory of advertising which is broadly accepted, in more and less sophisticated forms, in North America. Here advertising → think → feel → do.

4. By contrast the "weak" theory, originally expressed by Andrew Ehrenberg as ATR (Awareness, Trial, Reinforcement) is widely accepted in the UK. The strong theory is similar to psychological "classical conditioning" (Pavlov and his dog) whereas the weak theory echoes "instrumental conditioning" (Skinner and his pigeons) in that affect *follows* purchase. You will recall that the dog was trained through associating a particular action it would not otherwise have done, with rewards from the trainer. The dog knew before the action what the trainer wanted. The pigeons, however, learned by trial and error. They too associated rewards with actions but only as consequences of those actions. Thus the weak theory amounts to advertising's reinforcement of existing habits as distinct from change to purchasing behavior. Here advertising → awareness → trial → beliefs which are formed mostly from the actual product and service experience. Advertising has only a weak effect to reinforce habit or to minimize expectation/reality dissonance. Consumers like the product because they use it, not use it because they like it.

These are not mutually exclusive and there are many variations on these themes. "Involvement," for example, makes a big difference. A high involvement situation means that the brain is fully in gear, buying a new car for example. When the purchase is infrequent and important, the customer can be assumed to be paying full attention. Wandering down a supermarket aisle however, the autopilot is likely to be making the brand selections. Simplifying quite a bit, the AIDA model seems closer to the first situation and ATR to the second. Individual commercials may work in different combinations of these theories even with the same consumer. An occasional user of Kelloggs Cornflakes may gain information, change purchasing behavior to greater frequency and reinforce an existing Kellogg habit at the same time. Different advertising works in different ways on different consumers at different times.

> **Different advertising works in different ways on different consumers at different times.**

The black box approach is cautious since it does not attempt to understand what is going on inside our heads. The other three now seem to be fatally flawed. Advertising works through human memory. We receive input at one time and behavior changes at another. Alternatively, advertising reinforces behavior but that too is a memory process. The memory receives the inputs, transformed in some way, and any consequences flow from it. We now know far more about human memory than the crude separation of knowing, thinking and experience used by the advertising models above. Short, and long term memory, for example, work differently. In short, the academic marketing community will have to rethink their approach to how advertising works.

Driving all this research has been the need for direct measures of advertising effectiveness. Sales, price, and profits are impacted by too many other factors to be reliable measures for advertising. Consumer awareness and attitude measures have traditionally been tracked to fill the gap. These attitudes may refer to perceptions of product quality, whether they like it, or the packaging, style, heritage. The odds on purchasing are heightened by positive associations of the brand name. These associations, positives or negatives, are supposed to flit through the consumers' minds as they make a choice. But before advertising can go to work to improve these attitudes, the consumer has to know about, or be aware of, the brand.

The classic measure of awareness is obtained by asking respondents which brands came into their heads when a category was mentioned (this is known as "top of mind" or "unaided recall") and then prompting them with a list of the brands of interest. Adding the two percentages together gives "total awareness," however illogical that may sound. Modern research breaks awareness down further to many different dimensions depending on the associations being used as prompts. We do not need to worry about these here.

Attitudes are measured by consumer reactions to a battery of questions with answers usually on a five point scale. An example might be, "indicate on the scale from *agree very much* to *totally disagree* your response to the statement: Nike is the best shoe for top runners."

Awareness and attitude measures of the effectiveness of advertising will, however, be influenced by experience of usage and word of mouth from friends and acquaintances, both more powerful than advertising.

Breaking through the clutter of competing messages with such a weak force as advertising is quite a problem. Visibility is not just the adrenalin of advertising, it is also the rationale behind it. This is show business. Many believe that in advertising you should spend big or spend nothing; dribbling it out wastes money. But there are always counter examples to any such convention. In the Scotch whisky market, first Bells and then Famous Grouse built credibility through years of small displays which faded into the wallpaper. Nevertheless, the convention that fmcg brands should consolidate their advertising into solid punchy blocks has had some academic support. Conversely, a plumber just needs to hang out his sign where the householder with a problem will find it.

The balance of opinion at the time of writing, but do not take this to the bank, is that one or two ads per purchase interval is enough. In other words, if the goods are typically a weekly purchase, then ensure the consumer gets at least one but no more than two OTS (opportunities to see). The *volume* of advertising you are buying is measured by GRPs (Gross Rating Points). The volume measure is needed to establish value for money from the agency's media department (GRPs divided by the media cost). GRP is the product of *reach* (how many see the ads) times *frequency* (OTS or the average number of times seen). These mathematics imply that reach and frequency are interchangeable. The research, however, tells us that reminder advertising of established brands needs very few OTS. Spend the rest of the budget on expanding reach.

Within the fmcg convention, consumer response, i.e. sales volume, follows an S-shaped curve, (see figure 1.1). The main alternative has diminishing returns from the first advertisement – (see figure 1.2). Figure 1.2 has more research support but I do not believe it. The S curve is more elegant. The cost of advertising has been shown as a straight line in both idealized

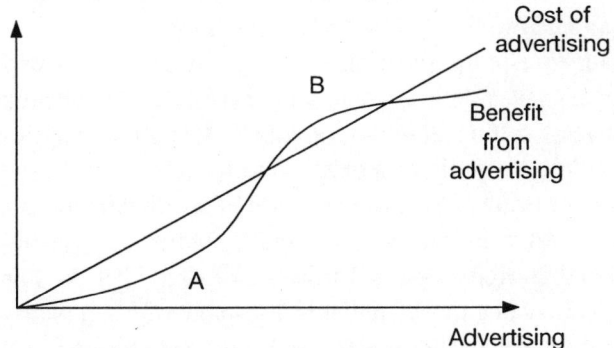

Fig 1.1   Consumer response to advertising

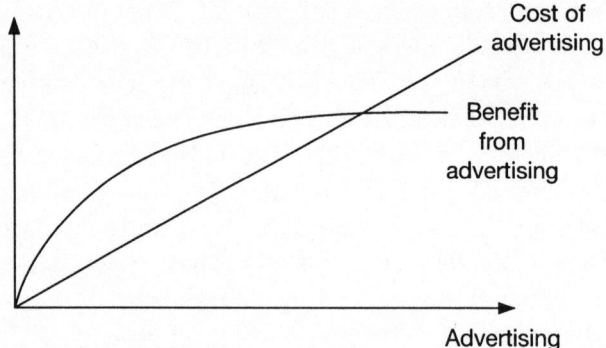

Fig 1.2   Consumer response to advertising

diagrams. Although discounts are available for higher spending, they may be offset by the need to use less efficient media as the budget increases.

At the beginning of the curve in figure 1.1, impressions are swamped by everything else in the media. Impact is limited. Spend more over time and there may be a breakthrough, shown as A on the diagram. Once the awareness impact begins, attitudes may begin to move and advertising becomes cost-efficient. At point A, it is beginning to achieve response at a greater rate than it is costing. Suddenly there is some impact that can be recorded for the advertising (and, if the client is lucky, for the brand).

The first turning point is not easy to find, nor is the second. B marks the stage where advertising starts to have declining returns. In theory, therefore, you should bunch your spending into peaks to target the consumer response peaks. In this model, spending all the budget to achieve point B maximizes both awareness and the positive benefit to brand attitudes. All you have to do is find the money and find the B spot! Where the budget is justified, spending should be concentrated into separate pulses each of which is targeted to hit B, with an intermission before the next pulse.

The consumer response function explains why advertisers will take space at famous events even though the costs per thousand are disproportionately high. A showcase setting should bring more attention, perhaps even glamor. Enough of a charge will create a buzz, so to speak.

The US Super Bowl is a classic example of an advertising "high": a burst of creativity, a burst of expenditure, and, hopefully, a widening circle of increased brand awareness and improved attitudes. That does not make the Super Bowl good value for money. It is priced out of reach of all but the few. Advertising during the 1995 US Super Bowl cost close to $3,000,000 per minute. One company, Master Lock, spends its total budget, each year, on just one Super Bowl ad. High visibility, high adrenalin, and doubtless a few seats and highballs for the top customers.

You will note that we have just argued round a circle. Master Lock's advertising is an extreme example of burst whereas the "two ads are enough" school believe in the drip approach. There can be no one generic solution: get your agency to present the case for each.

ADVERTISING AGENCY–CLIENT RELATIONSHIPS

Escalating costs, media proliferation, declining returns, and recession have put client–agency relationships under strain. In the UK the Rover car company rang warning bells by turning its business to one of its own executives who left to set up a new agency. The presumption is that the margins for a new agency business are narrow; it is easier to believe they "bought" the business than that they **The marketers must recognize that agencies understand advertising better than they do.** were better. The threat was clear and it was not just the money. If a marketer could do the agency's job, where would it all end?

Money is a chunk of the problem; results are another. According to the Media Audits' 1992 survey, 42 percent of UK advertisers think agencies are defrauding their clients to boost their incomes. The smaller spenders are the more suspicious; 72 percent would like to pay by results and 12 percent already do. The overall picture, probably alarmist, is one of confusion and dissent.

Once again the respective roles of advertiser and the agency are under review. How should marketers manage the advertising process? Clients are concerned with results more than process. Their first preoccupation is to find the right agency for their brands, and the right agency is not always the best agency even if "best" could be defined. For instance, small brands tend to sit more comfortably in smaller agencies. And some agencies are more effective in some product categories than others – something few will admit.

First, the marketers must recognize that agencies understand advertising better than they do. For one thing, they see a great deal more of it. They also see it off-stage without the tinsel and glitter of the sales pitch. Few clients realize the rejection and elimination that has already taken place before they get to see the show, especially where the client's judgement commands respect. Without respect, they may be shown any old thing.

Agencies are in love with advertising, but not with the client, and may well have an excessive idea of what advertising can do. Remuneration is directly geared to the amount of media space the agency persuades the client to accept. The scene for conflict is now set.

There are great relationships and lousy ones. What else would you expect? It is likely, though unproven, that great advertising comes both from great relationships and lousy ones, provided there is talent on both sides. Indifference is one killer. Interference is the other. Managing agency–client relationships, from the client's point of view, is a continuum from the extreme of "hands off" to the extreme of close involvement which I will call "meddling." Most clients fall somewhere in the middle but it is worth comparing the two.

In the "hands off" model, marketers select the most appropriate agency, brief their team thoroughly, agree realistic brand equity objectives and leave them to it. In the extreme form of the "hands off" model, the agency, not the client, decides the advertising campaign. No clients go that far, though they should. Whitbreads, the UK brewers, came close to this at one stage. They had enough trust to allow individual ads, within an agreed campaign, to run without prior approval where timeliness was critical. Such clients take immense pains with these first three stages to ensure that the right team is working on the account and they fully understand what outcome is required. More than anything, the marketer needs to be sure that the agency is committed to those results, as distinct from producing great advertising. Great advertising and results often coincide but the difference in orientation matters. To handle any internal doubts about that, part of the agency's remuneration should be switched to brand equity. The agency will be more or less rewarded than would otherwise be the case if they overtake or fall short of the brand equity measures. Good research (tracking studies) before and after the advertising will assess performance. Fresh objectives, mutually agreed annually, indicate areas for improvement; if no improvement occurs, you split. Either way, you might say, the agency is fired with enthusiasm. Bonussing systems similar to this have become popular in recent years.

In the "meddling" model, the focus is less on the briefing than the approval process. Naturally the marketer seeks the ideal agency, and briefs them, but the thought in the back of the mind is that client commitment only arrives when the campaign is approved. Thus the focus of their energies is on the approval system. Each level of marketing management insists on approving new concepts before the layer above see them. The marketing manager does not want to be embarrassed by the possibility of substandard work going to the boss. Every piece of agency arithmetic is double checked and the media buying is double guessed. The advertising industry, if that was ever a valid description, is full of ex-agency executives who make a living from advising clients how not to trust their agency. Sometimes their work is constructive, e.g. occasional audits of the relationship itself, but too often it is interference. For the bean counters, this is a fine way to break huge advertising budgets down to countable beans. I just do not want to fly with people who want to take the engine apart in mid-air.

Creative people are frustrated by great ideas being killed before the top decision makers, those most likely to recognize brilliance, ever see them. Safe or derivative advertising or no advertising at all is the likely result. Why should a 25-year-old brand manager whose only experience is in merchandising and promotions judge the work of top advertising professionals? The good advertising agency

> **Is a continuum from the extreme of "hands off" to the extreme of close involvement.**

keeps a brand healthy just as doctors take care of their patients. Would you fail to provide adequate information about the symptoms to a doctor and then subject your prescription to the same approval process as the meddling model of advertising? The more expert the doctors are, the more they know that you do not. Brief them thoroughly and then do what they say – or find a new doctor.

Every client–agency relationship finds its own pattern between these extremes. To some extent this is a battle of power: a strong agency much in demand can afford to be more dominant, however diplomatically they do that. Within clients, some delegate more to product managers; at the other extreme some, Pepsi Cola for example, have a global advertising department that calls most of the shots worldwide.

The amount of non-tax deductible entertainment testifies how seriously agencies worry about their relationships with clients. Maybe that lulls some clients into forgetting that it is they who are supposed to be motivating the agency, not the other way round. At the same time, clients need to involve junior management, if only for training reasons.

Clients love to grumble about their agencies quite unaware of the extent to which the agency grumbles about them. Some agencies now commission third parties to audit, annually or occasionally, client satisfaction and, in the process, ensure that the clients become aware of the problems they cause. This is good practice though expensive and time consuming. At the minimum, client and agency senior management should sit down together to review the relationship. Results should be compared against objectives and creative briefs. Each should ask the other how changed behavior, processes and practices could achieve better results and reduce hassle. Just to make it all more fun is wonderful enough.

BRIEFING THE AGENCY

Logically, this section should start with *choosing* the agency. Providing advice on that is as helpful as advising your children on selecting spouses. There are professional matchmakers, such as the Advertising Agency Register, and CD-ROMs for those who want to watch candidate agency showreels but not be approached. Some clients expect candidates to pitch with well-nigh final advertising recommendations (free), others will pay (as they jolly well should), and some agencies, if they think they are desirable enough, refuse to pitch at all. The prospect is invited in for discussions and to review the work they have done for others. Courtship involves doing your own fumbling to discover what works for you. More fumbling is probably better than less.

Briefing the agency clearly needs to take place both before and after the client and agency have selected one another. Confidentiality may be the determining issue. The process should lead towards a written "contract" even though some of the contents, e.g. expenditure levels (see page 24), may be varied later. The agreement should contain:

- Positioning statement including the target market, brand differentiation etc. (see chapter 16 "Positioning–Marketing's Martial Art.")
- Present and target brand equity (see chapter 2) measures and any other key indicators.
- Competitive equivalent figures and what, for planning purposes, they may be expected to do.
- What the advertising is expected to achieve.
- Creative limitations. In USA beverage alcohol advertising, for example, models must not give the appearance of being under 25 years of age.

Most agencies have their own fixed format creative briefs which they apply to all clients in order to get the brand problems into their own way of thinking. Whilst formats vary, the contents are broadly similar. They typically focus on the argument the ad should make, supporting reasons, and tone. This is conventional but wrong. If the client wants to stipulate what the ad should contain, why bother with creativity? An obsession with limitations and cunning use of the double negative ("this ad must not exclude our company logo in a prominent position") sterilizes advertising. Agreeing targets is essential whereas agreeing content is meddling.

> **Agreeing targets is essential whereas agreeing content is meddling.**

The brief is the cornerstone of getting quality work from advertising agencies or any other creatives, e.g. package designers. It should say *what constitutes success* but not what the answers should be. For example, it can say "total awareness needs to go from 73 percent to 83 percent" not "There should be a large bottle of our famous brand in the bottom right-hand corner because that is our house style." Of course, the agency should challenge the brand positioning statement and any mandatories, e.g. "thou shalt not use models under 25 years of age for drink advertisements." Creative briefs should inspire creative people to be creative, not put them off.

Creative briefs should inspire creative people to be creative.

Some believe that the briefing process should be in two or more stages: mega client (e.g. international or MD) briefs local/junior client who briefs the agency, i.e. the account team, and then they in turn work out a brief for/with their creative team. Sequential briefing has merit: the account group can be more objective, the creatives more professionally motivated. Against that, sequential briefing can lose in translation; "send reinforcements" becomes "send three and fourpence." On balance, one brief, agreed by all the relevant people in the same room at the same time, is better.

The debate may be long and acrimonious. The agency represents the sceptical consumer needing to be convinced. The brand's beauty spots, in its owner's beholding, are warts to the agency. When the talking is done, put the brief in writing and have everyone sign, provide palm prints, and give whatever incontrovertible identification will affirm agreement. Otherwise, the new advertising will be accompanied by an even newer brief, which, strangely, matches the advertisement to perfection. For the process to be effective, however, everyone has to *believe* the brief to be important – hence the signing ceremony. Time spent fighting over the brief is rarely wasted. If the frustrations of the process cause some lateral thinking and a great, but totally different, advertisement results, no experienced marketing person would be surprised.

Why is the brief so important? Is it not easier just to judge the advertising as advertising? Agencies see clients as long on rationality, if not downright pedantic, but short of more delicate sensibilities. Thus if they can be kept to signing off the brief, a business document, the agency can deal with the artistic stuff. Agencies now have "account planners" whose role, largely, is to analyze all the research and rational/commercial factors leading to the brief, i.e. play the client at his own game. This is a helpful development if only to ensure that briefing is thoroughly done.

Does the creative brief help the decision to accept the resulting campaign, or not? We will revert to that after considering budget determination.

HOW MUCH TO SPEND

When top UK marketing practitioners were asked recently what academics could usefully tell them, one of the most popular answers was "tell us how to work out how much to spend on advertising." The last thirty years have seen any number of Black Box enthusiasts run regression analyses to connect spend with sales. Winners of Advertising Effectiveness Awards demonstrate how their analysis predicted sales increases and experience proved them right. Those attempting to generalize from these results have mostly returned sadder and wiser. The Advertising Research Foundation in the US **Long held advertising wisdom that quantity is subsidiary to quality.** has found some light in the tunnel. Dr Lodish, of Wharton, and others reported some key findings in 1993. In about 50 percent of 389 tests, the quantity, or weight, of advertising did not appear to affect the responses (sales). Clearly such conclusions need to be examined in detail since, at the extremes, weight certainly matters. Their conclusion fits with long held advertising wisdom that quantity is subsidiary to quality. They also concluded that the wearout of advertising took about two years. Again the research must be context specific. In the tests they used, sales increased in the first year, year 0, by 22 percent relative to a control group. In the next two years, the research and control groups had the same advertising weight. The spillover effect was an increase in year 1 of 14 percent and 7 percent in year 2.

The net economic benefit of advertising, from the advertiser's point of view, indicates that 54 percent[1] is wasted although these findings have their critics. In other words, advertising is just less than an even money bet.

At category level, there is not much evidence that advertising increases the total volume of a mature market, i.e. once consumers know the products. There is little evidence for market share increase either. If everyone is advertising, they cannot all be adding market share. This is a fact of life that con-

---

[1] Magid M. Abraham and Leonard M. Lodish, "Getting the most out of advertising and promotion," *Harvard Business Review* (May–June 1990)
John Philip Jones, *When Ads Work* (New York, Lexington Books, 1995)

ventionally escapes product managers whose plans routinely claim increased share as the benefit from an increased advertising spend.

All these findings are distressingly similar: on average advertising has no impact on sales. Any number of advertising success stories tells us no more than the fact that some horses win races. Horses win rarely, bookmakers win mostly and punters always pick up the tab. Do not despair. The purpose of this chapter is to help you improve your odds.

In the first place, there is the maintenance argument referenced above, i.e. not to advertise causes volume decline. Secondly, innovation may well need to be advertised; the category result applies only to mature markets. Thirdly, advertising is associated with higher prices being acceptable to consumers. Given a choice between more volume or higher sustainable pricing, your accountant will settle for the latter (see chapter 19, "Pricing in Grandmother's Footsteps").

Against this background you should be wary of consultants with PCs sticking out of their pockets, claiming to divine the "advertising elasticity" of your brand, i.e. how much extra sales you will get from extra advertising. They may well be right. So might someone with a forked twig.

Quite apart from research evidence, or lack of it, there is a simple reason for this sweeping dismissal. The creative content has been variously valued at eight or ten times more important than the expenditure. How you can quantify the unquantifiable is beside the point that the creative content dominates the size of the budget. Researchers who omit this variable from their equations are, implicitly, assuming that all the campaigns included in their data have the same creative value. Other researchers worked back from the sales results in search of what was missing – hence the eight to ten estimate above.

> **The creative content has been variously valued at eight or ten times more important than the expenditure.**

Of course, if you knew the relative creative weight of a campaign before it ran, it would be simple to decide whether to accept it or not and how much to spend on it. Unfortunately formal research cannot *predict* results, as distinct from measuring them after the event. Formal research can help eliminate mistakes and thereby improve the odds.

Staying with the racing analogy, there are two tips:

1. Decide the bet (budget) only after you have seen the horse (campaign).

2. Bet on form: as the campaign proves itself, increase the stake.

While these may seem glimpses of the obvious, agencies press clients to identify the budget as part of the briefing process, not least because it affects media selection. Television typically has higher critical mass to get onto the steeper part of figure 1.1 (see page 18) than press or posters. Multimedia is likely to cost more than just using one. Competitive and agency pressures encourage a large budget now and not the gradualist approach of allowing form to develop. In theory, you could provide a guidance budget for briefing purposes and only make real decisions once the campaign is decided. In practice, few walk away from a stated figure unless financial circumstances have deteriorated in the meantime.

In rejecting "scientific" methods root and branch, there is no need to reject method as such. In practice, successful firms bring together intuition, experience, mathematical methods, and political power-broking to produce decisions from a series of human, sometimes very human, interactions. The most straightforward of these is the "huddle."

The aim is to match believable profit and brand equity objectives with acceptable budgets

The huddle should include the advertising agency and key players from all the interest groups, especially finance and sales. The aim is to match believable profit and brand equity objectives with acceptable budgets by eliminating the unlikely and incredible. Calculated advertising elasticities through regressions or whatever should be included alongside the following more primitive rules of thumb:

- Last year plus inflation.
- What the agency recommends less X per cent for vested interest/bias.
- Keeping up with the competition. "Share of voice" is the equivalent in media spending to market share.
- A fixed proportion of sales, or net sales.
- Next year's profit target less budgeted costs, i.e. what is left over.

This last is both the worst and the most frequently found in British and American companies. "Can we afford it?" is sensible enough but taken in isolation leads to progressive degradation of budgets.

Better to remember that both objectives and resources are there for the juggling: profits and brand equity can, to some extent, be traded off but not indefinitely. If profits always take priority there will be no brand equity and then there will be no profits.

The reason a huddle works is because a cluster of forecasts in response to each strategy builds up a "fuzzy logical" picture. No one can explain later *why* the targets for awareness, attitudes, sales, spending, and profits are right.

The fact that all the key players are comfortable with them, believe them, and can commit to them is enough. Of course, it does help to ensure that the objectives are internally consistent with each other and consistent with past experience.

DECISION MAKING: DOES RESEARCH HELP?

Tracking studies to measure awareness and attitudes pre- and post-advertising are basic good practice. So is commissioning all research independently of the agency. That excludes research the agency arranges to collect its own information or ensure its own quality control before client presentation.

A further basic principle should be the use of research to improve advertising productivity after client approval and before production. A brilliant idea can lose its shine with indifferent execution just as much as an ordinary idea can be effective with brilliant production. Historically, UK agencies were seen as more "creative" relative to the USA but the American agencies were ahead on production values. Lately, however, there has been so much trans-Atlantic interchange that the differences are now more cultural than professional.

Sensitive use of research at the mid-production stage will identify things which need improving. For example, cameras can track the movement of a respondent's eyes while watching an advertisement and show pupil dilation which indicates interest or attention. Surface brightness indicates attraction/repugnance. Portions of the advertisement which are shown to be "boring" can then be improved. Being strapped in a chair with all this gadgetry may not be what you do at home, but some claim that results testify to the improvements obtained through the use of such technology. Others claim it is hogwash.

> **Sensitive use of research at the mid-production stage will identify things which need improving.**

The key question about research is whether you research a new campaign prior to deciding, or decide first and use research to debug any problem areas, or hedge your bets by accepting the campaign subject to research. Should research make the decision?

Research should be used for illumination, not support. Most professional marketers will, if funds permit, research a major campaign, probably first with discussion groups and then with quantitative methods. Specialist research agencies can be called in to compare the performance of new concepts against previous research of other advertising at similar stages. With that support, the marketers will make their final decision about the campaign.

That is a fine way to have safe advertising – and kill off great advertising. To run a major advertising campaign with no research would be foolhardy, but poor results don't necessarily indicate a poor campaign. The reason may simply be that the consumer, in research, responds well to the familiar and poorly to the unfamiliar and challenging. Great advertising will be loved, eventually. Good research results should be taken as a warning.

ACCEPTING THE CAMPAIGN, OR NOT

In the "hands off" model, choosing the new campaign can be left to the agency. Basically, the client chooses the race, the agency chooses the horse and the client decides the size of the bet. All quite simple really. We will assume, though, that you have chickened out of that option. Everyone else does.

Thus you have chosen the "meddling" option, hopefully in less extreme form. Illuminated or otherwise by research, the campaign has been presented. The client team has commented in order of ascending seniority. You have noticed that everyone has said something good about the campaign and something bad. Whatever happens, they will be right. Now what? It is time for a decision, and the sheen of the long table is reflecting a dozen pairs of glinting eyes, all swivelled towards you.

You may believe that the agency should always be sent packing the first time since they can always do better if they try harder. This technique, where it works at all, has limited duration; soon the word gets out. Some agencies even present a straw campaign the first time on principle; it makes the real one look better.

Decision making is too subjective to define best practice. Nevertheless, there is much to be said for resisting hasty conclusions. Advertising with instant appeal may not mature well. Live with a new campaign for a few days. Put the roughs on a wall, perhaps. Agencies scoff, but taking the work back for the family to discuss is not so crazy. Then decide.

If your budget is small, you will have to choose between advertising it and researching it. Send the research agency packing. Your office or warehouse staff will give a more reliable response than the sales force, but do make the ads look like real ones, not roughs. Internal staff will tell you what they feel, while sales will be second guessing customer reaction.

Advertising decisions should be left to the consumer, not in research but in real life. In the meantime, one person's mature judgement, not the huddle or any other committee, should decide. A tingling sensation of acceptable risk may be that person's guiding factor. Establish the quality of the advertising before the quantity. Awareness and attitude targets can be achieved by numbers, by throwing money at the problem. Better is to see how the campaign opens. Most people quickly and accurately judge a campaign once it is on the street; few, if they are

Most people quickly and accurately judge a campaign once it is on the street.

honest, can do so before. When the campaign has established its productivity, the treasure chest can be safely unlocked.

Advertising works on "highs." Its great exponents can be impatient with pedantic details such as tracking studies and creative briefs. Brilliant insights arise in mysterious ways. "Famous advertising starts here" used to be written impressively on charts, as if to deny the value of anything so pedestrian as analysis. Today's tougher relationships are more professional, and rightly so.

The challenge is to reconcile that professionalism with the flights of fancy that create giddy patterns in the sky and capture the consumer's imagination, attention and respect. Great advertising flies as high as a kite. Feet on the ground, the string in control and yet the creative execution is pulling up and providing lift. Blue skies? Crazy? This is advertising; it should be.

Memo to file

Subject: ADVERTISING KITE HIGH

- What kind of advertising do you need? If high visibility and impact are important, then so are a burst of creativity and a burst of spending. If your resources cannot achieve critical mass, do not advertise.

- The agency cannot be overbriefed. When it is done, record and sign it.

- Focus on results, not advertising content. And pay (part of) the agency's remuneration based on those results, lest they forget.

- Manage the agency–client relationship professionally, including a formal review once a year. It is the client's job to motivate the agency, not the other way round.

- The "hands off" model is unlikely to be used but it is a benchmark:
  (1) Choose appropriate agency.
  (2) Define comprehensive objectives in joint creative brief.
  (3) Do not prescribe the answers.
  (4) Run tracking studies pre- and post-advertising.
  (5) Use research to improve performance next time.

- "Scientific" methods, research, or mathematics, should contribute to, but not dominate, the determination of budgets. Get the key players into a huddle and lock the door. Finalizing the profit and brand equity objectives and weight of spending, is an iterative interactive process.

- Use research to improve advertising, not decide it. Take good research results as a warning.

- Leave the campaign acceptance decision, if not to the agency, to one experienced executive, not a committee, still less chasing up and down the hierarchy. That person should consult widely and think long. If there is no tingle of danger, it may well be a boring campaign. Kites don't fly if they don't get the breeze.

2

BRAND EQUITY

The asset the marketer is building: the source of profit

Key issues
● What is a "brand"? ● The brand as a valuable myth.
Building brand personality ● Brand value and brand equity.
Separate concepts ● Brand equity assessment

WHAT IS A BRAND?

In the beginning, a brand was the red hot iron used for applying a mark of ownership. The burn was indelible and difficult to imitate. Today, brand owners use holography to distinguish their products from the fakes. Techniques change; the concepts remain the same.

A "brand" is not just a product on a supermarket shelf but anything which is distinguished from similar products or services. Thus Ivory Soap is a brand and so are Andersen Consulting and Safeway. Mitsubishi is a brand and Coca-Cola is probably the world's best known brand. The Roman Catholic Church is a brand of religion just as Shell is a brand of petrol.

> **A "brand" is not just a product on a supermarket shelf but anything which is distinguished from similar products or services.**

A "marked man" was a criminal or slave who had been branded with a hot iron. Branding has associations with infamy that still linger. Consumerists see brands as devices for raising prices; branding and marketing are confidence tricks. Cunning and powerful transnational corporations manipulate ordinary people, it is implied, to buy what they do not need at prices they cannot afford.

Naturally the same scene, from the other side, is reversed. The all-important consumer dictates whims and fancies to a supplicant marketer. The marketers' existence depends on their ability to meet consumer needs.

The truth is that these views need to be taken together. Of course the marketer is self interested, and so is the consumer. At the heart of marketing is the simple truth, to which we will have to return, that both parties can only satisfy themselves by satisfying each other. This is why marketing is a cooperative, win-win, game.

It is easy to get metaphysical about definitions, but branding, broadly defined, is the root of marketing. Strip away the posturing and a brand is revealed as simply the promise of the bundle of attributes that someone buys and that provides satisfaction. Plato, two and a half millennia ago, figured out that reality is all in the mind. We only experience "reality" through our senses. Thus reality, for us, is what we think and feel. Bishop Berkeley, two and a half centuries ago, wondered if the tree would be there if we were not. Beliefs equal reality until destroyed by experience. The last 30 years of research into how advertising works has revealed little more than that. He also told us that "truth is the cry of all, but the game of the few." He would have done well at J Walter Thompson.

As long as the consumer accepts the attributes of the brand, and enjoys the experience of using it, then that brand provides value. The attributes that make up a brand may be real or illusory, rational or emotional, tangible or invisible. A brand is a mnemonic for the consumer. It is easier to remember a single brand name than all those different product characteristics.

Every brand has one or more products. "Products" may be goods and/or services, consumer or industrial. Products today increasingly bundle goods and services together. A Toyota car sells as much on post-purchase service, or the lack of need for it, as the physical attributes of the automobile. There is also confusion between the terms *brand* and *product*. What was once a brand manager is now called a product manager. There are a number of threads in this particular evolution, one of which is a sensitivity to the negative associations of the term *brand*. Since Marlboro cigarettes spectacularly cut prices by 20

> **Every brand has one or more products.**

percent, and the shares by about the same, the lack of confidence in the brand concept accelerated, especially amongst marketers who react to any crisis by changing language. Chapter 3 "Category Management and Other Heresies" addresses this phenomenon and the modern heresy that marketing is not really about brands at all.

There are, however, two schools of thought about a brand, the *holistic* and the *added values*. The holistic model is:

Brand = Product + Packaging + Added values.

The added value model is:

Brand = Added values only, i.e. not the substance of the offering.

In this simple difference much confusion lies. While the holistic approach is common in the UK, the added value model is usual in the USA and, historically, has much to commend it. Products usually exist before they are branded. The cow comes before the brand. Recognition that the product is the most important part of the consumer package prompted the job title change to product manager. Definitions may be thought to be a matter of taste but adherents of the second view get themselves into a tangle when the logic is followed through.

The added value school, for example, led to British High Street banks treating branding and marketing as a wholly separate activity from the consumer service experience on the High Street. Advertising the bank's service fantasies, which contradicted consumer experience, did more harm than good, as Bishop Berkeley could have told them.

In many cases, consumers do not make a distinction between a product and the added values. They do not stop at the counter and decide to purchase a cola before considering which added values they identify with that morning. They buy a Coke. They are barely thinking about it at the time. The hand goes out for the whole damn thing. In other cases, e.g. cars, a purchase follows considerable thought but the consumer may still be unable to distinguish between the product and the added values. Attempting to separate the "real" quality due to product attributes from the "perceived" attributes of added values is not realistic. The human brain does not separate neatly into left brain (rational thought) and right brain (emotions). Whole people buy whole brands.

> **The whole provision to the consumer should be included.**

While the alternative definitions of the brand are controversial, no marketers deny that marketing includes the *whole* provision to the consumer. Marketers want to provide real benefits to consumers because that makes the job of selling so much easier. Products can be more clearly related to benefits than can brands. This book therefore adopts the holistic model henceforward.

The packaging on physical goods is apparent enough, but the packaging that wraps around services may be obvious or invisible. Avis has to be visible to travellers in unknown airports. The fascia, uniforms, and paperwork are designed to be attention-getting but also value-adding. The packaging of a radio station, on the other hand, will be negligible, but the station will still be attempting to add value and will have an equally strong identity in the minds of its listeners.

The holistic version of brand definition is preferred but before we leave the subject, there is one more way to look at it: in terms of the basic consumer benefits. In this view,

Brand = Functional + Psychological + Economic Benefits.

In simpler language,

Brand = Quality + Image + Price.

In this perspective, the marketer's job is to keep a balance between these basic benefits. A high price and low quality is no more satisfactory than a low price and high quality though the Japanese have taught us not to be too simplistic about that. To some extent these benefits can be traded off against each other (but be careful of "or" thinking) and to some extent they must be in harmony.

These three components provide one of the frameworks for measuring brand equity, as we shall see (see page 35).

THE BRAND AS A VALUABLE MYTH

The Oxford English Dictionary defines a myth as "a traditional narrative ... embodying popular ideas on natural or social phenomena." Primitive cultures use myths to create a link with the large and overwhelming world around them. In ancient Greece, more complex series of myths helped people understand society and themselves through projecting their own desires onto supernatural creatures. Myths can never really be described as true or false, they just exist in popular culture. A limited company has no tangible reality. It is as intangible as a brand. The law, however, considers a limited company to be a legal person and treats it accordingly.

Building brands includes the business of building myths cooperatively with consumers. This takes us into the anthropological wonderland of tribal symbols, values, badges, and rituals. Inaccurate though it is, let us shorthand it to myths. In the late 1980s and early '90s, young people adopted Doc Marten's footwear. The grunge look and boots offended parents and delighted peers simultaneously. Win-win again. Doc Marten was a myth created more by the user than the manufacturer.

Consumers want myths; they create them, enjoy them, and perpetuate them. Bronze Age people, being starved of television, attributed personalities to the trees, water, and rocks around them. They gave them names and fantasies. Rationally, they knew they were trees and water and rocks, but they wanted to personalize whatever they had to deal with.

A trip down a supermarket aisle is hardly the equivalent of dallying with Pan in some sylvan glade, but brands have personalities. Those personalities are created by users, the consumers, as well as by marketers. When building the myth, marketers will ask consumers what they think and then try to capitalize on the more positive aspects. What consumers think may, or may not, have come from any past marketing efforts.

> **Brand equity is shorthand for what a brand is worth.**

The idea of taking a piece of lime with Mexican beer was not originated by any brewer. The idea came from Tequila and just meant "Mexico" to consumers. When Corona found Californians doing it, however, they were quick to help the word of mouth along.

The added values that turn a product into a brand are most obvious when the same product is sold under different labels. It may be worth more to one consumer than another because of the fit between the brand's identity and the consumer's self perception. Some people will buy Gucci shoes because they are Gucci; others will think they are overpriced. The brand personality helps the consumer to get to know the product.

With computers, automation, emergent economies, and globalization our lives are overfilled with products clamoring for our attention and our money. Think of it as the world's biggest drinks party. Who are you going to spend time with? Those you know and like or those you do not? Those who seem attractive and compatible? Or the jerk who never remembers to repay the money he borrowed? Marketers ensure that their products are nicely presented and have personalities compatible with the target market.

BRAND VALUE AND BRAND EQUITY

The separation of brand from product becomes more important when considering the concept of brand equity. This is a 1980s term for the old idea that a brand has a value of its own, beyond the value that comes from the product. Brand equity is shorthand for the brand asset. For example, if Inter-Continental Hotels buys a suitable building from Bloggs City Centres, they will be able to charge more *and* give more satisfaction. The addition of the Inter-

Continental brand name has raised the value of the business. That is one way of measuring brand equity; there are a number of others.

Brand equity became a hot topic in the 1980s because companies were being bought and sold for the value of their brand names. Rowntrees went to Nestlé, Martell to Seagram, Kentucky Fried Chicken to PepsiCo. This triggered a fierce debate in the UK about whether such values should appear on the balance sheet. Not to include brand values would undervalue a company in the eyes of their shareholders and make it vulnerable. Shareholders might, in the heat of the battle, receive less than they should. Rank Hovis McDougall had their brands valued and listed them as assets.

To take a simple example, suppose company A has a net worth (or total assets less total liabilities) of £50 million. It finds company B, which may be worth anything up to £100 million in terms of future earnings to company A. After a competitive auction, company A buys company B for £80 million. Unfortunately, it only has £20 million of net assets on the balance sheet. The rest of the value is made up by some marvellous brand names.

If company A cannot include the brands on its balance sheet, the consolidated balance sheet looks like this:

Balance Sheet

	Before £m	After £m
Assets	60	80
Cash	80	–
Liabilities	(90)	(90)
Net worth	50	(10)

It would appear that company A has become insolvent and people in white coats will be coming for the directors. In fact, they have increased the value of the company by £20 million (£100 million earning power of the brands less £80 million paid for them). If company A *does* put the brands on the balance sheet (£60 million) then the apparent net worth will remain the same (£50 million) since the net assets plus the brands will equal the cash paid out.

This example is oversimplified but shows how, if brands are not treated as assets, the accounts may make smart buyers seem dumb. The arguments for including the *cost* of brand acquisitions is not the same as including the *value* of brands, or, indeed, any other assets. The traditional accounting convention is to show the *lower* of cost or market value but this has long been breached in the UK for property which has been upwardly valued on balance sheets in order to give a more realistic view of the company. The world is not yet ready to apply the same logic to brands.

Not only is the distinction between cost and value of brands important, but so is the distinction between brand equity and brand value, or valuation. Brand equity is the asset itself in the same way that a house is an asset. The value of a house may depend on whether the valuation is for sale or purchase, for insurance, or for probate. These values may all differ and none is the asset itself. You cannot live in a valuation. This partially explains the reluctance to put brand values on balance sheets. Which one will you use? Furthermore the fact that an asset has many differing values does not suggest that the asset does not exist. Sceptics, who have a difficulty with the brand equity concept, use the undoubted measurement problems to cast doubt on its existence.

> **In theory a brand's value is the capital worth of the premium it achieves over the equivalent generic product**

A house has no objective value but only what value the market indicates, i.e. what someone will pay. There are enough properties being sold at any time to give some confidence to the arithmetic; the exceptional highs and lows can be averaged out. Adjustments can be made for known differences such as garages or gardens. But even with all the data they have available, property valuers sometimes revert to an approach that seems circuitous to a layperson: estimated rental is grossed up by the expected percentage return on investment to give the capital value which then generates the rental.

Brand valuers have essentially the same problem as property valuers but with less data. Where a brand has been purchased, then the purchace price may become the "value" for balance sheet purposes. It may be the remainder after the other assets have been subtracted from the total purchase price for the business. An acquisition sets market value (= cost) initially but value will need checking thereafter.

In theory a brand's value is the capital worth of the premium it achieves over the equivalent generic product, i.e. the same thing without the brand name. The premium arises from four factors:

- Higher price paid by customers and consumers.

- Greater volumes sold.

- Greater certainty/predictability arising from consumer demand as distinct from sales push.

less

● Any greater marketing expenditure thus required.

Despite the importance and longevity of brands which can live forever, accountants will continue to debate whether, and if so how, brands should appear on balance sheets for years to come. The controversy has highlighted a fundamentally important concept for marketers: their function is not just to achieve short-term profits, but to increase the equities of the brands in their charge. *Brand equity is the storehouse of future profits from the brand.* It is what the brand has earned but has not yet paid out in profits.

BRAND EQUITY ASSESSMENT

We are not concerned with the technicalities of balance sheets but with improving marketing performance. A healthy brand will spin off profits for many years into the future but how do you check out the storehouse today?

The two main financial approaches are discounted cash flow ("DCF") and earnings multiple. Both mirror the thinking behind the sale or purchase of a brand and as such try to be market based. If such valuations were valid then the performance of the brand team could be measured by the increase in brand valuation plus the net profit for the period.

The first problem with DCF is deciding whose forecasts should be selected. The brand manager can hardly be judged on her own estimates, especially if she is skipping off to a new job on Monday. Equally, will the brand team accept some gloomy prognostication from finance? Let us assume the huddle from the previous chapter has produced some reasonable high and low estimates which all can accept. We still have the problem of subjectivity, i.e. the team judging its own performance, but the problem is worse. The forward projections include the profit arising from forward marketing efforts. In theory these could be separated but it would be difficult and it is not done. General practice is to extrapolate trends in a more or less sophisticated manner, adjusting for known or possible changes. This is fallacious: the storehouse today does not contain the profits from *future* efforts and expenditures.

The earnings multiple method has been popularized by Interbrand in the UK and is closer to real life. Brands and companies are indeed quoted and sold on the basis of the most recent net profits times a multiple from 5 to 50 to reflect expectations in a broad brush way. The more typical range is 10–20, as inspection of any daily page of equity prices will show. Clearly the action lies in the selection of the multiple since earnings are factual. Interbrand bring in a wide range of relevant factors in getting down to this single index. The methodology and the sensitivity of the result can be argued but this is not where the problem lies. The whole point of brand equity is that it is independent from profit: it is the other side of the picture, needed to

Brand equity is the storehouse of future profits from the brand.

provide balance. The sale of 100 cases of beans just before the year end which would otherwise have sold in the new year should increase this year's profits but decrease the storehouse by the same amount. In real terms the sale two days sooner or later is immaterial. Under the earnings multiple method earnings *and* brand value increase. The multiple is not sensitive enough to compensate and the

A growing brand has more equity than a declining brand with the same short term profitability.

earnings base will tend to drive both in the same direction. The same applies to advertising, negative to profits but positive to brand equity, or price promotions which are typically the reverse.

That both these popular methods are flawed does not mean they should not be used. They are better than nothing. More importantly, the attention to the brand's life signs, especially when outside consultants are involved, provides much of the focus management needs.

The concept of brand equity has not been around for long enough to allow measurement standards to emerge. A UK survey of leading advertising spenders revealed very little consistency except for two things: forecasts were not used and the need to measure the brand asset, by whatever name, was recognized. In any case the exact numbers are less important than the focus away from the immediate results onto the longer horizon which brand equity requires. However the arithmetic is done, a growing brand has more equity than a declining brand with the same short-term profitability.

Reducing brand equity to a single index, or value, is not yet satisfactory but there must be some n dimensional measure which will serve. How big does n have to be?

Some hold that market share and relative price, i.e. n=2, will serve. It is true that market share is like a flywheel: it builds speed slowly and carries energy smoothly from period to period. On the other hand it suffers similar problems to the multiple method in that it mirrors changes in profit rather than providing an independent measure. It is also prone to manipulation by marketers who change definitions of the "market." Do you measure Suzuki sales by share of the car market or the small car market? Pillsbury frozen dough has close to 100 percent share of the frozen dough market and close to 0 percent of the bread market.

Relative price (market share by value divided by market share by volume) is a great measure of the consumer's belief in the brand and especially the quality of the brand. Problems with market selection remain and there is some correlation with profit. Sustainability is the key issue: if the price has been hiked, profits are riding for a fall.

> **Relative price is a great measure of the consumer's belief in the brand and especially the quality of the brand.**

Thus n=2 will not do. My own preference is for n being between 10 and 15. Less than 10 gives insufficient comfort on sustainability. More than 15 is confusing. This is a matter of taste. Popular brand equity measures include the following, all with trends:

- Brand awareness – total and unprompted.
- Market share, either volume or value but consistently.
- Relative price, market share by value/share by volume.
- Awareness, either unaided or total but consistently.
- Perceived (by consumers) quality.
- Economic profit or other bottom line indicator.
- Market size, total value.
- AMP (advertising, merchandising and promotion, i.e. marketing) expenditure.
- Advertising as a percentage of AMP.
- Share of voice (brand advertising/total category advertising).
- Penetration, percentage of consumers buying in the last year.
- Loyalty, there are four ways of measuring this. One is percentage of requirements among users.
- Number of (product lines – stock keeping units).
- Percentage of sales in products launched in last n years (n can be three or five, for example).
- Some measure of distribution strength.
- Strength of retailer relationships.
- Pipeline inventory (i.e. stock sold into channels but not yet bought by consumers, quite a sensitive measure this as Marlboro found out).

- Leadership, i.e. rank in market.
- Percentage sales on promotion.
- Price elasticity.
- Actual quality, e.g. recalls, user surveys of satisfaction.
- Other image measures, e.g. fashionability, modernity.

The measures appropriate to each brand depend on the market. Brand equity of a university can be measured, in part, by the number of qualified applicants they turn down.

The other framework for analysis consists of the basic consumer benefits: functional, psychological and economic. These three dimensions can be assembled from the variables above but at the minimum, brand equity measurement should include: perceived quality, relative price and awareness as a proxy for the strength of brand personality.

How brand equity is assessed is far less important than the fact that it is, and consistently. The numbers do not matter but the trends do. So does consistency between indicators. If perceived quality and relative price are both up, book your holiday, but if relative price is up and perceived quality is down, start taking the Zantac.

An annual Brand Equity Assessment should challenge the prevailing wisdom and status quo about the brand. Caesar rode in his chariot with a slave whose sole purpose was to tell him that his feet were made of clay. Consumer values shift, and a brand has to keep pace. The more scientific marketers will want more analysis of positioning for the brand and the competition, more research into the particular attributes and associations, details of the individual products, sizes, how well they are doing, and how they fit. How much of this analysis is necessary and appropriate will depend on the brands, the company, and the amount of money involved.

Whatever the quality of the information and analysis, the discussion has to return to the brand as a whole. Is it thriving, surviving or dying? Brand Equity Assessment is no different in principle from an annual medical. You cannot just add up all the numbers. All the indicators save one may be great but if there is no pulse you are probably dead. A 110 percent average of health check indices did not save you. Ultimately, you have to step back and look at the whole brand from the consumer's point of view.

To its management, a brand should be an old friend; its eccentricities, and

An annual Brand Equity Assessment should challenge the prevailing wisdom and status quo about the brand.

perhaps its old-worldliness, can be overlooked. The objectivity to see what consumers see is not easy. It is what you pay advertising agencies for. Many now have their own patent ways of doing this. Young and Rubicam, for example, has trademarked "BrandAsset." As Professor Barwise has pointed out, accountants gain strength by sharing language while marketers insist on reinventing it. Y&R's methodology uses four dimensions for measuring brand equity which they collapse to two. "Vitality" is made up of "differentiation" and "consumer relevance" and the "stature," or magnitude, of the brand comprises "familiarity," or awareness, and "esteem." As mentioned above, Interbrand and other specialist consultants also bring objectivity with their expertise. Objectivity is essential whether it comes from outside or from inside.

When all the analysis is done, there are just two questions concerning differentiation and added value: Is the brand set far enough apart from its competitors? And, is it attractive enough to the target market? These are the drivers of brand equity. These are also the basic questions answered by a brand's "positioning" – the start point for marketing (see chapter 16).

Scientific methods for brand equity assessment provide even less help than for determining the size of the advertising budget. As the two subjects are interlinked, you may as well use the same "huddle." In other words, lock all the key players up together, including the agency, sales and finance, to consider all the evidence and decide whether the brand is strengthening, weakening or maintaining its health.

Memo to file:

Subject: BRAND EQUITY

- The most valuable equity of a brand is the mythology created by consumers. Go with that flow.

- A brand is a differentiated product to which the consumer ascribes higher values. From these the marketer derives higher profits. Think about a brand's personality as a whole. Taking it to pieces all the time may not reveal the essence. Is the personality attractive and distinctive enough?

- Brand equity is the storehouse of future profits but it is a today measure. You cannot measure the future; forget forecasts.

- Choose between ten and 15 brand equity measures and then apply them consistently. Trends matter; single year indicators do not.

- Ensure that the measures cover the three basic consumer benefits: functional, psychological, and economic, e.g. with perceived quality, awareness, and relative price.

3

CATEGORY MANAGEMENT AND OTHER HERESIES

Being distracted from the brand may be good business, but poor marketing

---

Key issues
● **Balancing brand portfolios** ● **The retailer's view**
● **Category equity** ● **Private label** ● **Heresies**

BALANCING BRAND PORTFOLIOS

The term "category management" originated, as did so much else in marketing, with Procter and Gamble in the late 1980s, though the idea of optimizing a portfolio of brands in the same product category is far older. Take laundry detergents, for example. Tide, Ariel, Cheer, Vizir, Oxydol and Daz all belong to P&G. They are made of similar ingredients, cost similar amounts, and do similar things to clothes. If P&G rationalized them down to a single brand, Unilever's competing detergents would increase their share of market and profits. If, on the other hand, P&G maintained all their brands and let them fend for themselves as if they were all independent, they would take share from each other as much as from Unilever.

Category management is, ideally, the organization of brand positionings so as to maximize the aggregate brand equities and profits from the company's brands in that category. Proponents of strategic marketing go further and deploy brands to block competitors and prevent them gaining strength. In both cases the unit of analysis is the category rather than the brand.

The first two sections of this chapter deal with the two strong roots of the concept: the positioning of brands relative to one another and the customer's point of view. Then we consider whether the brand owner should provide competing products under the retailer's label. This is known as "own label" or "own brand" in the UK and "private label" in the US. Retailer power has grown steadily and the necessary efforts to accommodate them have led marketers into what some consider loose thinking. The final section seeks, controversially, to separate orthodoxy from heresy. Every company needs to decide for itself where to draw the line between customer satisfaction in the long-term interest of its profits and its brands and appeasement which it may regret.

> **Category management is, ideally, the organization of brand positionings so as to maximize the aggregate brand equities and profits from the company's brands in that category.**

If your business does not have more than one brand per category, and most do not, skip straight to the private label section or just amuse yourself with heresies.

The mechanics of category management may be simple or complex. In a duopoly, i.e. a two-company market as detergents sometimes are, the two portfolios usually end up neatly opposing each other brand for brand. The most common differentiation is on price, classically traded off against advertising. Those consumers who want lower price and less psychological benefits get a choice of two, one from each company, and so on up the price scale to the most premium.

If gentleness is a key benefit or cold wash or the latest piece of genetic engineering, the two companies will match each other to the extent that volumes and margins make such niches profitable. Every so often, minor brands are rationalized out, leaving the other company with the odd niche or two to itself but, overall, the market shares remain as steady as the front lines in World War I. In this game of chess, the brand pieces are aligned black against white. Without conscious category management, internecine strife is all too likely.

Where there are many competitors, optimizing the portfolio is more complex but still necessary. Planning for each brand in isolation takes no account of the knock on effects of, for example, repositioning or pricing strategies on the other brands in the portfolio.

Sophisticated "what if?" packages on PCs are becoming available to help deal with these consequential calculations. You should consider not only your own moves but the competitor and retailer responses. The crucial arithmetic may also be done with pencil and paper. As with so much in marketing the devil lies not in the detail but in thinking the unthinkable. For this a team of iconoclasts and a couple of scorers is more valuable than the latest IT.

The steps you should consider are:

● Identify the positioning and strength (brand equity) of each of your own and the key competitor brands.

● Where are the areas of waste, i.e. where are your brands hurting each other rather than competitors'?

● What are your realistic options?

● What may retailers and competitors do (a) in any case (b) in response to your moves?

Perceptual mapping, (see chapter 16, "Positioning – Marketing's Martial Art") is a useful place to start. If the positioning statements have been well analyzed they will reveal the key reasons consumers buy the brands, e.g. for detergents gentleness, technical advantage, cold water washing, value for money. For cars, it might be space, reliability/engineering, style, safety, and performance. The most important of these consumer factors form the axes. Plotting where each brand lies according to its ratings on those dimensions shows how "close" brands, yours and theirs, are to one another. More than two dimensions are hard to visualize. Some dimensions may be important to other brands but irrelevant to you. Cadillacs will never win on cost per mile. Think carefully before you dismiss them. The best new angles are never obvious.

> Planning for each brand in isolation takes no account of the knock-on effects of, for example, repositioning or pricing strategies on the other brands in the portfolio.

The mid-point of each axis on the perceptual map should be the point of optimum demand by the target market. Game theory shows that, if there are simply two brands, both should occupy this central positioning on each dimension. If the other brand has taken a non-central position, take the centre yourself. Hence the duopoly solution above. If a third brand comes along, where it goes makes no difference, so long as it is far enough from the other two. After that optimal territories fall as you would expect; you try to crowd the opposition and keep your own brands in as much space as possible.

Of course, few companies have many brands in one category. The usual pattern is a premium brand and one or two cheaper brands sometimes called "flanker brands." Their main role is to absorb price competition, thus allowing the premium brand to maintain its higher price. In the vodka market,

Popov is owned by the same company as Smirnoff. It is not advertised but it is sold at a lower price to match other domestic cheaper vodkas. When they indulge in promotional activity, Popov will do so similarly. Copying the others accentuates the differentiation of Smirnoff.

All these maps plus those following your own and competitor moves, and those then again after the responses to those, will more than cover the walls of the six-star hotel to which you have wisely repaired to deal with category management. By now you will need whichever form of stress

The usual pattern is a premium brand and one or two cheaper brands sometimes called "flanker brands."

therapy dictated the choice of the hotel. The scorers may or may not be happy to be left to reduce all those maps to present value profit and brand equity calculations. Somebody has to do it.

Very few companies have real category management problems and even fewer approach them in this way. With a single brand in a category, or a premium and a fighting, flanker, brand, the problem barely arises. Brand positioning is still necessary but not category management in the sense of this section. It may be necessary, however, for dealing with customers (see p. 50).

Where there are multiple brands in a category and the company has choices to make, a special task force more typically considers options over a period of months rather than as a quick part of the brand planning process. Category management is a strategic issue and a more deliberate process may be appropriate. One way or another, the brand managers should participate.

THE RETAILER'S VIEW

Publicity for P&G's category management, compounded with the new shelf management software, soon prompted retailers to re-examine their own thinking. These programs calculated the share of shelf to be allocated to a category, and only then divided that share between brands. This was nothing new but it was more formalized. The retailer wanted to maximize the profit return, as always, by linear foot of space; brand loyalties were irrelevant.

The early forms of these programs led to some daft solutions. In the mid-80s, one of the Canadian Provincial Liquor Boards calculated that about 70 percent of their profits came from whisk(e)y and about 70 percent of that came from one brand. In a vast store with 2,000 different product lines, 49 percent of the total display space was devoted to this single brand. The experiment was not a success.

The programs became more sophisticated but retailers recognized that neither they nor their computers had the time nor the expertise to optimize the shelf allocation. This required real understanding of the consumers' needs. The same skills that brand owners used to balance their own portfolios were relevant to balancing the retailers' shelves.

To oversimplify the detergent example, suppose there are two manufacturers and no private label. Suppose further that 50 percent of sales are on technical merit (washes whiter/more effectively), 15 percent on kind to clothes, 10 percent on cold wash effectiveness, and 25 percent on price. The initial allocation would match those percentages to ensure all needs are met and shelves need refilling at the same rate. So far we have not had even to consider brands.

The secondary stage is to determine which brand is the leader against each reason to buy. The same brand may win on more than one. Factoring in the different profitabilities, to the retailer, affects not only space but which shelf it will be on (eye or ankle level). The software will do all the space, volume turnover, and profit calculations.

Thirdly, the analysis needs to consider the different sizes on offer from suppliers and demanded by the customers of that particular store.

Finally, there are the softer marketing issues, consumer choice and the perception of choice being two separate issues. In the large segment, technical merit, two brands will be offered and profits will probably rise. In the smallest segment, cold wash, offering a second brand will probably reduce retail level profits and there would need to be a compelling reason, e.g. extra discount from the brand leader, to do so.

This simplified example illustrates what has to be done. The order of the decision-making varies; sizes can be allocated before brand, but the key point is that the retailers have persuaded the brand owners to do this analysis for them. Why should brand owners burn up their own overheads to do the retailers' job for them?

Some believe that category management heralds a new dawn of partnership between brand owner and retailer. Others consider that wishful thinking. "Closer to the customer" can be a mixed blessing. Lou Stern, of Northwestern, likens partnership with large retail chains to romancing a 40-ton gorilla. How close do you want to get to that?

There are three reasons why marketers with strong brands should influence retailers through category management discussions:

1. The manufacturer that most influences shelf setting is best placed to gain share of facings, gain the most valuable shelf situations, and thus market share.

2. Seeing things from the customer's point of view, and using the customer's language, are not just good manners, they are good marketing.

3. The more retail buyer attention is occupied by you, the less will be left to
   give your competitors.

Figure 3.1 illustrates the domain of tolerance, assuming perfect knowledge
and communications, that the retailer has
for manufacturer self-interest.

   The y-axis shows the profit advantage
from the shelf setting around the optimal
point B. The x-axis shows the supplier's
share of shelf space. To get close to 100
percent share of shelf, the necessary dis-

The same skills that brand owners used to balance their own portfolios were relevant to balancing the retailers' shelves.

count to the retailer would wipe out the supplier's profit. Between points A
and C, the shelf setting makes little difference to the retailer but considerable
advantage to the supplier. Thus the area between A and C is the "domain of
tolerance."

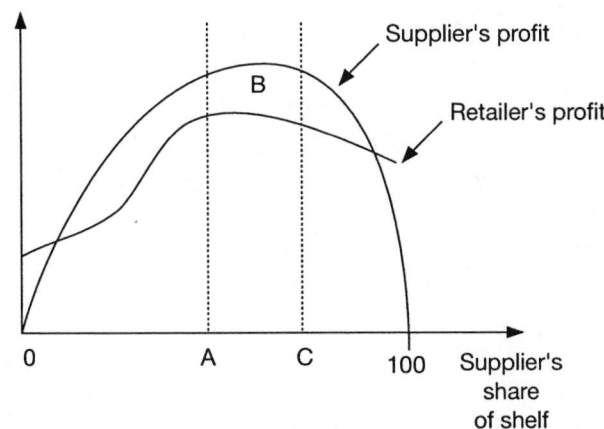

Fig 3.1   Domain of tolerance

   Translating the feasible shelf settings into profit advantages for retailer
and supplier requires computer calculation. Pencil and paper category management of the overall brand portfolio may be possible for the supplier
because there are usually few valid options. When we get to the retail store,
however, where the different shelves, facings, and sizes of all the products in
the category have to be taken into account, this is no longer feasible. Fortunately, PC packages are widely available.

CATEGORY EQUITY

If there is "brand equity," is there "category equity"? Unfortunately, this is a complication. Most marketing brand equity measures, as distinct from brand valuation, are *relative*. Market share, share of voice, relative price, awareness, perceived quality, and other attitudinal indicators are all relative to other brands in the same category. To compare brand equities in two different categories, some way to multiply each brand's equity by its category equity needs to be found.

For example, your brand may be the best brand of muffins, 60 percent share and very high perceived quality and relative price. If the muffin category is losing favour, compared to bread products, the real worth of your muffin brand is declining too. This gives rise to the thought that your company has to "manage the category image" as much as, if not more than, the brand's. This is a slippery slope toward marketing heresy.

Consider two alternatives:

A. Your brand dominates the category, as perhaps your brand of muffin does with 60 percent share. Or as Guinness dominates stout.

B. Your brand does not dominate.

In the case of A, your definition of category is too narrow. You have no worthwhile competition in your sights. Without that threat, marketing may become lazy and boring. The brand (and the category) will decline. The answer is not to manage the category but to redefine it. Give yourself a new challenge. This is particularly true when the brand is the category, e.g. the California Fruit and Nut Marketing Board generic campaign. We will assume for a moment that fruits and nuts do not come from any other place so that the "brand" has 100 percent share of its market. In its positioning statement (see chapter 16) it must define its main competitor, i.e. from whence is its new business coming?

> **If a major brand within a category can again become vibrant, the category's image will improve too.**

In the case of B, your competition will benefit more from any category management than you will. There may be new competition as, if you are successful in improving the image of the category, new entrants are that much more likely.

In practice, the reverse works quite well. If a major brand within a category can again become vibrant, the category's image will improve too. The image of cinemas, for example, went south in the 1970s. No one ran a come-back-to-cinemas campaign to restore the category or, if they did, it was so useless I missed it. What happened was that individual outlets and chains multiplexed, improved their facilities and products. Customers returned to them as individual operators, not because someone had managed the category.

Guinness never lost sight of the fact that they were promoting the brand, not the stout category. They have applied the brand name to bitter (ale) and now lager. Even so, their revitalization of the stout category brought in competition, from Murphy's and Beamish, where none had existed before.

In short, category equity exists as a concept – but forget it.

PRIVATE LABEL

So far we have excluded private label considerations. Some companies make handsome profits through the supply of products under the retailer brand name. Northern Foods supplies Marks and Spencer's St Michael brand, Geest supplies Tesco and Sainsbury. The Cott business in Canada supplies colas and other soft drinks. McBride has become successful in supplying UK own label household products. They are thus part of the retail brand marketing operation, "symbiotically" in the language of Northern Foods. The quality of private label goods has been increasing both in reality and consumer perception. "President's Choice" was developed by Loblaws, a Canadian chain, as premium private label and is now carried by chains in the USA and Europe.

It is thus a mistake to see private label supply as being outside marketing, i.e. just manufacturing. The brand name may be owned by another company but they are involved in marketing as much as if it was their own. Chris Haskins, CEO of Northern Foods, argues more so because they have to sell "through" their customer using his facilities. The private label supplier must understand consumer needs every bit as much as the brand owner, perhaps because only the product, package and price tools are available.

The private label supplier incurs less marketing costs, notably advertising, but that is offset by lower prices. Costs may or may not be lower than the manufacturer's brand operations depending on economies of scale, both raw material buying and logistics, and quality.

The pressure for private label is partly cyclical. In a recession, the consumer, and thus the retailer, becomes more price conscious. At the same time, demand falls and the producers have surplus capacity. The retailer's sales of private label increase and the retailer seeks not only cheaper prices, creating an auction, but a broader range of private label products.

The manufacturer has the possibility of supplying private label *or* own brand products. The vexed question is whether to supply *both* private label *and* own brand. Here are some of the classic reasons for doing so:

- Maximizing the share of retailer's supply will allow you to become the category leader and thus be the main adviser on category management, as above. Not to supply this key part of the retailer's strategy will exclude you from this position.

- Increasing volumes can increase any buying and logistics economies of scale.

- Category dominance brings its own rewards, e.g. in dictating prices and margins.

- The plant is underutilized. Private label will have minimal marginal costs as the plant is already paid for.

- Given these low marginal costs, private label business is profitable.

- Private label organizations are market, not brand, oriented. Brands are dying whereas top quality, customer responsive, service is the future.

- If a firm refuses to supply private label when the retailer asks for it, reprisals across the board may follow. A weak brand may only maintain its position on shelf if the firm agrees to supply private label as well.

- Supplying poor quality private label will show how good the branded quality is. Retailers know about this ploy. Today they seek product quality to match, or exceed, branded quality.

- If you cannot beat them, join them. Private label accounts for more than 30 percent of food sales in Germany and the UK and about 20 percent in France. It is growing in Europe and the US and no category is proof against it.

And here are some classic arguments against:

- When consumers discover, as sooner or later they will, that the firm supplies private label alongside their own brands, the credibility of their brands will suffer. Kelloggs take this seriously enough to advertise the fact that they supply no private label. Mars took a firm line against private label until June 1995 when they announced in the UK that they would make some grocery products available.

- The organizations and production systems suitable for brands and private label are different. United Biscuits tried to solve that by having separate companies in the group competing against one another. Predictably the private label company, which would leak a new technology to their customers as soon as the

> **The vexed question is whether to supply *both* private label and own brand.**

branded company marketed it, proved more profitable than the branded company. They tried to hold up releasing new technology but that is tough to do. "Predictably" because the benefits of advertising take time to show through whereas the costs are immediate. The two companies have since merged, largely under private label management. Whether UB brands can survive in this environment is a moot point. Short term they have done well. UB has a 50 percent market share – impossible if they had kept to brands. The branded share of market has been falling by 20 percent p.a. whereas UB's biscuit division has grown at about 10 percent.

- Filling surplus capacity is a temporary phenomenon that becomes permanent, like taxes. Sooner or later, new plant is needed and to walk away from private label supply will antagonize the customer.

- The problem of surplus capacity is cyclical. It is more profitable in the long run to brazen it out.

- On the other hand, if there really is a long-term surplus of production capacity, e.g. beer in the UK, then private label is no solution. What we gain in auction today will be taken from us in auction tomorrow. Private label profits will spiral down.

The debate in brand companies, about whether or not to supply own label, is liable to become heated. The device of supplying own label in categories where brands are weak but not in those which are strong may be rational but is seen as appeasement. Once supply has started, it will only expand. Once you provide private label for one retailer, how can you resist others? Once you do it in one category, how can you refuse private label in your strongly branded categories? You cannot lose, they say, part of your virginity, nor can you get it back.

The profit arithmetic is usually in favour of private label supply (if not there is no issue) and the strategic arithmetic, for those companies with big investments in brands, against.

Here are some ways out of the box:

- Address the total capacity problem. The cognac producers in France do a wonderful job regulating supply to demand.
- Subcontract the private label to another. Since it was marginally profitable, if at all, you may make the same margin, satisfy the retailer, and not compromise your dedication to your own brands.
- Offer the retailer a new flanker brand, uniquely for that chain if need be. At least you will end up owning any brand equity that arises.

While some companies may find ways of spanning brands and private label, United Biscuits, for example, most should decide whether to fight the private label movement or to adapt to it, even if brands are abandoned. Instant coffee and petfoods provide examples of how this can be done. Nescafé fought off a UK threat from private label with higher quality and, surprisingly, higher prices. Consider:

- Enlivening the category with product improvements, extensions, advertising, and promotions.
- More professional consumer understanding of product needs and propensity to pay for quality.

HERESIES

At this point, heresy looms. To remind those whose grasp of ecclesiastic history may be a bit faded, heretics were burnt or otherwise put to painful death whereas unbelievers were treated as potential customers, fêted, and regaled. It seems a bit harsh that those who agree 99 percent with your own views should be treated so much worse than your outright opponents.

Category management in its original form is entirely consistent with marketing designed to maximize brand equity. The supplier's portfolio should be aligned precisely to ensure that the aggregate brands' equity is maximized through as little internal waste as possible. Similarly, gaining retailer attention and trust to maximize the shelfage available to your own brands is wholly beneficial.

In practice, the category macho polemic overtakes fundamentals, rather as it has above. Category dominance becomes a goal in its own right. Market share, dangerously equated with brand equity, becomes the key measure irrespective of prices, consumer perceptions, and even the brand names being used. Market share for own label *weakens* brand equity not only because brand share has to go down by the same amount but

> **Market share for own label *weakens* brand equity**

also because the dynamics of the market turn against brands.

What happens, in recessions especially, is that the sales function achieves increased power relative to the specialist marketers. We need sales today, not tomorrow, and we had better cut the advertising budget to ensure the bottom line. Better still, let us raid the marketing budget to pay for the price promotions we will run in the name of category management. Politically correct?

In adopting category-speak for customers (good), sales management uses it internally (not so good). Very soon, a case is a case and the raison d'être of marketing (differentiation and advantage) has gone out the window.

There are two other heresies we should consider while we are on the subject:

1. Marketing is about customer satisfaction.

2. Marketing is about achieving profit results. We have the product, throw more or less promotion on the fire to produce the bottom line we need.

These are both heresies, as distinct from untruths, because they are mostly right. Customer satisfaction is important but it is not enough. Likewise consumer satisfaction. Likewise achieving profits.

Marketing involves doing all these things at the same time and raising brand, not category, equity.

Memo to file

Subject: CATEGORY MANAGEMENT AND OTHER HERESIES

- When the brand plans are ready for review, check their positionings to ensure they are fighting the competition, not themselves.
- Understand how your largest customers manage their categories. What software do they use? Then use that understanding and language to gain shelfage within their domain of tolerance (see figure 3.1).
- If you really do "own the category," then the category becomes the brand. Redefine "category" to include those you will take business from.
- If you think you own the category, but do not, building the category creates opportunity for others. If you do dominate the category, redefine the category. On the other hand, building your brand will also build the category.
- Private label is a strategic decision which it is difficult to reverse. Private label just to fill short-term manufacturing shortfall is a bad decision. A total industry overcapacity will not be solved by moving deck chairs around. If you decide the private label route is best for your company, go for it. Do not attempt to ride both horses.
- If you elect to stay with brands and come under pressure to supply private label, look at more creative options for the customer to source those needs whilst reinvigorating your branded activity.
- Talk categories, think brands.

4

DISTRIBUTION CHANNELS

The rate of change of shopping habits and distribution possibilities is easily overlooked

---

Key issues

● **Channels are changing to follow the consumer. They need constant attention** ● **Disintermediation: the number of steps in the process are getting fewer** ● **Critical mass is needed to maintain the "head pressure" on each stage of the distribution** ● **Channels are for information as well as product but they do not have to be the same** ● **Channel relationships. At any level the customer is even shorter of time than money** ● **Efficient Consumer Response (ECR)**

In this chapter we will focus on the "distributor" being any merchant, including the retailer, in the chain between manufacturer and final consumer. Thus the chain is: manufacturer → importer → wholesaler → retailer → consumer. In practice, there may be more or fewer stages; we consider that under "Disintermediation and Critical Mass" (see page 61). Importers and wholesalers will be more top of mind to start with and we will conclude with retail considerations. In practice, the roles of all intermediaries have more similarities than differences.

CHANNELS

The term "channels" for distribution is neat. When business tides are high, any channel will do. Yet, beneath the surface, the shifting of invisible sands may well have changed the safe route to the market. When (tidal) recession strikes, you may be left high and dry.

The links between supplier and an importer can make their partnership seem as integral as marriage, or it can be as casual as an annual order and invoice. A distributor is not just an outlet but a partner. Classically, a major supplier/importer partnership involves emotional bonding at many levels. Such relationships, built up over many years, can be destroyed in a month when economic realities reveal changed patterns of trade.

Where the brands are complex or of high image, major distributors will be expected to contribute much more than their basic economic functions of breaking bulk and reselling. An importer typically creates and executes the local marketing plan as part of the whole. Local knowledge of the marketplace is referred back to be integrated into that total marketing plan.

In 1980, there were many wine and spirit distributors in California. By 1990, there were effectively only three. Why? Historically, California had been treated as three regions: north, south and the inland valley. Each area had its own set of wholesalers trading with the US importers and manufacturers. Three events then occurred: retailers merged to form state-wide chains, the US wine and spirit trade consolidated at the supplier level, and California set aside its "fair trade" legislation which set minimum margins for retailers.

The newly powerful retailers then pressured the wholesalers of each brand to pitch for their business on an all or nothing basis effectively shutting out all but the largest wholesalers. The resulting consumer discounts undercut their retailer competitors. Consolidation took place both at wholesale and retail levels.

Consumers were impressed by the value for money now available from the chain stores and, subsequently, from the price clubs. In the USA, club stores grew by about 20 percent in the early 1990s while other grocery outlets stagnated. Armed with the appropriate plastic card for their price club, any consumer could buy the brand leaders at low, low prices. Driving miles to get this benefit seemed not to bother many Californians: home to a Southern Californian is a place on the freeway.

The number and roles of intermediaries in the channel from manufacturer to consumer vary by product category and country.

The Food Marketing Institute forecast that "alternative format" retailing, mostly clubs, would grow from 21.3 percent in 1991 to 41.4 percent in 2001, though this second wave will be driven more by the new "supercenters", more like European hypermarkets. The club format has lost momentum for a number of reasons: novelty wear out, no new stores are needed, unattractive shopping experience, heavy pantry investment. Research shows that price savings are offset for the consumer by the greater volume purchased, and then used.

The number and roles of intermediaries in the channel from manufacturer to consumer vary by product category and country. Some are simply buying and re-selling. Others undertake marketing activities. Meanwhile, retailers are building their own brands in competition with the suppliers whose goods they carry.

Even so, there are four trends in distribution:

1. Consolidation by retailers and brand owners forces those in between – the distributors – to merge or quit. This is because the more powerful brand owners, with broader portfolios, can afford to undertake tasks previously provided by their customers. Likewise, major retailers, such as Walmart in the USA, do the same to their suppliers in reverse. Thus firms such as Walmart and Procter and Gamble do not just link directly but integrate. This was the origin of ECR which we review below (see page 67). P&G maintains a team on Walmart's premises continuously monitoring replenishment and other marketing needs.

2. Road and other transportation links are improving. Information flows are becoming much faster. Both these forms of improved communication shorten the effective distance from brand owner to consumer, and allow the number of links in the distribution chain to be reduced. This is called "disintermediation," if you want to be fancy about it. Bypassing your own customers is a delicate business not usually trumpeted in advance, but the benefits of information technology and improved inventory control include less stock sitting on shelves, less out of date or stale product, less double handling and better prices for the brand owner and/or consumer. A further benefit can be the quality of information for the brand owner (see page 64).

3. Brand owners integrate forward (i.e. towards the consumer) in order to control consumer pricing. Europe has seen great strides towards ownership by the big brand companies of their distribution systems across the whole EU, so that distributors cannot disrupt prices in other countries. Few developed countries still permit brand owners to enforce retail price maintenance, but the stronger and more consistent the line to the retailer is, the more consistent the consumer price will be.

   At the same time some retailers have integrated backwards; supermarkets in particular have taken distribution control away from manufacturers. Even where these retailers do not use in-house distribution, distributors are becoming captive.

4. Perhaps the most subtle trend is the shift created by changing consumer time availabilities. Today, many people are intensely busy, or wish they were. Managers work longer hours, the retired go back to work, the out of work seek it or create it in other interests. The 19th century concept that you only worked to enjoy leisure is long gone. There are so many forms of leisure now available that people go back to work to relax. The consequence is that people use their time in different ways: marketers and retailers respond to that.

Some believe that the greatest contribution to business productivity has not been motor vehicles or aircraft or mechanization/automation or computers, but self-service. Self-service doesn't just mean pumping your own petrol or collecting your own food from the counter; IKEA, the vertically integrated international furniture retailer, successfully gets people to assemble furniture themselves. Curious as it may seem to the rest, some consumers enjoy taking on DIY projects or taking over the services of selection and delivery which the retailer once provided. It has changed the shape of retailing. Traditional banking was surprised that customers would rather stand in the rain to take cash from the machine in the wall than wait in line to be ignored by the clerk behind the counter. Whether the aggregate shopping time has increased or not, the patterns have changed.

The car is a factor. So are cultural shifts of values, such as more men shopping, both partners working, flexible hours, and work locations. Sunday shopping, so long resisted in the UK, has become a fact of life because both partners work. Some like to shop together as part of their shared leisure experience; alternatively the shopping role is assigned one way or the other. Retail offerings say much about the local culture. Supermarkets in Germany are often functional to the point of parading cheapness. Affluent Germans, and few people are more affluent, make a virtue of price consciousness. The USA may have the widest variety of retail choice: there are around 50 different retail formats which offer food. Some attract those seeking price (clubs); others are premium and proud of it. Byerly's in Minnesota, for example, offers a luxury supermarket format with space, comfort, and beautiful food presentation. Excellent service ends with the delivery of the goods to the trunk as you drive the car out. One word of warning: be careful about segmenting shoppers by retail format. Most of us use one format for quasi-leisure, another for price, and a third for convenience. Furthermore, a store that is just convenient to one may be offering luxury to another. Those who live in Knightsbridge in London may use Harrods Food Halls but would not dream of buying anything else there.

Another factor is the computer chip. Installation that was once a skilled task is becoming replaced by an LCD display which tells you what to do next, in any global language. Cameras and microwave ovens may have started it. Shopping trolleys, for example, can have screens to help you find your way around and keep track of what you are buying.

Today, shopping is possible seven days a week and 24 hours a day. Personal shopping is supplemented by every other medium. In a hotel or an airport, you run the gauntlet of the shopping arcade to get to the room or the plane. Duty Free shopping does not exploit duty savings so much as the time available in the airport or in flight. The new airports in Denver and Pittsburgh are shopping centres as much as plane connectors.

> **Channels are changing because consumers' use of time is changing and because they have less time to spare.**

When consumers visit a price club or cash-and-carry, they are using their time, which may have no price ticket, to replace a retailer's time, which has. Channels are changing because consumers' use of time is changing and because they have less time to spare. Retailers, as we shall see under ECR (see page 67), are in the same fix. The brand owner keeps ahead by adjusting logistics systems, packaging and even products to fit the growing channels. Special packs are made available for price clubs with two objects in mind: to provide greater bulk to meet the ostensible raison d'être of these "wholesalers" and to differentiate their prices from those of other outlets.

Once a year, usually as part of the planning process, it is worth taking time properly to consider each stage in the distribution channels. Better still, go out and look at them. How can convenience for the customer be improved? In other words, where will the consumer be that can be transformed into a "shopportunity"? Perhaps that requires rethinking or repackaging the product. How can IT make usage easy for the customer? If you can take some more hassle out, you can probably take some more money out.

DISINTERMEDIATION AND CRITICAL MASS

Channels are getting wider but shallower. As the variety of "shopportunities" increases, the number of stages in the distribution chain is reduced as communications and product handling become more efficient.

The primary role of a wholesaler was to buy in bulk, hold inventory, and ship onwards in smaller units. Manufacturers had neither the knowledge, nor the facility, nor the information to undertake this role. Over time, some distributors, perhaps importers and retailers more than wholesalers but that depends on the sector, became valued as sources of local knowledge. Their ideas on how to market the brand were as good as, if not better than, the brand owner's. Three types of traffic therefore have to be separated out:

1. Physical logistics. Transportation, inventory, sales order processing, breaking bulk all have to be undertaken by someone.

2. Information to and from the market. The importer undertakes the sales role, sometimes advertising and PR too. More than that, the distributor is the source of knowledge about the competition, shifting channels in that part of the world, changing consumer behavior.

3. Decision making. Brand owners can make all marketing decisions themselves, delegate many to distributors or share the process.

Technology has made a huge difference to the first of these and some difference to all three. Production can be geared more tightly to consumer needs. Mass customization makes the car to the end user's specification. Garment makers produce rails of clothing that go directly to the store that ordered those styles, sizes, and colours. The shift from rail to road means that goods go door to door and get there just in time. Bespoke Levis are now delivered ten days after the measurements are taken at the store.

In economic terms, each stage in the chain creates value for later stages, adds costs and takes out a profit margin for the distributor. Technology is making it possible to add the value upstream, i.e. at the manufacturing stage. That and pressure on prices at the consumer end conspire to encourage the brand owner to disintermediate, i.e. cut out a stage, or even two. In making that decision it is important to consider not just the logistics costs but also the impact on information flows and decision making. Retailers are also working back and forcing suppliers to cut costs aggressively as more and more of their function is taken over.

> **Each stage in the chain creates value for later stages, adds costs and takes out a profit margin for the distributor.**

As traditional channels consolidate, new ones open up. The three decision areas for the brand owner remain the same, and are possibly even more critical:

1. Should you choose a smaller specialist or a larger generalist distribution house?

2. How much control over a distributor is necessary, realistic, or wise? The distributor itself needs to feel in control. Indeed, how much mutual dependency, true partnership, should exist, i.e. how much control should the distributor be allowed over the supplier?

3. To what extent is it desirable, or viable, to bypass intermediaries and deal directly with retailers, or consumers?

The "critical mass" concept may help. This is defined in terms of a brand portfolio rather than a single brand. A portfolio with critical mass has enough clout with the customer to gain respect, or at least serious attention. When all the major UK brewers had their own soft drink portfolios they had distribution in their own pubs but little in the retail chains. They did not have critical mass. Putting Coca-Cola in the portfolio, as one of them did, transformed their strength. Critical mass gains access to major buyers.

Anton Rupert, through the Rembrandt tobacco business in South Africa, achieved control of an international empire of such names as Rothmans and Cartier through multiple stages in the shareholding hierarchy. To have control of one level requires 50.1 percent. If the company is valued at £400 million, that will cost £200.4 million. Control can be achieved for only £100.2 million, however, by having a 50.1 percent controlled subsidiary purchase the 50.1 percent. Rupert carried this logic into longer chains of subsidiaries so that he was able to control a huge empire with relatively small investment by the ultimate holding company.

> **A portfolio with critical mass has enough clout with the customer to gain respect.**

This mirrors the critical mass problem for the small brand owner. If that brand goes directly into the portfolio of a vast distributor it will disappear from view. It does not have critical mass. However, if it has critical mass in the portfolio of a specialist import company which in turn has critical mass with the distributor, all is well. If critical mass is defined by a 10 percent share (not a bad yardstick), then a manufacturer with a single brand having a 1 percent share will not have critical mass. On the other hand, if the same manufacturer has a 10 percent share in a distributor's portfolio which also has a 10 percent share, critical mass may *just* be reached.

Thus the need for critical mass *increases* the number of stages needed for effective distribution whereas the modern trends in logistics, information, and decision making tend to *reduce* them. This conflict is one of the reasons for brands being acquired by large companies. In theory, the critical mass can be established by the reputation of the ultimate owner. When Procter and

Gamble bought Vicks, the OTC (over the counter) remedies business, there was no longer any doubt about its critical mass.

Critical mass is the threshold of power for the supplier. Below this threshold there is no power. Above it, there is the opportunity for constructive partnerships or for time-wasting positional plays. In both the UK and the USA, the increasing power of the top retailers has weakened the bargaining strength of suppliers. In the high volume categories, retailers may only need the brand leaders and their own labels or own

> **Critical mass is the threshold of power for the supplier.**

brands. Retailer power, however, has been created in part through the provision of ever larger shopping spaces with ever wider ranges to fill the ever wider shelves. This has led to some stores making it easier for small suppliers in some categories to fill specialist needs at the same time as mainstream suppliers are finding it more difficult. No one ever said it was simple.

INFORMATION

Running silently through all these issues is the need for information. Distribution is one of the basic four Ps of marketing: place. It is critical to know where the consumer is and is going to be. The channel has to finish where the consumer is and then present the brand in the best possible way. With computer cash registers, the retailer collects huge volumes of data on each brand including when it was sold and the price paid. Through syndicated services, higher levels of the distribution chain can access the same data.

The idea that producers can cope with information about every transaction concerning their brands all over the world is absurd. Some means of reducing the data to human proportions is essential. The point is that information no longer has to run through the same channels as the product. Double handling information is as wasteful as carrying boxes. Key facts, by default or intent, are likely to go missing.

When reviewing distribution channels for brands, it is worth making a parallel consideration of information. How does information get from consumer to brand owner? How could it do so better, faster, cheaper? How can market information be enriched?

The idea that the distribution database is fully open to the brand owner may strike both with equal terror. Most of us keep our clothes on to protect the public, not just to keep warm. At the same time mutual dependency needs to be matched by some trust in sharing information before it has been excessively processed. The distributor needs to know what is coming from the brand owner almost as much as the brand owner needs the plain unvarnished facts of the marketplace.

The role of the distributor is far more than just that of a merchant forming one of the links between consumer and brand owner. Whether fully independent or a subsidiary of the supplier, the distributor has separate objectives. The distributor has its own margins to worry about, own costs, and independent goals; competing distributors have to be kept out. Whatever other parts of the marketing mix they may control, each distributor reaches its own conclusions on the best balance of volume and price, typically not the same as the distributors next door. For this reason the traditional relationship is based on territorial separation at the national or wholesale levels: one distributor deals with one market.

Changing consumer buying patterns and increasing distributor consolidation are altering that relationship. A distributor may have more clout with traditional retailers but specialists, duty free shops for example, may need separate attention. A large part of a distributor's role is service, and new retail sectors can be penetrated through distributors already servicing those outlets. Increasing retailer sophistication in some sectors is reducing distributors' traditional clout; in the new car business, distributors are now little more than transportation experts.

> **The distributor needs to know what is coming from the brand owner almost as much as the brand owner needs the plain unvarnished facts of the marketplace.**

Indeed in the car business, the showrooms should represent the personality of the cars they sell. In UK practice they sell an increasingly wide variety of brands, for the reasons above, with decreasing involvement with the manufacturer. At least, the brand owner has not effectively communicated how the brand's personality should be presented and the retailer is as much concerned with the showroom's own, not necessarily consistent, brand image. The consequence is that the marketing opportunities at showroom level are not maximized. Daewoo, the Korean car manufacturer, have recognized this and, partly to differentiate, persuade the car buyer that the relationship is direct. They have integrated distribution in order to strengthen its branding.

Friction will increase if more than one distributor services one marketplace. Partitions by customer segment, as was clear in California, are eroded by the customers themselves. Those buying cheaply will on-sell to others. This factor was a driver of EDLP (every day low pricing) by brand owners in the USA. Whether or not on-selling results in further distributor consolidation, more of the marketing mix reverts to the next highest level of the distribution chain. The rationale for the distributor's existence (keeping marketing close to the consumer, cost/efficiencies) is then also damaged.

CHANNEL RELATIONSHIPS

Marketing, and especially international marketing, can be expressed as the management of relationships between the brand and the various members of the distribution chain, including the final consumer. We consider relationship marketing in chapter 25 but it is worth noting here that much of the research seems circular. Business success is correlated with successful business relationships which include trust as a key factor. It would be a bit surprising if these did not hang together but that does not mean that trust leads to success. It is more likely that failure leads to distrust. All we can really conclude from this work is that good channel relationships are usually a necessary, but not sufficient, prerequisite for business success.

Another way of looking at relationships is implied by the previous section: who has the information and how well is it shared? In the beginning, a distributor will know far more about the market than the brand owner. Assuming the brand owner has found the right distributor, decisions should largely be taken by the distributor. Over time the brand owner learns, especially when there are many distributors all passing back different experiences. Distributors are aware of their own expertise and are not necessarily anxious to share it with suppliers who, once they have learned how to do it may disintermediate them with extreme prejudice. Herein lie the seeds of distrust.

Good channel relationships are usually a necessary, but not sufficient, prerequisite for business success.

Evaluating distributor performance is as subjective as any other personal appraisal. Your own hirings may have halos whereas those you inherit have more apparent failings. Fellow subsidiaries of the same organization can be especially unattractive, since they have little dependency on the international brand manager. Large corporations, with hired hands coming and going, have a bigger problem in this area than family businesses where the relationships can succeed through generations of friendship. Multilevel contacts are the norm, not least in order to maintain continuity.

The Chinese believe that you should build the relationship first and good business may result. Even if it does not you still have a valuable friendship and that matters more in life than business. In the West we tend to do the business first and a relationship may grow as a result. On balance, the Chinese route is the more plausible though it makes heavy demands on the fledgling business in choosing which relationships to develop and waiting for cash to flow.

Managing distribution channels calls for considerable understanding of marketing, marketplace information and interpersonal skills. These take time to build and should rarely be thrown away. At the same time, recognition of the developing trends in distribution require that channels be seriously reviewed on a regular basis. Performance may be fine but if retailer and consumer purchasing habits are shifting the sands, new channels may have to be cut.

EFFICIENT CONSUMER RESPONSE (ECR)

In the UK, Electronic Data Interchange ("EDI") was originally developed as "Tradanet," as a means to reduce paper flows between suppliers and customers, and specifically to reduce the matching of orders, delivery notes, invoices, and payments. Tradanet was a logical extension of universal article numbering (bar codes) which enabled independent companies, for the first time, to identify each other's SKUs (stock keeping units).

In other words, firms originally had only their own proprietary product identifications which made shared identification impossible. The receiving firm had to recode the arriving products. Bar codes provided "universal" (there is one set for North America and another for Europe) identities. With those, electronic media could now transmit delivery notes, invoices, credits and allowances without the need for paper or clerical intervention. Tradanet was piloted in the UK in 1984 and launched in April 1985. By handling all these communications electronically, a vast amount of paper and clerical time can be saved. EDI was thus relatively more attractive to larger firms, where the start up costs could be spread across a wider portfolio. Today, EDI is a reality for firms of all sizes as their customers expect this service.

The perception that the distribution chain could be more efficiently organized, using data networks led in the USA to ECR.

The perception that the distribution chain could be more efficiently organized, using data networks led in the USA to ECR. The main attractions were more efficient replenishment through sharing information of inventories at all stages of the pipeline and smoothing promotions' "spikes," i.e. the very high sales during price promotion at the expense of continuous supply. In 1993, 16 leading manufacturers, wholesalers and retailers in the US food industry estimated that $30bn could be saved just in the grocery sector through better coordination.

Many of the companies that led the USA ECR initiative have since addressed the situation in the more complex EU market. The problems here will be greater due to the lack of EDI standards and differing national regulations. France, for example, has one of the strictest regulatory environments in the world.

While ECR is a new term, the partnership concept, with its sharing of information, has long existed in Japan and also in the clothing industry where it was known as "Quick Response." Here close cooperation is needed between retailer and manufacturer to meet often short-term fashions without leaving excessive inventory in the shops when the fashion, or season, changes.

In essence, ECR seeks to share information and sees logistics as a whole. The waste taken out of the system (the $30bn) can be spread equitably between consumer, retailer, wholesaler, and manufacturer. The emphasis on the consumer in the title is to square this horizontal (across competitors) and vertical (up and down the channel) cooperation with US competition authorities.

Thus ECR not just automates the information flows that exist but requires a new "philosophy." In other words, firms are being asked to cooperate in order to use common standards and measurement systems.

It may be helpful, at this stage, to take an example of ECR, focussed, as most of this section is, on the retailer.

An ECR case study

Golden Cat Corporation uses software to help predict sales taking into consideration promotions, bad weather, and numerous other variables and also to provide for continuous replenishment. This system cannot happen without EDI and it includes data swaps with key retailers so all mail and fax orders have been eliminated. Golden Cat wanted to help themselves deliver the best product for the consumer, and also help retailers make more money.

In one supermarket with $4m cat litter sales, category profits doubled to 4.9 percent following the changes. They changed mix of items, cut the number of SKUs held, ran just-in-time delivery of inventory, and sold product before it was paid for. Internally Golden Cat now has retail sales teams comprising of individuals from different functions (logistics, sales, marketing). Key to this outcome is the interpretation of the information that was already available to the supermarket management but they did not have the resource to analyse nor communicate the conclusions to their suppliers. By using the supplier specialists, as part of their team, to review the information and consider alternative formats, the information could be translated into actions for both supermarkets and suppliers. At the same time, those results guided the suppliers towards more effective management tools, i.e. information synchronized with their customer's management information.

Golden Cat now plans promotions and merchandising six months ahead, working from the same side of the desk as the retailers and changing the nature of the relationship. The market is now moving so that retailers focus on selling well rather than buying well, i.e. pulling customers into the store rather than pushing the merchandise onto the shelves.

ECR benefits and problem areas

ECR should not be seen strictly as an effort to improve efficiency in the grocery industry, as its ultimate goal is to use IT and closer relationships between distributors and suppliers not only to minimize costs, but also to maximize consumer satisfaction. Four key benefits should result from full implementation of an ECR program.[1]

> **Its ultimate goal is to use IT and closer relationships between distributors and suppliers not only to minimize costs, but also to maximize consumer satisfaction.**

1. **Store assortment.** Improved Category Management: what to put on the shelf, applying category specific information to merchandise management such that it improves category productivity and profitability. As the example above illustrates, the specialist skills of suppliers allows supermarkets more precise comparisons, e.g. averages for the category section rather than the whole store. Increased sales and gross margin per retail square foot and inventory turns should save the equivalent of 1.5 percent of dry grocery sales.

[1] See the ECR report produced by Kurt Salmon Associates Inc and published by the Food Marketing Institute in Washington D.C., January 1993.

2. **Product replenishment.** Replenishment at least cost for the total system and based on actual and forecasted store/consumer demand rather than ordering to meet forward buying discounts or other conventions which have arisen to take transactional advantage of the intervening market. All suppliers know their own sales but sophisticated information technology and cooperation is needed for suppliers to track point of sale ("POS") volumes and channel inventories. The total expected savings are equivalent to 4.1 percent of dry grocery sales, together with a reduction in inventory levels of 40 percent, from 104 to 61 days.

3. **Promotion.** Better measurement of promotion success through the use of actual scanner data to hold retailers accountable. Supplier reimbursement of retailers based directly on POS volume data would reduce processing and validation expenses. There is also the potential to eliminate inefficiencies such as forward buying and diverting (overbuying during a supplier promotion to sell in another place), both major problems with current promotion practices. These inefficiencies take the form of "spikes" on flow of supplier sales and, to a lesser extent, consumer sales. The frequency and regularity of price promotions in the USA, coupled with greater storage space, has led to consumers only buying when a promotion is available. Thus production and logistics are overworked during the promotion cycles and idling at other times. ECR is a strategic attempt, like EDLP ("every day low pricing"), to remove these cost inefficiencies. The total expected savings are equivalent to 4.3 percent of dry grocery sales.

4. **Product introductions.** A team approach between retailer and manufacturer should develop products that anticipate and respond to customers' needs and demands. Under old systems, sales information was so slow that initial sales were only available after the introduction had been rolled out. With modern IT, small tests can be quickly reported and grossed up to national equivalents before too much waste occurs – the great majority of new introductions fail. This also, of course, requires a degree of trust between suppliers and retailers, e.g. to ensure that figures are not manipulated. Savings are equivalent to 0.9 percent of dry grocery sales.

Problems with ECR include:

- Cross-docking of anything other than straight pallets is an added cost service. (The fork lift truck introduced pallet loading, each taking around 40 cases depending on the category and case size. Conventionally a pallet contained identical cases. ECR requires the original supplier to make up pallets of mixed cases for the end retailer which are cross-docked by the wholesaler, i.e. moved from one vehicle to another without change, entering the warehouse, or paperwork).

- Partnering that involves the appointment of one supplier as category manager can reduce the level of communication with other vendors in the category. Since the category manager is *primus inter pares*, each major supplier vies for that position and can provide good reasons for the retailer not to select another.

- Although 40 percent of projected savings are marketing related, marketers have rarely been involved in ECR deliberations.

- Beverage suppliers feel that the cost of complying with the ECR requirements has been slow to justify its benefits.

- ECR requires critical mass, i.e. enough suppliers to take part. In other words, the benefit from standardized systems, be they IT or physical distribution, only arise when standardization occurs. Procter and Gamble and Quaker Oats are using ECR with their largest retail customers but it requires horizontal cooperation (across suppliers) as well as vertical (channel).

- ECR demands a holistic change management program (re-engineering) with buy-in by all functions and individuals. This is, perhaps, the most interesting issue.

CONCLUSION

This chapter has been about ensuring the brand is any place the consumer may want to buy it. Coca-Cola have long sought universality for their brand's distribution: "within arm's reach of desire." For luxury goods, a rider should be added: any place consistent with the brand's image and personality. I doubt, for example, that it would help Häagen Dazs to have its signs outside seedy back street grocers.

To achieve ideal distribution, the whole of the channel has to be managed, not just the input and output ends.

Memo to file

Subject: DISTRIBUTION CHANNELS

- Distribution channels are reducing in depth but increasing in width. The number of steps to the consumer is reducing but the retail options are increasing. So is a brand's likelihood of being stranded. An annual review as part of the marketing plan should put new markers on the changed channels.

- Much of this is driven by convenience: fitting in with life styles. Buying and delivery when it suits the customer – at every stage in the distribution chain.

- Consider, when reviewing channels, three issues separately: logistics, information flows, and allocation of the components of the marketing mix, i.e. who decides prices, advertising, packaging, promotions.

- Ensure that each level of the distribution chain has critical mass with the next level down to maintain sales pressure.

- Whether distributors are within the same group or independent, treat them equally as partners, and seek to be treated as such.

- ECR, or the equivalent in other sectors, formalizes what technology can do to yield profit from cooperation, not competition. But the technology cannot release the money unless the channel relationships are right first. Manage them actively.

5

EXTENSIONS AND BRAND FAMILIES

Brands are becoming more complex assemblies of products and sub-brands

---

Key issues
- **Brand and line extensions** ● **Extension considerations: cannibalization, fit, brand stretch, brand revitalization**
- **Brand families** ● **Pruning** ● **Extension management**
- **Portfolio management**

BRAND AND LINE EXTENSIONS

"Brand extension" means the use of an existing brand name on a product in a new category, whereas "line extension" refers to its use on another product in an existing category. Neither covers new sizes, shapes, and colours. Thus Virgin Cola was a brand extension whereas Pepsi | **The financial incentives to extend are considerable** Max was a line extension. For the purpose of this section it is easier to refer to both as brand extensions as the distinction need not delay us.

The financial incentives to extend are considerable, especially just after a brand has been acquired. The investment has already been made and the franchise with the consumer exists. Gaining distribution is relatively simple. In the 1980s, brand extension reached cyclical peak and financially driven firms sought to exploit brand equity. The odds against new brand success, reputed to be 40–1, become closer to evens if the additional product itself performs well. The idea is not new. When Cavenham Foods bought Bovril in the 1960s, Chicken Bovril appeared soon after. Heinz made a virtue of

57 varieties a generation earlier. Since the dawn of branding, equity has been maintained, and built, by moving on with new products and gracefully discarding the old as they fall out of favour.

At the same time there are risks. Too many products under the same brand name can dilute the prestige of the name. The French call it "vulgarization;" the Pierre Cardin name was diminished from high to low premium by excessive exposure and extension over a ten-year period. Extensions can also endanger the essence of the brand. Does the addition of lemon and orange flavours to Perrier bring its fundamental purity into question?

Extensions are usually considered as new product categories at around the same relative price premium. The price of a Lacoste shirt relative to its commodity equivalent is about the same as any other Lacoste item. But when the name is licensed out to different companies, such a policy is threatened. Christian Dior suits became low-priced relative to its perfume ranges, with damaging, but since rectified, consequences.

There is another type of extension which may be more acceptable in Hispanic and Japanese cultures than in Anglo-Saxon markets: extending upwards in price whilst remaining in the same category. Whisky marketers have found it difficult to persuade British or American drinkers to buy higher qualities within the same brand, whereas Japanese expect to find a ladder of safe steps so that they can trade up and up as they become more affluent. The premium level of whisky indicates seniority. However, the portfolio that is harmonious in Japan may be less so in the USA. What is true for whisky is not true for all categories. Nescafé succeeded in persuading British consumers to trade up to Gold Blend. The product advantages were tangible. Holders of American Express cards are invited to trade up to Gold and Platinum.

Marketing, as ever, is specific to the context of country, product category and timing. Accordingly, while marketers try to standardize individual products globally, the whole brand may need to remain more flexible. Selective national brand extensions are one way to market globally while meeting the needs of individual markets.

EXTENSION CONSIDERATIONS

1. A line extension is likely to draw business away from the existing product portfolio. *Cannibalization* is measured in various ways: "market share of the existing brand if the extension had not been launched less what it turned out to be" may be theoretically correct but is impossible to measure.

Usually we just take market share before the launch less market share of the existing brand (ex extension) after launch. Sometimes cannibalization can be negative: the publicity surrounding the launch of Mars ice cream caused the original chocolate bar to *gain* share. There is some evidence that line extensions do not take share disproportionately from the original products with the same brand name, as might be expected, but evenly across all the brands in exactly the same proportion as if it was an entirely new brand. In particular, an extension will take from similar product formats rather than its own brand siblings. For example, the introduction of each further brand of compact laundry detergents took share from other compacts, not from the other products with the same brand name.

2. The new products must *fit*, and ideally reinforce, the brand positioning either where it is or, better still, where it is going. The brand has a relationship with the consumer. Will the extension strengthen that relationship? The quality of the extension must be at least as high as the original. While most marketers are sure their experience can distinguish a good "fit" for a brand extension from a bad, the evidence is that their individual responses vary markedly. We are all expert in determining fit, with hindsight. Ricoh copiers are a good fit for Ricoh cameras as both transfer needle sharp images.

3. Another way of expressing "fit" is rationality. While not essential, positive perceptions are less likely to be disturbed if the extension makes sense. The lack of a "reason why" is one more hazard for the product to cross. The Virgin extensions were less hazardous than they appeared. Records to airlines to cola to vodka are big steps in product terms but the target market and brand personality were consistent. Style can be, very nearly, all.

4. An extension may be a way of making the existing advertising budget more productive by covering more products. How far can the brand, or the advertising come to that, stretch? The wider the variety of products the more diffuse the brand personality and advertising has to be. It is like elastic: everyone knows there is some point at which it will snap. No one knows where that is, until afterwards. Crystal Clear Pepsi seemed like a good idea at the time and yet the lack of colour was a stretch too far.

5. The incremental effect of the extension, which is almost always positive, is not as important as how the whole brand looks after the event. This is not just looking at cannibalization. There are three options: extending, launching the new product with a new brand name, and using the same extra resources on the existing portfolio. What are the effects on brand(s)

equity, and total profits, from each course of action? The cumulative effect of extensions may be to dilute brand equity. Somehow this needs to be tracked.

6. Additions demand more time and effort from the sales force and everyone down the distribution chain. The effect may be to cannibalize one or more existing products or to bring new interest in the whole range. Clearly the net effect needs to be positive. It might well be the right time to prune the dead wood. Where the 1980s saw an explosion of extensions, the 1990s has witnessed range pruning to concentrate on the winners.

7. The new flag carrier, e.g. when Persil detergent took over from Persil soap flakes, is not at all the same as yet another variety, e.g. a new flavour of cat food. The difference is between revitalizing the brand and just broadening it which may, or may not, add to brand longevity. Extra width is not always good for health but it may keep others out. Occupying retail shelf space may not help the brand but it shuts others out. Nevertheless, this is not where the big money is. Much of chapter 17, "Product Satisfaction," deals with this.

8. The best extensions increase brand equity by moving it toward the desired positioning and/or moving the positioning in a healthier direction. For example, the whisky extensions mentioned above not only made more profit when cannibalization happened, they also improved the image of the whole range. Extending upwards beats extending downwards.

BRAND FAMILIES

As brands extend, the measurement of brand equity becomes complex. How do you measure the perceived quality of Sony when it appears on myriad products from televisions to local cinemas? Worse still, a "brand" may be a composite of personalities: Kellogg's Special K is quite different to other Kellogg cereals wrapped in calories. Special K is almost a brand in its own right. Nestlé paid many millions for the Rowntree brands, notably KitKat. Now the Nestlé name appears boldly on the KitKat pack. What does that do for the brand equity of (a) Nestlé, (b) KitKat? Answers to the nearest billion Swiss Francs, please.

The balloon analogy may be helpful: the greater the distance between the balloon and earthly reality, the bigger "footprint" it has but the air is thinner and it has to be larger and have greater lift. The balloon, of course, is the brand: the higher it is, the more abstract its values have to be. The more products it carries in its basket, the more lift it needs.

Thus the apparent attraction of the megabrand (just one advertising budget) is offset by the increasing size of that budget. These megabrands do not get the relevance or differentiation provided by unique products and have to achieve ersatz differentiation through advertising. This option is not as cheap as accountants would like it to be.

> **These megabrands do not get the relevance or differentiation provided by unique products**

Again we see cultural differences between Japanese companies, where the *keiretsu* names like Mitsui or Mitsubishi carry great reassurance for the consumer, and some western fmcg giants, where the corporate name would send consumers straight to the list of preservatives.

Where brand names are all tangled up in some hierarchy and where they spread across a proliferation of products, there can be no easy answers to measuring brand equities. As the numbers become more confusing, the concept of brand personality becomes stronger. The marketer has to start by considering the extent to which these brand and product interrelationships reinforce one another or compete. Then the team can consider whether each brand personality is strengthening or failing. The principles remain the same.

PRUNING

In principle, pruning is just negative extension. Mirror images should apply and yet it is not symmetric. The incremental calculation tends to favor the addition of some SKUs (stock keeping units) so long as they are priced higher than marginal cost. The reason for this is that incremental steps for product addition are small whereas the incremental steps for the addition of production and overhead facilities are usually large.

Of course, heroic assumptions can be made to justify additions or deletions of products. We have noted how extensions and rationalization tend to move across industries in waves of fashionability as marketers copy each other.

> **Extensions should usually be incremental while rationalization should be rare but comprehensive.**

We witness this lack of symmetry in pricing too. Generally you should increase price in small, inconspicuous steps but flaunt large decreases. Similarly, extensions should usually be incremental while rationalization should be rare but comprehensive. This makes it easier to package up the tail for sale to someone else, as Seagram and United Distillers did in the USA.

The reason for this is that the overheads must be disposed of along with the products if the savings are to be achieved. Rationalization is required in order to reduce the number of sales forces. An alternative is to *avoid* investment in new plant or facilities through rationalization of the less profitable SKUs.

Usually driven by profit, marketers should consider the implications for brand equity. The increased focus may well be positive and offset any profit shortfall.

EXTENSION MANAGEMENT

Extension policies may be easy to agree; implementation is not. A poor fit well presented within the style and personality of the brand may work better than a perfect fit clumsily introduced. Taking a brand extension to market involves participation by many managers. Harnessing combined experience, or corporate learning, should maximize its chances, but do nodding heads around a table indicate true agreement or the after effects of a fine lunch? The subtlety and subjectivity of brand extension make it particularly vulnerable to misleading research and false consensus.

Marketers should also be clear about the risks. At the very least a brand equity assessment should be made using pessimistic forecasts.

It can be worth sensitizing management to these risks by playing an extension-testing game before any decision to extend the brand. Specialist consultants and academics will have variants of this game on computer disks, but the basics are simple enough. A set of possible extensions are created for well-known brands. Each respondent is then asked, separately, to score the extension on quality of fit with the main brand and likelihood of success both as an extension and overall, i.e. the net of cannibalization or other negative impacts on the rest of the business. Finally, the respondents are asked to identify brand extensions by competitors which have proved either beneficial or prejudicial to their businesses and ascertain why.

The purpose of the game is simply to highlight to those concerned what the factors are and the divergencies (if any) in their separate opinions. Agreement, naturally, is no indication of being right; all it shows is that when the actual decision is made, any apparent consensus should also be real.

PORTFOLIO MANAGEMENT

In considering extensions for an individual brand, most managements will also be thinking of the whole portfolio. At any point in time, they have expertise with existing brands, products, and customers. They can elect to develop that expertise into new directions or deepen their knowledge. Figure 5.1 considers brands and products. As the firm moves from top left of the diagram to bottom right, their expertise declines and their exposure/risk increases.

Product category

	Existing	New
Existing (Brands)	Line extension	Brand extension
New	New brand development	Diversification

Fig 5.1   Extension options – brands and products

Figure 5.2 is a similar analysis for products and customers. The top left box, market penetration, is the area of greatest safety but has diminishing returns. Sooner or later the firm will have to develop new products and/or new customers. Current thinking, with its focus on "core," regards diversification as risky: the firm should develop one dimension at a time.

Products

	Existing	New
Existing (Customers)	Penetration	Brand extension
New	New users	Diversification

Fig 5.2   Extension options – products and customers

Figure 5.3 translates 5.2 into a US Smirnoff example. The previous product line was strictly domestic vodka. New products for existing consumers were Citrus Twist (flavoured with citrus) and Black (premium, Russian made).

Products

	Existing	New
Existing	Red label Penetration	Citrus Twist Black
New	In bar sales	Singles Non-alcoholic mixers

Customers (row label)

Fig 5.3   Smirnoff Vodka – US example

"Diversification" was represented by non-alcoholic mixers and "singles," both aiming to be more appealing to new drinkers than traditional vodka. Market development, in a sense, was also a factor here as mainstream Smirnoff, as the creator of the vodka market, had few new consumers to find. The problem was more to bring lapsed users back.

Some observers believe that Smirnoff has been more successful with product development than diversification or market development. While this may be the pattern typical for other brands in Smirnoff's situation, that is far from being a rule.

Memo to file

Subject: EXTENSIONS AND BRAND FAMILIES

- How well do the products reinforce the brand? Are there others which could be more positive? Brand extension is not a patching job but long-term alignment of a brand's personality with products which strengthen total brand equity over time.

- Brand families embrace many different products and linked names on the same products. This complicates brand equity, especially equity measurement, but it does not change the principles. How well are the brand personalities and products working together? How are their life signs?

- Extend incrementally but rationalize dramatically to reduce blocks of overheads at the same time.

- Develop extension and portfolio management skills ahead of extensions. New products and consumers demand new skills.

6

FAILURES BRING SUCCESS

The only true failure is the failure to try: experimentation should be encouraged

> ### *Key issues*
> ● **Recognition of the importance of failures to corporate learning. Ways to benefit** ● **Keep failures small but encourage experimentation**

Managers in some companies regard failure the way a rodent is petrified by a snake. As a result, immobility guarantees the very result they want to avoid. Blame corporate culture not the manager.

Their different treatment of failure is another area where Japanese culture gives its marketers such a start over Westerners. They see failure as an instructive step towards success. Failure is not shame or to be swept under the carpet with unseemly haste. Carpeting in Western offices, however, is well cushioned.

Toshiba launch more failures than their US competitors launch products in total. Each failure is a prize to be taken back into the company and for the reasons to be analyzed. The whole total quality movement stems from this enthusiasm for tracking errors back to their sources. Try that in the UK or the US and the meeting room will be empty. Association with failure is career threatening; credibility is damaged. The process that caused the error needs the correction, not the blame. The Christian Church latched onto the concept of being against sin, but in favour of sinners, 2000 years ago. Maybe we lost it as part of Puritan intolerance.

Failure is recognized by educators as the key to learning. Most of us learn by doing, not by reading the instructions. In the process, we get it wrong.

Rather than admit to that, some teachers compound the cultural problem by trying to protect children from failure. The sense of failure, we are told, leaves deep and indelible emotional scars. It is impossible to fail some examinations; the worst possible result is to pass with an E grade. No wonder young marketers have difficulties. To reach such eminence, they have been outstandingly successful in classes where failure was unknown. Now they want to try things in order to learn and to gain experience. They try their new ideas on seniors and colleagues who say such concepts have already been tested and failed or fall outside corporate acceptability. Soon enough, the tyro marketer stops getting such dreary advice. Is not marketing the business of continual controlled innovation? Then comes the threat: "Yes, you can try it if you insist, but be sure it will succeed before you do."

> **See failure as an instructive step towards success.**

Wiser educators and managers distinguish between small failures and large ones. An infant learns about height by falling off a chair. Falling out of a window may be more instructive but even less career enhancing. For one of Toshiba's many launches to fail in the market is no more than falling off the chair. A Western company, in the effort not to fail at all, may research a product long past the optimal launch date. The eventual launch falls out of the window. New Coke, extensively researched, is an example.

Creating the environment where small failures are encouraged in order to provide the raw material for success is not just fixing the culture. Business practices need to be changed too. Experimentation has to be made possible. In the ice cream business, trying a new product out in the market should be easy. If the business cannot handle small-scale production for testing, it should. At the other extreme, Boeing will not build new aircraft for young managers to play with. Experimentation has to take other forms. Creative organizations make space for failures with low penalties and each achieves it in a way compatible with the business.

In the 1960s, IDV discerned that UK consumers admired sherry that was pale and dry but actually preferred it to be sweet. Croft Original was born and succeeded. The same logic was promptly applied to table wine: consumers admired red but drank sweet. No sweet red table wine existed in any volume. Docura was created, researched well and proved an instant disaster in the market. The failure was analyzed with the conclusion that the source, Portugal, was a mistake and that the tannin content was excessive: it clashed with the sweetness. Two years on, a red Hungarian wine, St Stefan, was launched with a better liquid. The pack and the source were still wrong. It was not just any red wine that consumers admired: it had to be French. The late '70s saw Pierre Picard, a Vin de Pays with special dispensation from the French authorities to allow sweetening with grape must (juice). Sugar is not allowed. Still too much tannin. Finally, Le Piat d'Or hit the jackpot and became far the most successful table wine in the UK.

There are three morals from this tale:

1. Research is an unreliable guide to marketplace performance.

2. Failure is instructive.

3. Keep the failures small. None of Le Piat's predecessors cost much.

Once eventual success is achieved, the stepping stones of failure acquire nostalgia, even affection. In hindsight, their value is obvious. What about beforehand? Enthusiasm for failure can be overdone. Failures are genuine, authentic mistakes. Preparation had not been skimped. The launches were not taken lightly. Those concerned were mortified by their lack of success and would have much preferred they had never happened. How, before the event, do we distinguish diamonds from coals? They are made from the same substance. You may as well face up to the fact that you cannot predict. Experimentation needs to be built into corporate culture.

The value of a mistake is the amount it adds to corporate knowledge. If the corporation has already spent a small fortune to discover that square wheels do not roll, allowing a new manager to make square wheels will not win any prizes for leadership. Yet, no organization can distinguish what it knows for sure from its collective prejudices. All it can do is to ensure that any innovator is aware of past experiences before the innovation gets to market. Encouraging experimentation does not mean protecting mavericks from internal doomsters. If they cannot weather the doomsters, their product is unlikely to weather the greater hostilities of the market. The trick is to leave the ultimate decision to the mavericks and then protect them from the consequences. The firm will never learn from failure if those who make mistakes do not stick around to add that failure to corporate learning.

Senior management should provide the maverick with an acceptable list of excuses from which to choose, in the event it goes wrong:

- The boss said it would not work. He has never been right before.
- The idea is just a little ahead of its time.
- The profits to the rest of the range offset this loss.
- The cost was fully provided out of *last* year's profits.
- This project has really energized the R&D function.

- What we have learned from this failure makes success now more likely.
- The Chairman's wife suggested this idea at the last Christmas party. What else did you think we were talking about?

If none of these will work, you are working for the wrong company.

Is this subversion in jest? Partly. Failure should not be a solo activity. The reference to the individual maverick above was misleading. As again is apparent from Japanese successes, the marketing process should be collaborative. Marketing is a team job. The assessment of what can add **The value of a mistake is the amount it adds to corporate knowledge.** to corporate knowledge can only be collaborative since that is where the knowledge resides.

Some say that the only failure is the failure to try, but reality is more subtle than that. Maintaining standards, doing things as well as the organization knows how, are basic business skills. Sloppy work deserves no excuse. Encouraging well-directed failure is not permissiveness, and is certainly not a deviation from clear focus on skills and objectives. It is a determination to build on those skills.

If an organization does not have a failure culture, what can it do? Sudden proclamations on the virtues of failure may not be believed, or lead to some remarkable disasters if they are. Announcing a policy of allowing failure, and then sacking the first manager who does so may be recognizable organization behavior, but business schools advise against that sort of thing. Changing culture head-on is itself as likely to fail as not. History is not encouraging on this point. Changing reward systems (i.e. what triggers bonuses) has a better track record.

It is easy to welcome failures in theory; in practice they are uncomfortable. What can you do in practice? The informal lunch is one route. The value of the "Educated Lunch" is discussed in chapter 12. CEOs who are prepared to break bread with their juniors and swap failure stories have already cracked the problem. Any CEO is bound to have had more failures, and with any luck more amusing ones, than junior marketers. The steps from talking to learning are not so great. What is a top manager if not a teacher?

The recognition of the importance of failures to learning and ultimate success is more than just the encouragement of experimentation. To try is not enough; what is learned from the trial is what matters.

Marketing is not just an analytical science. Any successful marketer will acknowledge the significance of luck. The successful give luck a better chance to happen. Excessive research, long delays, and bureaucracy are reducing the opportunity for luck to strike.

Napoleon did not want clever generals, he wanted lucky ones. Lucky ones are prepared to risk failure. The faster the plan → experiment → measure → corporate learning → plan cycle goes around, the more often luck gets a chance.

Memo to file

Subject: FAILURES BRING SUCCESS

- Ongoing success requires continuous experimentation.

- Recognize that small failures are an inevitable consequence, however hard we try to avoid them.

- Ensure managers try hard to avoid failure by fully using corporate learning thus far.

- The only failures that should be punished are the failure to learn and failures of excessive size. Do not fail big where you could as well have failed small.

- Applaud, even reward, learning from failure, but not the failure itself.

- Speed. The rate of learning is what keeps you ahead of competition.

- Luck. Invite consistently unlucky managers to get lucky some place else. Whoever said life was fair?

7

GLOBAL MARKETING

National borders have declining importance to marketers

Key issues
● Multinationals are going global. Why? ● Global marketing may utilize more effective segmentation than national boundaries ● Not Invented Here, the central challenge to international marketers. Kill it or be killed by it ● Organizational issues. Divide and rule? Internal competition? Transfer pricing. Shared learning.

GOING GLOBAL

Does it pay to be global? Not necessarily.

Global marketing became an issue from the time Ted Levitt published *The Globalisation of Markets* in 1983. His point was that people around the world were more alike than different. Modern communications were increasing universality. The world was becoming a global village. Marketers would make more money, he claimed, by concentrating on the similarities and forgetting the differences.

Outside the high tech industries, this was not the general experience and other gurus were quick to react. Philip Kotler, author of the main MBA textbook[1] on marketing, argued that marketing was all *about* differentiation, distinguishing consumers' needs and your brand in such a way that value and profits could be established. To ignore differences would ignore the very roots of marketing. Companies needed to see things in multinational, or

[1] *Marketing, Management, Analysis, Planning, Implementation and Control.*

better still, multilocal terms. Coca-Cola wrote to agree with Kotler. Yet by 1992, Peter Sealey, Coca-Cola's Senior Vice President, Director of Global Marketing, addressed an international conference on "Global Beverage Marketing: Getting Ready for the 21st Century". Coca-Cola is now perceived by many to be the archetype of a global marketing company.

| **"Think Global, Act Local"**

Similarly, in 1987, Procter and Gamble did not consider itself to be a global company. Five years later, it did.

Those five years marked a major shift in thinking towards global marketing. Since then common ground has emerged around the cliché "Think Global, Act Local" though that can be translated to almost any combination of local and global marketing authority. Even in the same company.

Levitt saw the world as a single market place for which there is a single marketing plan, with uniform programs, and a single coordinated production and distribution system. Products are made wherever the customer delivered costs are minimized. Everything is standardized; decisions are centralized. Focussing on that main chance would indeed cause a company to miss opportunities for non-standard demands but the efficiency savings would offset the lost profit. Few companies fully meet that definition, but many lean towards it. Ford, for example, aims to meet Japanese competition by using its geographic base to produce world cars.

Is there, then, a global consumer demanding a global product? I very much doubt it. The consumer's mind discounts differences where it expects to find differences. Scots know Germany is foreign before they get there. If their favourite breakfast cereal is in a different package in German supermarkets, are they less likely to buy it when they get home? Over the course of ten years, Absolut vodka grew from launch to a dominant position amongst premium vodkas in the USA. At the same time, it was sold at a discount in Canada. There was a three thousand mile, well-trodden border between Absolut priced at 60 percent more than Smirnoff on the American side and 20 percent less on the Canadian (and in Canada, the brand did not sell). If brand consistency mattered, it did not show.

The main drivers towards globalization are usually seen to be:

● **Costs.** For some industries, e.g. cars, globalizing production can indeed save money. Making one advertisement for the world should, in theory, be cheaper than separate ads for each country. In reality, once an agency knows it is a global ad, the production costs escalate dramatically. Ask BA what Maurice Saatchi charges for theirs.

● **Speed of new product roll out.** Procter and Gamble launched their two-in-one shampoo/conditioner as Pert Plus in the USA and then under the Vidal Sassoon brand name (called Wash 'N' Go in the UK and some other markets) in about 40 countries in the four years 1987–91. Unilever took more than ten years to introduce Timotei, a similar product, to the same number of markets. P&G today would consider one country a month to be too slow. Now that communications are so fast, your competitor will have the results of your test market as fast as you have. As you know, to copy your brand in the same market would be a "me-too." To copy your success in a country before you get there, as IDV did with Malibu, is a "me-one." To avoid this, global companies research, and then roll out, their new products in parallel, not in series.

- **Competition.** As a general rule, where the competition has globalized, you probably have to follow. Unilever had to globalize, or at least regionalize, in those categories where they were up against P&G, but not the others.

- **Quality.** The world car is a *better* car. Each engineering culture from around the world will contribute what each considers important. Each country's consumers will insist on their particular foibles. Americans, for example, have to have cup holders in their cars so that they can drive, throw money into toll booths, and drink coffee at the same time.

- **Media.** Print and electronic media are now hooked up to satellites with footprints bigger than single countries. They have at least regional, if not global, space to sell, and advertising agencies are there to help them.

- **Central overheads.** The central driver towards globalization is the need to justify central overheads. This is not quite as cynical as it may sound. If all the business units were wholly oriented towards their own markets and heedless of the wider world, how would central management add value to the business? It would simply be an unnecessary cost, and the group would be better broken up and sold off; no wonder CEOs are keen to proclaim global tendencies. In fact, the central function adds value not only through cross-fertilizing best practices from one unit to another, but also through the growth of corporate learning in the process. Achieving the benefits from commonality needs central leadership.

Is it more profitable to be global? For some, e.g. Ford, it probably is, but only for a very few. Any company with a single HQ where virtually all decisions are made, airlines or Japanese companies being examples, can be global. Most already are. Australians invented the "born global" concept because exports, even for start-up ventures, looked more appealing than the domestic market. From Sydney, the whole world looks about the same distance away. For multinationals, however, the costs are considerable. Decision making which seeks to preserve any kind of country autonomy, i.e. consensus, involves endless meetings and airfares. Autocracy may be quicker and cheaper but may miss the critical local detail. For most multinationals, going global is a painful evolution with regionalization a convenient staging point. In the long run, they know some balance between global and local authority makes sense. "Authority" because we are not talking marketing as such but who makes the decisions.

> **Going global is a painful evolution with regionalization a convenient staging point.**

SEGMENTATION

Some see multilocal and global as ends of a spectrum. Every market can be treated as completely the same, or as completely different. To find a rational middle position, you can plot the economies of scale against the benefits of bespoke attention to each market. The benefits of scale are not just in engineering and production. R&D in pharmaceuticals, for example, needs the widest possible sales outlet and the least possible internal duplication. News media, both electronic and print, share their collection, collation and editing costs. Partly or fully standardized material is beamed for local printing or broadcasting. Murdoch and Conrad Black clash worldwide. The BBC competes with CNN. Murdoch ditched BBC in order to team up with China News. The multilocal to global spectrum does not tell the full story. A global marketer treats the world as one marketplace and one source of supply.

National boundaries are just a form of segmentation; the global company can segment in many other ways. So long as the advantages of variety outweigh the costs of production and reaching the consumer, the global marketer can compete in as many niches as it chooses. With the automation of more and more intelligence into production lines, it is possible to match consumer choice quite precisely with output. At the end of that rainbow mass customization provides individual customers with their bespoke product from a central automated factory.

Global production, or not, is a matter of arithmetic; global marketing is a matter of personal identification. International marketers may identify more with the executive traveller segment, of which they are part, than with the population of any single country – especially if the marketers spend more time in airports than in their home country. Either all consumers are similar enough to be considered globally or they should be segmented into manageable separate groups. In theory, the individual differences within any one segment should be less than the differences between segments. "Total Research," a US market research company, divides people into six segments: Rationals, Self-Gratifiers, Status-Seekers, Fast-Trackers, Functionals, and Conventionals. They claim these operate worldwide. The marketing manager for any segment needs to be close to that segment both psychologically and geographically.

> **The marketing manager for any segment needs to be close to that segment both psychologically and geographically.**

We review the pros and cons of segmentation in chapter 27. In practice, few companies see it that way. More typically they go through this evolution:

- Domestic.
- Domestic plus exports. Assume the foreigners want the same as the domestic market and adjust the products only if you have to. IKEA assumed that their furniture, so successful in many European countries, would be fine in the USA. Only when sales flopped did they discover that beds, for example, needed to be larger.
- The overseas operations grow in function (accounting, marketing, perhaps production) and independence. Ultimately they become multinationals with "barons" running the countries as personal fiefdoms.
- As recognition of the need for global thinking grows, the painful evolution begins.

Thus national segmentation was never the conscious choice; it just grew that way. As we look back from the future, however, country boundaries will seem just one of a number of possible ways of segmenting the global market. To the extent that language and cultures continue to differ, that will continue to be a good option.

International brands can carry more status and therefore price. International branded whiskies, rum, and vodka have been growing in Europe when local spirits have been falling. The "imported" label still adds value in the USA.

One conclusion is that, measurable or not, some products fit the global dimension better than others. New technology is new to everyone and therefore has global marketing propensity. Food and drink, however, are traditional products imbued with local cultural associations. How true is this? Are not Big Mac and Coke universal food and drink brands? Protagonists of global marketing argue that young people are less culturally rooted; what may be meat and drink to their elders are acceptable facets of American culture to them. Most examples also have counter-arguments and rationalizations made to fit. Some products do globalize better than others; in particular the more premium brands, relative to their immediate competition, are likely to internationalize more readily. Ignore the nay-sayers. Only trial will expose them to that possibility though it is wise to do some qualitative research country by country to save embarrassment. Some names do not travel well: "Durex" means socks in Mexico and condoms in the UK. No doubt this explains the reputation of Latin lovers.

NOT INVENTED HERE

You would have thought it pretty obvious that the marketing perspective of the manager depends on that manager's altitude. When just about level with the marketplace, the immediate surroundings have more prominence than the distant and the contour of every local hillock and depression dominates his landscape. Some 33,000 feet up in the intercontinental Jumbo it all looks nice and flat; furthermore it looks much the same. The colors change a bit from green to brown. The international manager makes a note to remember local differences. Then the third type of manager is submerged by the market, cannot see a damn thing, and has to do it all by feel.

When these three managers get together they are all market-oriented but their minds' eyes see three landscapes. In particular, the aerial view reveals only similarities; the others see only differences. From this simple variation in perspective arises the central obstruction to international marketing known as Not Invented Here (NIH). The traveller brings successes from other markets to teach the locals; the locals use those examples to teach the travellers about the (differences of) their market. In the worst case, neither learns anything from the other. Yet both are doing their best to help. It does not take long to degenerate **Penetrating NIH barriers in order to share that learning is most of the challenge.** to the point where each side believes that the other is being deliberately obstructive or high-handed.

This NIH phenomenon is more obvious between companies in the same group than between independent brand owners and national distributors. In the truly arm's length relationship, contractual uncertainty or just common courtesy demands that each at least pretend to listen carefully to the other.

Global marketing barely rates a chapter in most marketing textbooks because globalization has far more to do with organizational behavior, human resource management, and information systems than marketing functions. The core of an international airline is not the planes or the facilities or the engineering or the brand image, but the information systems and the knowledge the staff possess. Penetrating NIH barriers in order to share that learning is most of the challenge.

Here are seven ways which are supposed to deal with NIH:

1. The simplest is old-fashioned **autocracy**. It worked well for Alexander the Great and it works fine now. Under Ed Artzt in the early 1990s, P&G's effective decision making became much nearer the top than Unilever's. Mars can achieve rapid roll-out because Forrest Mars' executives know who owns the business. Those who forget can pick up their checks on the way out.

2. **Stronger regionalization**. Boston Consulting Group reviewed the role of regional management in 1991. Many see that as at least an interim step before globalizing. France has more in common with Germany than with Namibia.

3. **Involvement**. As BCG suggest, good modern practice is to involve national managers right up front with the beginnings of innovation. This can be done without creating teams. Being present at the birth is supposed to encourage feelings of parenthood. The involvement in innovation can be followed by parallel research in the lead markets; sequentially now takes too long. For many companies this requires a cultural shift away from secrecy to sharing information, and especially information about innovation, as soon as possible.

4. A "**lead countries**" policy gives each national CEO/company some international marketing project. They know that NIH barriers can be raised or lowered on a reciprocal basis. To progress one project needs acceptance of others.

5. **Measurement and reward systems** can be adjusted to penalize NIH and reward the open minded. It is a nice idea; I do not know how to do it.

6. **Multinational teams**, cross-functional or cross-border or both. Idealists believe that you simply have to make up teams from different countries and let them solve the problems. Forget it. Most likely the national NIH will reproduce itself in microcosm with politics in the team. If it does work, the team members that change opinions will be marginalized by their colleagues when they get back. Given a common objective and motivation (preferably including financial/career), bonding should occur

and more creative solutions ought to be implemented more effectively but at least one study[1] casts some doubt on it. The authors found that greater diversity within the team impeded innovation. What it helped was the external communications between the team and the rest of the organization. There were differences between team members and outsiders over measuring performance. More importantly, everyone may have been too quick to judge. More diverse teams have more difficulty getting going but may also be more successful if given enough time.

7. **Manager rotation**. Teamwork is no instant panacea for new product introduction; P&G did not maintain it long in Europe after their successful launch of Vizir laundry detergent in Germany, which was NIHed in the UK amongst other countries. Travel and other costs inhibit long term and long distance. Task forces for other purposes, of course, are most effective in multinationals. A longer term approach, for example that used by Japanese business, is to rotate managers across functional and geographic boundaries so that individual experience is broadened and informal networks are created. Before expatriates became so expensive, American and European multinationals did more of this. By developing a whole corporate culture in this way, the benefits of diversity are created even though it takes much longer.

I doubt there is any easy solution to NIH. Its problems are compounded because it is a disease, typically, of the organization's most talented, most creative, most driven executives. The very forces that cause them to achieve the impossible and to bring others with them are the stuff of NIH, self-belief in particular. No organization will wish to eradicate those attributes in favour of grey conformists.

Two policies may help:

1. Recognition that global marketing is more about learning than teaching.
2. One sight is worth a thousand hearings. Rather than tell the locals in country A about the great promotion in country B, fly them there to see it. It costs no more for the local to fly to B than for the international manager to fly to A.

The significance of electronic information systems for global marketing is not yet widely understood. It will be, probably the hard way. Global marketing, to be successful, requires shared decision making which in turn demands improved communications and information – in other words, global learning.

[1] Ancona, Deborah Gladstein, and David E. Caldwell "Cross functional teams; blessing or curse for new product development," *MIT Management* (Cambridge, Mass., Spring 1991)

GLOBAL MARKETING ORGANIZATION

Within the marketing mix some elements are more global, i.e. more standard, than others. On a global to local scale a typical rank order is as follows:

Variability of Marketing Mix Elements

Most global/standard	Brand name
	Product
	Packaging
	Positioning
	Advertising strategy
	Price relative to key competitors
	Advertising execution
	Absolute pricing
	Promotions
	Customer service
Most local/variable	Personal selling

In any particular company, the extent of standardization across national boundaries will vary, perhaps even from brand to brand. What is certain is that any form of global marketing requires leadership. In a single brand, worldwide business, leadership is supplied by the line managers. Multibrand companies need some form of multidimensional structure, even though the "matrix" as a term is perhaps out of fashion. Shell, who may have introduced the concept to large companies in the 1960s, officially buried it 30 years on. Someone, somewhere, should be in charge of each brand if there is to be any coherence, any active and consistent management of its brand equity. Shell is highly focussed on a single brand name. Companies like Grand Metropolitan have dozens to worry about.

> **Any form of global marketing requires leadership.**

Responsibilities have to be shared, or turf divided, between global, regional, and national management. The most highly globalized companies need only a global marketing department and local sales companies. The most multilocal companies need a global brand coordinator with very limited powers. In between, pity the marketing manager in a country with both regional and global brand managers making demands in addition to the local hierarchy.

Almost any such solution seems confused to an outsider since it requires reconciling the unreconcilable: the decision-making autonomy of each level of the hierarchy. The corporate culture, not the structure, determines whether sharing is compatible with individual manager motivation. Structure is more visible than culture, yet it is corporate culture that determines whether any global marketing formula will work. If it encourages partnership and sharing, it will survive the problems of language and ethnic differences. So too will strong autocratic leadership, though it remains to be seen how long such an approach can deal with the subtleties and varieties of the world's marketplace.

Conversely, there are plenty of opportunities for global marketing organizations to fall apart. Why share information when to do so weakens your position? Why do any-

> **Culture, information, and shared learning are the keys.**

thing which does not maximize the profit of your own unit? Internal transfer prices from one division to another are a classic area for dispute; so is the responsibility for the investment portion of the marketing spend, i.e. that part which will not earn its keep in the current financial period.

Strong international information systems and shared knowledge bases are symptoms of an organization that has already largely solved the corporate culture problem. To get there, country and brand managers' objectives, appraisals, and accounting systems may have to be re-aligned to encourage cooperation rather than competition. Not all CEOs accept that. Many believe that the best results will come from a healthy competition between top managers and their business units. To a very limited extent that is true; but in general, cooperation is more important.

The purpose of management information is motivation and action. Who cares whether the numbers are right if they prompt the right responses? The concerns with detail and independent accuracy so important for financial accounting may be less helpful for international managers needing to find shared directions. Central management can seem like it is sending down tablets of printout from the burning computer to Moses waiting in marketing. Many an international manager has been struck down by laser printer. Keep taking the tablets and you may be all right, but it is more likely that their weight will drag you down. Global companies need fast and light information, especially consumer information, that can promote effective marketing action on a wider scale than ever before.

The attention in this section has been on fmcg. In some ways the opportunities and benefits of globalization are stronger for services, notably financial services, and capital goods. But the principles remain the same: culture, information, and shared learning are the keys.

The landscape metaphor used three perspectives: high above, at ground level and from below where the market had to be sensed by feel. The global marketer has the opportunity, not open to the others, for true *vision*. In looking at the brand positionings around the world, the common element, the *essence*, of the brand should be observable. I am not here talking of the full positioning statement, target consumers, and all that, but the central raison d'être of the brand which, if it appeals in one place, should appeal in another. Neither should this be confused with the way that essence is manifested. Smirnoff's essence worldwide is "Pure Thrill" but you will not often find that as a copyline. Local marketers have to interpret the essence in the context of their own culture. An essence is something very simple that can be written in five words or less.

When Cadbury had a UK success with Wispa, and it was huge, they naturally wished to reproduce that success in the USA. Wispa is, roughly speaking, their brand leading Cadbury's Dairy Milk with air blown into it. More taste, less calories, less chocolate, less cost and more profit. The USA plant cost multimillions before they discovered it had flopped there. Why? The *essence* of the concept was "Your favorite chocolate but lighter and nicer" (OK, that is seven words). In the USA Cadbury's Dairy Milk is not their favorite chocolate, Hersheys is. They should have matched Hersheys and aerated that.

If you can persuade your Group HQ that:

- Internal cooperation, partnering, is a better idea than arm's length competition;
- Management figures should encourage it, e.g. double counting so that both the country *and* international brand team are seen to achieve the full profit;
- The worldwide brand champion should be the guardian of the *essence* of the brand, notably the positioning, and the locals should be allowed room to interpret that within the spirit of partnership;
- Bonuses should be based on total profits, not the unit's share of them;
- Information databases should be accessible by all;

then global learning can begin. Global marketing will follow closely behind

Memo to file

Subject: GLOBAL MARKETING

- Rightly or wrongly, large international companies are going global. If your competition is likely to do it successfully, you should do it first, but incrementally if time allows.

- Of the many drivers to globalization, the strongest is likely to be the need to share learning from market to market.

- And from that, a simple global vision. Write the essence of your global positioning in five words or less.

- International marketing traditionally segments consumers by national borders. Global marketers can segment along other dimensions if that targets their needs better. Global does not necessarily mean universally standard.

- Research markets in parallel to speed up roll-out, not in sequence. Otherwise your successes will be subject to a "me-one" strategy by your competitor.

- Successful international marketers recognize the differences but profit from the similarities.

- Forget structure, planning, analysis, and bureaucracy. Global marketing requires an internal culture and information systems that foster shared corporate learning.

8

HERITAGE MATTERS

Consumers buy brands they trust

Key issues
● **The importance of heritage for knowing where a brand belongs ● Introduce a brand as you would a person: establish shared experience ● Then maintain it**

BELONGING

Heritage matters to a brand. A traditional category, such as whisky, leads consumers to expect traditional brand values. A modern category, such as electronic audio equipment, may need space age dynamics. Even so the user wants to know the provenance. What track record does the manufacturer have?

Before we can come to terms with the individual, we want to know where that individual fits in. We are establishing heritage. For marketers, there is a need to build heritage as well as building the brand itself. This will allow the brand in time to fit comfortably into the consumer's mental portfolio of friends.

Unless we can track a valuable picture from artist, step by step to sale room, authenticity will be in doubt and price reduced.

A new brand in a traditional category is likely to need the same kind of veneer of age as an old master, but the marketer may decide to take the riskier route of obvious contemporaneity. The choice between old and bold will determine consumer acceptance. The brand will need some differentiation, preferably in the product itself; the consumer is being invited to abandon some other tried and trusted brand in favor of the new one. It is asking a lot to expect the consumer to accept a novel heritage too. In traditional categories, old is more likely to succeed than bold.

Even in non-traditional categories, a second-hand heritage may still be preferable. The question is still the same. What context can we give the brand personality to help the consumer welcome the new brand? Familiarity can breed consent.

While the introductory phase is crucial, heritage considerations encompass all marketing programs. A brand compromises its heritage at risk to its birthright. Bombay Gin, the premium US imported gin, was conceived for the US market in a Chicago night club at some unmentionable time in the morning during the reign of Queen Elizabeth, not Queen Victoria even though she features on the label.

> **There is a need to build heritage as well as building the brand itself.**

Bombay is packaged to reflect traditional British qualities. The picture of Queen Victoria, and the other of British Colonial India, are not false claims. If we the consumers thought about it, the trappings would be clearly trappings. Yet we have no wish to do so for we are participants in the game. In a sense, all the brands we use are our friends. We know some are cheap, some pretentious, some a little out of date, but they are our friends. But as marketers, we have to rationalize that loyalty. In this case the gin is easily distinguishable and has substantive product advantages. The Bombay packaging simply adds value to any display of drinks in the drawing room.

Retailers regularly re-create their fascias, logos and other designs to meet the mood of consumer fashion. What is historically accurate blends with what might have been. Chris Macrae[1] recounts that the association of tartans with their clans has little to do with covering the knees of ancient Scots and all to do with a visit of the George IV to Scotland in 1830. The Scots needed instant heritage. Queen Victoria and Walter Scott may have gone on to do more for Scottish history than history ever did.

Marketers tread a careful path in order to maintain both accuracy and shared fantasy without trespassing into deceit. Americans invented that fine old British firm, Crabtree and Evelyn. There are examples all over London: Penhaligons, Richoux, and pubs that were once modern and are now traditional (check if the beams are plastic). If the trend continues, London will become more fictional than Euro-Disney. If consumers favor traditional values, marketers simply follow with traditional packaging.

[1] Chris Macrae, *World Class Brands* (Addison Wesley, London 1991).

INTRODUCING A BRAND

There is an uneasy balance of heritage with innovation. Each marketer has to determine the line between good present-ation and manipulation. To select the appropriate attire or cosmetics for a party is simply good manners. That is presentation. To have people believe you are a bishop when you are not is manipulative. So can you dress as a bishop at a fancy dress party?

Every brand introduction should maximize the extent of shared experience.

Marketing is context specific. It is also subjective. What is manipulation to a consumerist may be presentation to a consumer.

Linking a brand more closely to consumer experience is a valid marketing tool. Every brand introduction should maximize the extent of shared experience. This is why brand extension is so much easier: the heritage and shared experiences are already established. Of course, if the new member of the family turns out to be a black sheep, the rest will suffer.

Introducing a brand is little different to introducing a new acquaintance at the party – dressed conventionally enough to be accepted yet with enough individuality to be noticed. Quality beats cheap but true class does not mean snobbish. True class puts everyone at their ease. A new brand must bring something special to the party or at least be amusing. And finally we want to know their provenance: what do they do? Who do they know, or rather who already knows them? To whom are they related? Perhaps life should not be like that but we want to "place" people before we can accept them. Another reason why brand positioning is so important.

Part of the introduction process is establishing shared experience. Sampling Mars Ice Cream was not just about trying the new product. It was extending the consumer's experience with Mars and it was bringing the Mars Ice Cream experience into the consumer's portfolio. Thereafter they "knew" Mars Ice Cream.

MAINTAINING HERITAGE

The consumer is comfortable with the familiar, so why innovate? To meet the consumer's wants, you should continue with whatever now exists. In "Nova-tion" (chapter 14) increasing satiation builds both the demand for innovation and the pace. Yet familiarity has to be maintained.

The brand name, the logo, the use of colours, the style of the advertising supply a large part of that. In "Product Satisfaction" (chapter 17) we discuss the need to reverse the Salami Principle: instead of taking small slices off quality, add small slices of improvements. The same concept applies more widely than just to the physical product or service. Heritage can be reinforced by constantly referring back to the brand's traditional values *at the same time* as innovations are taking place. That can be done on the packaging, with PR, through advertising, or at point of sale.

Detergents use this technique constantly. When Daz introduced its cheaper refill packs, the benefits were advertised with a hark back to the traditional Daz advertising of yesteryear.

At any point in time the brand should appear to be consistent, familiar and possessed of the same old high standards. Yet all the while it should be improving its competitive position.

In this marketing paradigm, innovations are focussed, one at a time, on where the most improvement can be achieved for the least cost or perceptible change. These elements may not all be reconcilable. If a big

> **Innovations are focussed, one at a time, on where the most improvement can be achieved for the least cost**

fix is needed, then it will have to be provided. The nature of the change will determine whether it should be flagged to the consumer or not. For example, "new, improved" may be a fine addition to a detergent carton, but not to a bottle of Johnnie Walker Black Label; Johnnie Walker packaging does change, but it does so discreetly.

Whether silent or overt, the change should be narrow, allowing all other components of the brand to retain their familiarity. The marketer may wish to stress either consistency or improvement; yet both are important. In the debates about change, newer managers are classically pitted against those with longer service. To see winners, losers and compromisers as the outcome is wrong. The consumer needs to be resold both what is to be changed and what will stay the same. To do that, stand in the consumer's shoes.

Memo to file

Subject: HERITAGE MATTERS

- Do not launch a new brand without building the right heritage to make the introduction to the consumer. Good manners matter.

- When choosing party clothes for the brand, consider not only first impressions but whether the brand is likely to fit in with the consumer's other friends.

- What provenance do you wish the consumer to associate with the brand? Who else uses it, will affect its acceptability?

- Maintain that heritage consistently through future marketing programs. From the consumer's view, what feels right?

- Change incrementally in small but frequent steps. Otherwise drastic, and therefore dangerous, measures will become needed.

- At each step, sell the new within fresh reinforcement of the familiar. Innovation is essential for the future but the old established values pay the bills today.

9

INFORMATION SYSTEMS SURVIVAL KIT

Marketing information is going from drought to deluge – how to cope

---

Key issues
● **Marketing has moved from data famine to data glut, if you can resource it** ● **Manage information or be managed by it. Complacency begets crisis** ● **Time is the thief** ● **The reasons why marketers do not have IS** ● **Developing expert systems. Progressive automation of routine** ● **The survival kit. Practical IS policies**

DATA GLUT

Once upon a time, marketers could expect intermittent sales figures, Nielsen and other market research data, records of their expenditure, and precious little else. Today, their offices have information pouring out of every orifice. Hundreds of public databases, syndicated, on-line market research, consumer panels and databases, customer records, and internal databases add up to glut. Managers may be stimulated, or swamped, by the new excess.

Both neophytes and computer literates need a survival kit. Whatever their situation now, an information avalanche is just waiting to fall. Maybe it is already falling. The prime cause of this is the electronic till.

Every marketing chain ends with a consumer's cash or cheque or plastic card. All those trillions of transactions were never before recorded. Today, every purchase, every pairing of consumer and brand can be held on a database if someone thinks it is worthwhile – what was bought, the date, time, price, where it was in the store, whether it was on promotion and what it was purchased with ("combos"). On the consumer side, who the buyer is, where you live, how much is spent, details of your family, and your credit rating can all be electronically preserved. Concerns for privacy will increase legal restraints on use, but the information is there.

> **Today, every purchase, every pairing of consumer and brand can be held on a database if someone thinks it is worthwhile.**

Information systems professionals came late to an understanding of the needs of marketing. Perhaps the complexity of marketing requires more sophistication and hardware capacity than other functions; payroll, accounts, distribution, production, assets recording are all more amenable to numeric processing. Such transaction based systems had clear payoffs which were easy to measure. The importance of information to marketing was recognized, but the provision was lacking, except in job lots. Internal sales statistics were geared to differing territories. Forecasts could not be reconciled. Research suppliers each did their own thing and supplied reports measured in inches. Nothing fitted together.

That has now changed – at least in theory. All the data now exists in electronic format and all formats can be reconciled. Research companies will supply their results in any format you like. Internal IT specialists struggle to integrate data onto shared databases. If the only sources were the traditional internal sales and expense figures and external research, the problem would be manageable. That is just the beginning:

- Retailer and wholesaler files are open to you as part of Efficient Consumer Response. Promotions can be tracked on line.
- Store level data has always been available, albeit intermittently, but now selected consumers are recording their own individual purchases, waving wands over bar codes. Information from these consumer research panels is available on tap.
- Customer care lines (see chapter 25, "Relationship Marketing") are recording what they glean from their discussions with consumers.
- E-mail and other networking, e.g. Lotus Notes, make information available from peers and colleagues.
- Visual images are stored digitally so that you can review advertising and packaging around the world.
- External suppliers want to sell you their databases and software – and so does Head Office.

Of course, few companies have the money to pay for all this. Just as well.

MANAGE INFORMATION OR BE MANAGED BY IT

Information specialists, and the military, have long distinguished between data, (the raw material) information, (data transformed into a usable format) and intelligence, (what is learned from the infor-mation) (see figure 9.1).

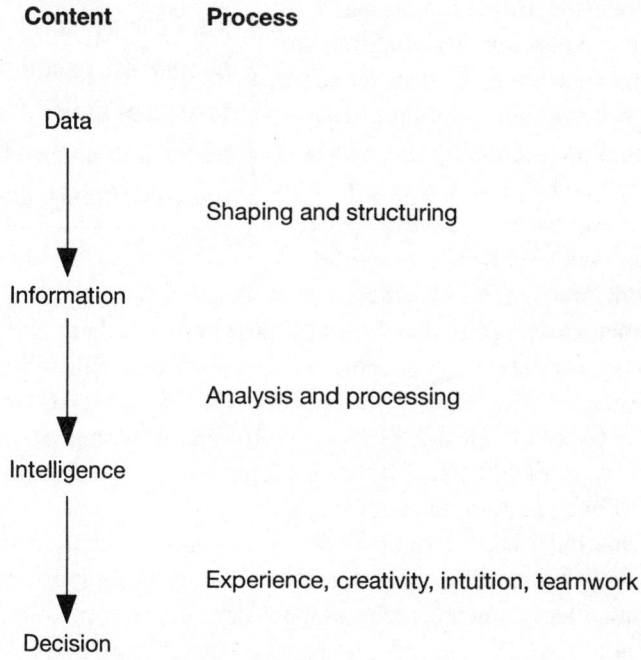

Fig 9.1 Processing data into decision

Rationalists believe management should be like this. In practice, decisions are not infrequently made before any data is in, let alone processed. Infor-mation is used to support preconceptions. Marketing managers are not alone in spending time and money to find the evidence to get the proposal through peer and senior review. If it does not get through, it is discarded. Rosemary Kalapurakal studied supermarket managers' pricing decisions, in midwest USA. These are tough and realistic people. They monitored the prices of their competitors, and reacted strictly rationally? Prices are hard data, not really open to debate. Kalapurakal's findings showed otherwise. If the price research accorded with their expectations, it was used and accepted. Other-wise, its validity was challenged.

To make the point, I exaggerate just a bit. These were just tendencies;

people are rarely so consistent. Nevertheless, it is important to be aware that managers behave like consumers. Rationality is only part of the story. Just as consumers, under the weak theory of advertising, absorb information *after* the buying decision, so managers also make the decisions first and allow information to affect their *future* behavior – especially if the decision was wrong.

Designing the way a manager will see information sets, to some extent, the way it will be used. Either intentionally, or just through unconscious assumption, the layout of a page or screen formats the order in which the mind will assimilate what is presented and the direction in which it leads. More than that, the way information is presented influences not only the decisions reached, but also the way we go about our jobs. To a large extent, we react to what we see and hear.

> **Marketers finally have choice, they should take charge of their information needs and ensure that it is *relevant, timely*, and *selective*.**

Few companies recognize that the way their computers shape and structure data for their managers also shapes the decisions that will ultimately be made. Incremental changes to systems refine what is already there but will not cope with today's nuclear explosion of information. Competition through the next generation will be substantially determined by the skill with which companies harness and use the data available.

The information used by managers determines the "orientation" of a company. One well known blue chip American company equipped all its top management with computer screens well before this was commonplace. Visitors were impressed. Walking around revealed that they all carried the stock market prices. Less impressive. Other companies are fixated by the daily takings or by quarterly profit forecasts or by production out-turns. None of these are *marketing* companies, in our sense of the word.

Marketing companies are fixated by the equities of their brands, by their relationships with immediate customers and ultimate consumers, by quantities in the distribution pipelines, and, most of all, by the quality and the perceived quality of the brands. They know that if they get the brand equities right, profits and cash flow will take care of themselves.

In this section, we have observed that information does affect managerial behavior but not in the linear fashion rationalists would like to believe. Information shapes the way we see the world and the way we do our jobs. Marketers who allow the data glut to dominate their screens will become increasingly confused. Now that marketers finally have choice, they should take charge of their information needs and ensure that it is *relevant, timely*, and *selective*.

Before considering how to do that, we need to make some space. Expert systems may appear futuristic, we are some way away from computerizing the brand management function, but the basic concept has application now.

TIME IS THE THIEF

Some 90 percent of bespoke software projects take twice as long as expected and therefore cost twice as much. Money is one reason why marketers do not have all the systems and data support they would like but time is a bigger one:

- Creating a new system today will not provide benefits for a year or two. Most marketers expect to have moved on by then.
- Most marketing departments have been delayered and downsized. The work to be done has, if anything, grown. The data glut means more work, not less. The assistant brand managers, and secretarial support, of yesteryear have gone.
- The immediate drives out the longer term (Gresham's Law).
- Doing something is quicker than agonizing about why you are doing it, still more what information you should really have and how it should all be organized.
- Any new system has its own learning hill that has to be climbed before the benefits accrue. I could save a lot of time on the PC I am using to write this if I had time to read the instructions. They are still clingfilmed.
- Computers, more than any other time saving machines, steal more time than they save. Marketers have got wise to this.

Most firms solve the time problem by assigning marketing systems development to a different team than the line marketers. After horrific experience of systems analysts failing to understand marketing, experienced marketers are usually assigned. Before you can say giga-byte, they go native. They forget what marketers do and start designing systems for what they *should* do.

> **Computers, steal more time than they save.**

This is a classic marketing piece of Zen: if you computerize what exists, waste and inefficiency are set in stone. Systems last longer than people. At least new brand managers are not bound by the flawed thinking of their predecessors, unless that is built into the system. Furthermore, a multinational, or multi-SBU, business has units doing things differently. Most agree that, given the time, trouble, and cost of creating any system, there should be only one "best practice." Furthermore, systems has a training role: systematizing what exists inhibits future development.

On the other hand, if the system represents what *should* exist, who is the arbiter of that? Some build systems from marketing textbooks and, horror, economic theory. Others ask the marketers what they want. Marketers are no more accurate in describing systems products that do not exist than consumers. Others again discover what the "best" marketing companies have and imitate that. Benchmarking narrows the gap with the leaders but it also ensures you never catch up.

We return to solutions to this conundrum below. For now, the uncomfortable truth is that line marketers have to be fully involved even though they do not have time to be fully involved.

DEVELOPING EXPERT SYSTEMS

Any analysis that can be routinized, can also be mechanized. And it should be. The idea that routine analysis is the marketer's main function, is nonsense. Machines analyze now, and more so in future, better than people can. On the other hand, relationship building can only be done by people. Marketers should be in the field building brand relationships, not sitting in front of a PC. Computers are tedious things to have relationships with. They should have relationships with each other. Networks, in fact, are part of the solution.

Analysis, in marketing, should find the unexpected and track the differences down to their source. This is satisfying work for those who enjoy holding magnifying glasses over computer printout, but it is by no means heroic. Expert systems begin with identifying the expected range of numbers beyond which the computer should tell you what happened and why. Not really why, of course, so much as the specific source of the discrepancy. For example, sales of the 100cc size are 21 percent up because of a surge in Cleveland. Even if you do have a computer that could interrogate the sales person in Cleveland, relationships demand that the brand manager makes the call.

A finished plan sets out the new year's sales volumes, market share, marketing expenditure by at least the Four Ps (see page 4), and, one hopes, profits. Whatever level of summary is printed up for managers, the computer can break spreadsheet sales into fine detail by week, by SKU (stock-keeping unit), by major customer, by area. That was four dimensions; easy for the machine but impossible for you and me. It can do the same for brand equity measures and any other number simply by extending the last year's details into the plan year in such a way that the totals reconcile. The details will not be perfect but they will be near enough. Fuzzy is fine.

As the year progresses, actual results are matched up with plan and previous year figures. Variances are explained by breaking the figures down to the next level of detail, or the next again, until the source of the discrepancy can be identified. It is at this point that many information systems fail. Forecasts prepared by other departments may not match those from marketing; lower levels of detail may not be available; comparatives may relate to the previous organization structure. Eventually someone will produce that great inanity: "the plan was wrong." The answer is not to complicate the planning process to reconcile all these different numbers but to simplify it in two ways:

1. Include fewer numbers in the plan: fewer to agree and fewer to key in. A plan should have brand equity and key P&L numbers, not much more. Let the machine automate the explosion from summary to detail.

2. Plan as a team, not separately. Then there will be only one set of forecasts and other numbers.

This much can, and should, be done today. The brand manager should collect the daily list of exceptions and make contact with those who would like to discuss them. There is no need to come into the office; his laptop should be able to take them off any phone line.

This is the groundwork for expert systems, but just a start. In some firms in the USA, it is happening now. Marketers should note, mentally or in writing, how they handle information they receive.

The more routine is taken away the more time there is for relationships and creativity.

Some they ignore, some they need to file where they can retrieve it, some causes action like the Cleveland figures. Once the consequence to certain information becomes predictable, it can be routinized and then mechanized. Now the machine is beginning to do what the brand manager does. It is becoming an expert. Some may see this as a threat but really it is a release. The more routine is taken away the more time there is for relationships and creativity, the fun parts of the job.

Those companies who have moved to daily exception reporting, but not beyond, may be in a worse pickle than those who have not started. The daily action list drives out both creativity and any opportunity for the longer and broader view. Time is the thief. Top management needs to ensure that trends and other analysis are mechanized but that will not necessarily add value.

The competition's computers are doing the same thing. Time must be released for marketers to do what machines cannot.

Expert systems should not be designed in great leaps forward but in small incremental steps. Once a piece of routine has been identified for addition to the marketing support systems, a few simple tests are required:

> **Time must be released for marketers to do what machines cannot.**

- Is this "best practice"? Would the organization's other marketers take the same action if faced by the same information?
- Is the effort in programming it worthwhile?
- Is the consequence something that needs a personal touch in order to build brand relationships? Some supermarket groups maintain full service counters even where self-service would be fine. The human contact adds values to the functionality.

We are not far from being able to prepare full marketing plans without any human intervention. Some presume they must already be written this way. If we took expert systems to the full extreme, this is where it would lead.

There are dangers here. Planning is the process which should encourage managers to learn: if they left it to the machine they would learn nothing. Producing mechanical plans to compare with the real ones is good practice which some companies are nearly doing. Quite where the pain of planning is necessary for creativity and where it should be relieved, is not obvious.

On the other hand, the convenience of having expert systems which could calculate the outcomes from alternative strategies has been demanded for many years. The "what if" facility, with transparent assumptions that can be challenged, would be a boon without compare.

THE SURVIVAL KIT

Data glut is here today or just around the corner, depending on the resources of the company. The components of the survival kit are:

- **Think the future but develop incrementally.** The occasional blue sky session, every year or two, to establish what marketers would like in an ideal world is cheap and easy. Avoid consultants, because they will try to turn the vision into business. The world of IT is awash with hardware, software, groupware, and X-ware suppliers only too happy to strut their stuff.

A shared vision of how brand management, i.e. marketing, could be ideally served by information systems is necessary to eliminate dross and ensure that each incremental change is *directionally* right. Systems cannot change direction as easily as people, and systems last for years. Resist the temptation to turn the vision into reality in one massive project. Grandiose concepts have an appalling record.

- **Use the vision to prune, as much as you increase demand.** Looking at all the new toys on offer is bound to whet the appetite even if one does have to wait till some future Christmas for Santa to visit. In many companies, for marketers just to be demanding more IT support is progress indeed. Some realist will ask about cost but, more importantly, what are the toys now in the cupboard that do not appear in the vision? What are the systems, data, information, reports that are produced today because somebody once wanted them but which are not wanted now? Those can be junked at once, possibly saving money but, more importantly, time. Most companies have swathes of nice-to-know, but ultimately irrelevant, data that can be eliminated.

- **Use the blue sky time to develop and share the "information iceberg."** Figure 9.2 is not an ink blot test. It is an iceberg.

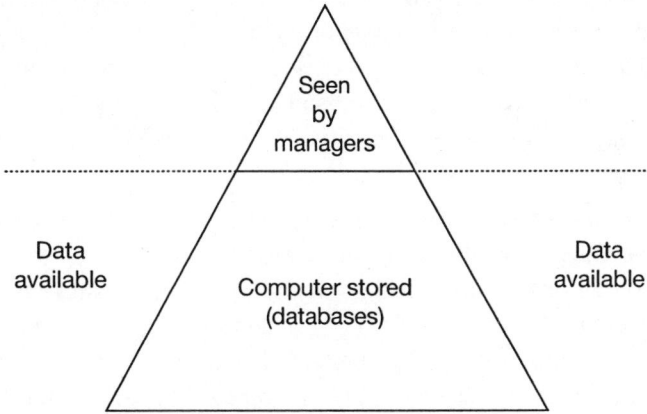

Fig 9.2   Information iceberg

The metaphor highlights three components: the visible tip of information you routinely want to see, the 90 percent the computer needs to hold in order to drill down to answer "what if" questions, to explain variances, and to track in detail, and the surrounding waters. Some of the surrounding waters may be added to the berg; some of the berg will fall away but this process should be gradual. Numbers are rarely interesting in themselves, the trends are. Constantly adding and dropping data from the database plays hell with comparatives. The blue sky event will be productive if all participants, after the toy parade is over, draw up their personal proposals for the three categories and then they are shared. In a large group, they would have to be shared across a number of such events. As a rule of thumb, the visible part should be equivalent to the numbers that appear in the annual marketing plan. The surrounding waters are the candidates for junking.

- **Forget "integrated systems."** Data needs to be integrated into shared databases to ensure accuracy, consistency, and efficiency for multiple users. That is distinct from trying to integrate the systems that manipulate those data. Integrating systems is trying to complete a jigsaw puzzle with missing pieces which keep changing. Systems are now cheap, certainly cheaper and more reliable than bespoke programming. If it fits the business and meets the needs, buy it. They can usually be customized quite simply – the equivalent of shortening the sleeves. If it still does not fit, it is smarter to change your business practices to fit the system than vice versa. The programmers probably based the system on a company ahead of yours anyway. The problem arises when the supplier aims to sell a whole range of systems all mutually compatible but incompatible with everyone else's. Software suppliers try to lock in their customers today just as hardware suppliers used to. We cannot here descend into technical debates about the architecture of databases. IT is not quite as simple as I am holding it out to be but the counsel remains: share and integrate data but use disposable systems.

- **Match systems with individual jobs, not organization structure.** Organizations never cease fiddling with their structures as they accommodate the changing needs, skills and expectations of their management. IT can never keep up if the organizational structure is imprinted into the system architecture. Individual jobs, however, change slowly. The title of a brand manager may alter every week but the job has not varied much in twenty years. Sales vice-presidents also need more and better information than before but what they are trying to do has changed slowly. Job-centred systems follow their managers around and withstand organizational change.

- **Information should be a commonwealth.** New information should be contributed to databases accessible to all. Confidential information will have to be partitioned, but how confidential is it really? More harm is done in large organizations by concealing information than by sharing it.

- **Information is the blue print for the job.** Perhaps the wave of delayering, downsizing and re-engineering is over for a generation, but most organizations will continue to review what each function is supposed to achieve and how that role should be performed. The specification of job-centred systems provides the opportunity to answer both of those questions. Whether we are what we eat or not, managers are largely what they read. What is provided, and how, influence how the function is performed. For example, trade or customer marketing specialists have been developed to provide better marketing for sales and immediate customers by separating that role from the traditional brand manager who is thereby left free to focus on the consumer. Specifying the information needs will specify the jobs.

● **Systems assurance.** This huge increase of information, programmed analysis and machine intelligence is creating a dependency. Companies already exist where the only asset truly crucial to their business is the information system. Airlines and credit cards are examples. With the increased richness of market data, look for information systems to become increasingly crucial to marketers in all sectors. Systems failures may be a mild irritation today but they will be catastrophic tomorrow. This is not the place to review the conventional strictures about data and information management. Suffice it to note that information systems need to be safe and certain. Check out annually whatever procedures your specialists tell you are foolproof. They haven't met Fred.

● **Do not leave serendipity to chance.** When all is done, planned information needs will never turn out right. Redundant information will still be there and the *really* important question will remain unanswered. All we can do is to organize the bulk of information needs in such a way as to gain, not lose, discretionary time for the manager. A principle use of this excess time is to let serendipity happen, or rather, get into the circumstances in which it can happen. Conferences, market visits, challenging suppliers to produce new information are all serendipity opportunities – if they are made to be.

RELEASING MANAGEMENT FOR WHAT MATTERS

Not all marketers will share this vision of the information explosion. Some will see it as threatening, others will be over enthusiastic, others again will be passively resistant. Unkind things will be said of those who set new system developments going and leave before the disasters strike.

The pace of development will be dictated by competition, not in the IT world but in yours. The technology is already here. Marketing success does not depend on analysis; it is a valuable contribution but it is not the key. The more important components are

The more important components are creativity, innovation, and putting it all together, or synthesis.

creativity, innovation, and putting it all together, or synthesis. Marketing has far more to do with managing relationships between brand, consumers, and customers, than with numeric analysis. To release marketers for what really matters, machines have to take over analysis and information must be reduced to exception reporting. This should not shackle managers to a daily round of chasing up statistical anomalies but should take over analysis and the routine decisions that follow.

Information systems have to be survived before they can be harnessed to realize that future; a future which allows marketers to leave the paperwork behind and get back to the marketplace.

Memo to file

Subject: INFORMATION SYSTEMS SURVIVAL KIT

- Control the information explosion before it or your competition blows you away. Two stages help: blue sky visioning (more to eliminate redundancy than to choose new toys) and "iceberging" the information available.

- Iceberg it into three groups: top of mind information (probably the key brand equity and P&L variables in the brand plan), the support database for computer tracking and analysis, and the nice to know information you should let go.

- Computers are better analysts than brand managers. Mechanize analysis, and then consequential decision making, incrementally. Use that process to liberate time for marketers to do what *really* adds value.

- Share data, and planning, but provide systems by individual job function. Information helps blueprint the role.

- Assume that Murphy was an optimist. Information systems are becoming crucial to marketing. They fail only where the experts have not anticipated the failure. Review assurance once a year.

10

BEYOND THE J CURVE

Trends and forecasting

Key issues
● **Trends and forecasting** ● **The angle of credibility is an index of the change that has to be believed** ● **Unexplained upturns in plans should not be accepted** ● **Brands may be myths but marketing is not magic** ● **The causes of trends need to be understood first**

TRENDS AND FORECASTING

Figure 10.1 shows the sales history and forecasts for brand X in the 1960s.

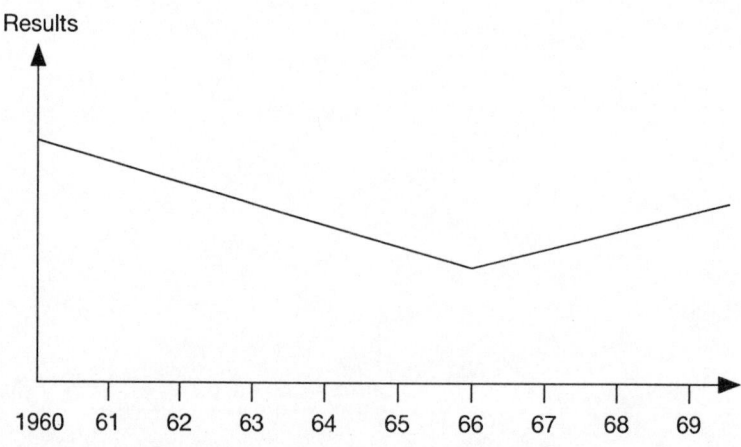

Fig   10.1   In what year was the forecast made?

What was the year when the forecasts, i.e. the plans, were made?

You can confidently answer that question without knowing the brand, the market, the environment, or any other circumstances of that time. The "hockey stick" is a popular name for the phenomenon that follows.

The scene is the boardroom. It is marketing plan presentation day. In the long list of signals which trigger sales of stock options (new corporate offices, awards for business success, record levels of Group CEO benefits) the marketing department's use of elaborate computer graphics, rather than simple overhead transparencies, must feature high. This is such a day. If it can be done with mirrors; it is about to be.

In professional tones worthy of an undertaker, the newly appointed brand manager describes how sales, market share, and profitability have been sliding steadily. The sympathy of the audience is won immediately. They made this appointment and they want it to prove correct. Predecessors (apt word) somehow avoided the issues. The speaker has arrived in the nick of time to rescue the situation with courage, candour, and objectivity. The hitherto unspeakable is now to be spoken. Some 30 screens later, the audience is clear that things are bad, they are going to get worse, that investment is needed but that the eventual upturn will bring rewards beyond their ken (Ken being the Finance Director).

Figure 10.2 shows the all purpose "J curve," which is slightly more believable than the hockey stick, because the downward trend is only gradually arrested and turned around. Compare this with figure 10.1.

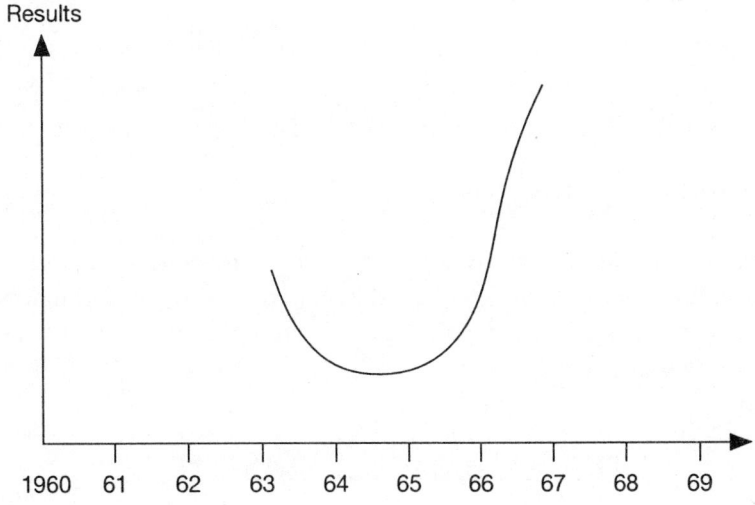

Fig 10.2   The J Curve

This well-orchestrated presentation carries the audience towards the happy ending they all want to believe. Reversing the trend was why the appointment had been made. The advertising agency, sales management, market research all testify that they believe this plan. Key customers have been pre-sold.

To question the euphoria of the moment seems poor timing at the least.

The forecast could be true. Blind faith is a powerful force, especially when you have run out of other ideas. The J curve has particular attraction for those who do not expect to be around when the long-term benefits are supposed to roll in. But it could be true because repositioning brands, advertising, and much of the most important structural work takes time to show the gain. Maybe past investment really is about to pay off.

Maybe the business is cyclical: you can drop the J in figure 10.2 into the business cycle in figure 10.3 and the forecast seems reasonable. The same curve with a different past (figure 10.4) strains credibility.

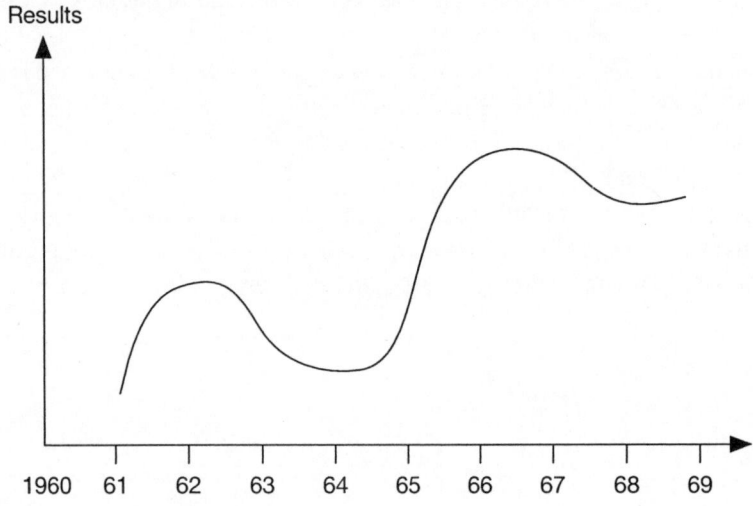

Fig 10.3   J Curve in one context

Therein lies the clue to getting beyond the J curve: there needs to be another way to see the same data. Before we address this problem, it is useful to quantify the extent to which any marketing plan with which you are presented is intrinsically believable.

THE ANGLE OF CREDIBILITY

This should really be the "angle of <u>in</u>credibility" but that would be less polite.

In the original, hockey stick, situation, the angle is the number of degrees between the trend so far and the forecast (see figure 10.5).

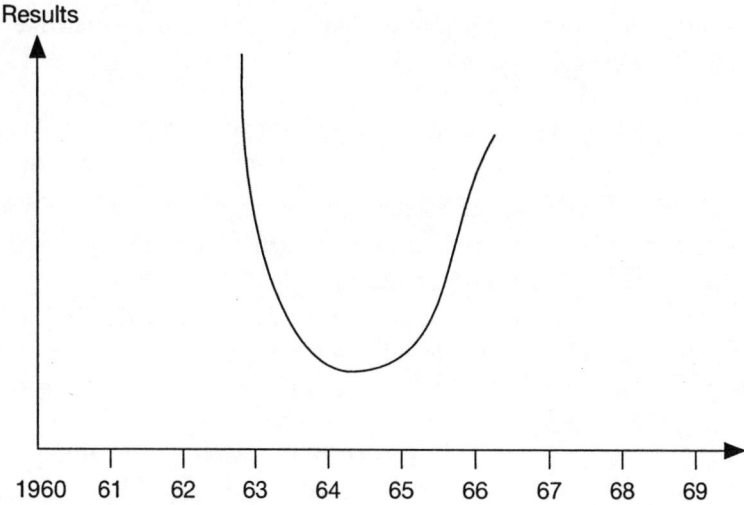

Fig 10.4   And in another

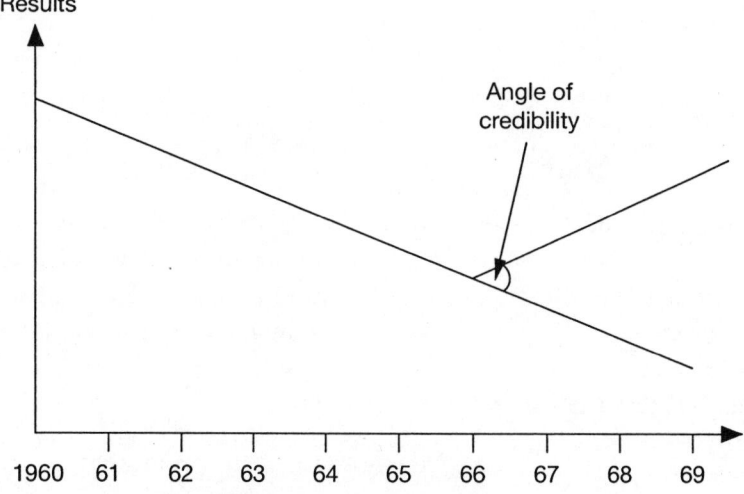

Fig 10.5   Angle of credibility – straight lines

The general formula for the angle of credibility where both the history and forecasts have unchanging trends, i.e. two straight lines as in figure 10.5, is:

$$\text{Angle} = 90°(T_f - T_h)$$

where T_h is the historical trend
and T_f is the forecast trend.

If sales are going down 15 per cent p.a. and, according to the plan, are about to go up 10 per cent p.a., the angle is:

$$90° \times \{10\% - (-15\%)\} = 90° \times \{10\% + 15\%)\} = 22.5°$$

Obviously, if the historical and forecast trends are the same the angle is zero. For cautious planners, especially if the historical trend is highly positive, the angle will be negative, i.e. very credible.

When we switch from linear trends to the J curve, however, the maths get too complicated for this text. Consider this pattern of sales for the past four years:

	Decrease on previous year %	Improvement on last time %
1959	11	
60	11	0
61	10	1
62	8	2
63	5	3
64	1	4

Sales are indeed declining but trend is turning around at an accelerating rate. It is quite reasonable that sales next year will be up and that they will grow at 10 per cent thereafter. Obviously the improvement acceleration will run out of steam at some stage. All we know now is that something is causing improvement.

Thus it is reasonable to believe:

	Increase on previous year %	Improvement on last time %
1965	4	5
66	10	6

You will have a forecasting package on your computer to do this extrapolation stuff for you or you may have some maths PhDs locked away for this eventuality. Failing both, just draw the historical sales on graph paper and freehand the curve onwards. Likewise, freehand the forecast curve back a bit. Whatever your technology, the principle remains that the credibility gap lies between extrapolated trend line and the actual forecast.

> **The credibility gap lies between extrapolated trend line and the actual forecast.**

If you cannot be bothered with all that, then take the angle of credibility to be the approximation:

$$\text{Angle} = 90°(T_f - T_h - A_h)$$

where T_h is the historical average (straight line) trend for the last 5 years,
T_f is the forecast average (straight line) trend for the next 3 and
A_h is the acceleration effect.

Figure 10.6 shows the historical sales up to points A, B and C and the forecasts thereafter. As it turned out, the forecasts were spot on. (Drawing only one curve makes the illustration easier). Clearly, if you were at point A, the angle of credibility would be very great whereas at point B, the angle will be less and at C less again.

	A	B	C
Actual date	**1.1.64**	**1.1.65**	**1.1.66**
T_h	–9%	–7%	–4%
T_f	+4.3%	+8%	+10%
A_h	+6%	+10%	+15%
	(1+2+3)	(6+4)	(10+5)
$T_f - T_h - A_h$	7.3%	5%	–1%
Angle	6.7°	4.5°	–0.9°

Thus the turnaround does not have positive credibility until the turn of 1965 to 1966.

That this methododology is not strictly correct in mathematical terms is beside the point. Credibility cannot be calculated with any precision anyway. The purpose of this yardstick is to provide a benchmark to ensure that a plan is specifically assessed in terms of its turnaround capability. The question "what is the angle of credibility of this plan?" is a precursor to looking at the likelihood of the actions proposed creating the change expected.

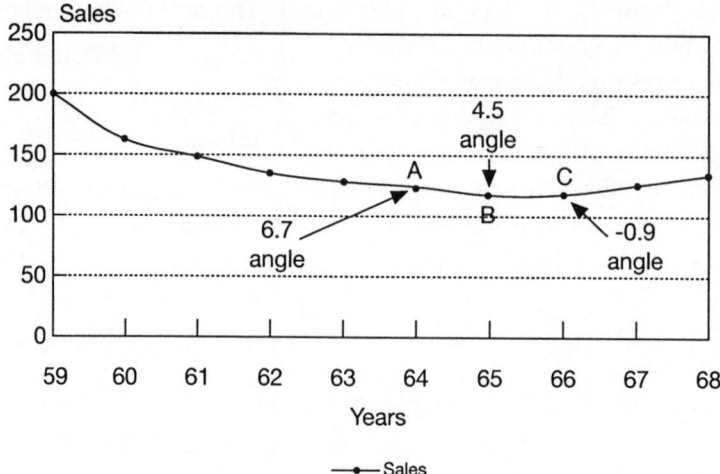

Fig 10.6   Angle of credibility – curvilinear

If the angle of credibility is near to, or less than, zero, then a plan much like the last should be fine. Otherwise, some major changes have to be made. Are they enough? Can they have the necessary impact within the time frame forecast?

CHANGING THE PARADIGM

If the basic thinking is much like last year's, a significant change is unlikely. One of the problems of revolving brand managers is that the people change but the thinking does not. Of course, they all think they are different. So do the peas in the pod. The problem is exacerbated in those companies who bump their product managers up brands in a sort of pecking order by marketing expenditure.

Product managers A, B, C, D etc. spend descending sums and thus product manager A is the senior. When the best new job comes along, A gets it, B takes A's job, C takes B's, and so on. D in the new job has to be different to C, to impress top management, just as C was different to B. Since they all went to the same sources and were hired by the same system, it is odds on that D's innovation will look remarkably like B's was.

A large angle of credibility from this type of stable without something remarkable leaping out of the page is, quite simply, enough to reject the plan out of hand.

Maybe a set of considerations is missing. It is tough looking for what is missing when you do not know what to look for. One candidate is the assumed market that the brand is competing in.

The fascination some have for market share is strange. Consumers do not buy categories, they buy products and brands. Markets, or categories, are groupings artificially brought together by marketing managers and retailers. Note that retailers define categories largely by where the products go on the shelf and which buyer buys them These categories may or may not be the same as those used by the marketing manager. These may be either those that the research company uses for their data, e.g. Nielsen, or the category specially defined to make the brand plan look good. If locally made products are strong and your product is imported, the marketer may elect to show market share as a percentage of imported goods.

> **The most important step, when faced by the need for a high angle of credibility, is to consider whether you can change the category.**

The exclusion of the consumer from determining category is not strictly true: some would argue that consumers define markets through substitution. If Daz and Persil both do the same thing the consumer will accept one or the other but not both. However different consumers substitute different things (soap for detergent for some but not others), some substitutes are acceptable sometimes but not always for the same consumer (private label is OK when you are not serving others) and high levels of disposable income have undermined the idea that the consumer has to *substitute* at all. A packet of wine gums is not a substitute for a packet of cigarettes except in the sense that it is hard to suck both at the same time.

While it is not strictly true, it is true enough that managers define categories; consumers do not. Thus the most important step, when faced by the need for a high angle of credibility, is to consider whether you can change the category, i.e. change the paradigm or change the way of thinking.

Take Lucozade, for example. Beechams sold ethical drugs, over-the-counter drugs, and Lucozade as a pick-me-up for convalescents. Faced by a galaxy of new formulations, boring old flavoured glucose and water was a pale and sick remedy for pale and sick people. Market share remained a healthy 100 percent but sales did not look so good. Convalescence itself is outmoded; if you get tea and a biscuit after your operation you are doing well. Beecham changed the market definition, i.e. the paradigm. Lucozade was now to be positioned as a healthy drink for the already healthy. As the drink for athletes to restore energy, what could be better. Daley Thompson personalized the brand's switch from wimp to Britain's decathlon hero. The investment was made; the J curve materialized.

If a brand is declining, there must be some reasons. What are consumers using in its place? Check the brand health indicators. If the diagnosis is not clear, maybe you have the wrong indicators. If you are changing the paradigm (market or whatever), what is the evidence this is valid? If you are moving from a moderate to a dramatic increase, how quickly can this happen? Generally, changes in brand equity are slow to impact.

If you do not already have a neat little test market that supplies the answers, ask the consumer. Focus groups should not be used where you don't think you have the answer, but who needs rules? Throw in some random other prompts to your problem brand and see how they talk about brand usage and how consumption patterns are changing. How do other countries use the brand or its product equivalents? One way or another the neat box used to serve up the J curve in that presentation has to be torn apart so that real reasons for the upturn can be found.

Memo to file

Subject: BEYOND THE J CURVE

- It is worth extrapolating trends in the course of evaluating a plan.
- The extent of fresh thinking must be as great as the angle of credibility.
- We all want to believe in happy endings but do not be carried away.

11

KAMIKAZE AND GUERRILLA MARKETING

What marketers can learn from the military

Key issues
- The conflict paradigm or marketing as warfare
- When flanker brands become expendable (kamikaze)
- Avoiding competition until your brand is big enough to win (guerrilla marketing)

THE CONFLICT PARADIGM OR MARKETING AS WARFARE

Of the three ways of thinking about marketing, conflict is the most fun – at least for those of us who still hanker after playing soldiers. Competitors are the "enemy," sales people are the infantry and advertising is the artillery. Market share is the measure of success. The troops are rallied by calls to arms at the annual sales conference. Morale is fussed over and fraternization with the enemy results in termination. Those nice people over in HR become the firing squad.

The idea of using military thinking in business, what we now call "strategy," is hardly new. Socrates is usually credited with that insight and I dare say it is much older.

Von Clausewitz[1] defines war as "an act of violence intended to compel our opponent to fulfil our will." In this model there is only one opponent. One of the problems with the warfare paradigm is that marketers have at least four "opponents":

[1] Karl von Clausewitz *On War* (London, Penguin Classics, 1982; originally published by von Kriege, 1832).

- Consumers who want to buy the products.
- Customers throughout the distribution channels.
- Internal members of your own organization who have different priorities and objectives.
- Competition to whom the paradigm usually refers.

Ries and Trout[2] get around the problem by defining competition as the enemy and consumers as the ground being won or lost. Neat but not a full answer.

This picture is not far from the way Procter and Gamble and Unilever laundry detergent marketers see each other, or Coke people see Pepsi's. In a duopoly, market share gains reflect quite well who is winning. In fact, detergents are not quite such a duopoly as people imagine. The worldwide shares of P&G and Unilever add only to 44 percent of the global market, 24 percent and 20 percent respectively. In Europe they are larger. P&G (32 percent) overtook Unilever (23 percent) partly because Unilever allowed its country barons (see chapter 7, "Global Marketing") to hold up innovation.

In 1994, Unilever decided to hit back in a big way. They spent around £100m on a new plant to use a magnesium-based catalyst accelerator to remove stains at lower temperature. The line extended their main brand in each country – a dubious decision in itself but inspired by their previous compromise of innovations by using less popular brand names, i.e. tired old brands. The idea then had been to minimize risk. Now they were determined to reverse trends and go the whole hog. Andrew Seth, the UK CEO of Unilever's laundry products was quoted as saying "it's the most significant thing we've ever done" (*The Economist,* June 11, 1994).

Everyone in the industry had been aware of this new additive (weapon) and the dangers of using it. Persil Power's (Omo Power's in Holland) launch was quickly followed by P&G's disparagement. Law suits were instigated but the truth was that Unilever had made a simple mistake equivalent to a military disaster. The short-term financial losses have not been revealed. The damage to the Persil brand was greater because Persil has long been positioned as the *gentler* product as well as "washes whiter." It continued as soap flakes long after the rest of the industry had switched to detergents to preserve this positioning. Since then, advertising has walked a narrow line to preserve this paradoxical pair of advantages. Persil Power with its single-minded bid for strength abandoned that positioning (hill in the military analogy) and failed to secure the new one.

[2] Al Ries and Jack Trout, *Marketing Warfare* (Singapore, McGraw Hill, 1986).

While this book argues that competition should be second, in marketing thinking, to cooperation, it is essential to

- Stimulate innovation. Competition provides the benchmarks your brands have to *beat*.

- Stimulate the market. Nestlé's entry into the US frozen dough market in the mid-90s enlivened what was a near monopoly. It became more interesting for consumers and grew as a whole.

- Stimulate management and sales people.

In a duopoly, such as those above, the conflict paradigm works well, as one company's gain is largely the other's loss.

Against that, the conflict paradigm, otherwise known as "strategic marketing," has some problems:

> **In a duopoly, the conflict paradigm works well, as one company's gain is largely the other's loss.**

- The win/lose nature of competitive thinking is flawed. Marketing is not a zero sum game but win/win.

- Preoccupation with the competitor is the wrong orientation: satisfying immediate customers and final consumer may require them to prefer your brand to the competition but that is incidental. Fixation with competition can cause companies to forget customers altogether.

- Competition is expensive. The most common example is the price war in which prices are lowered not so much to please the consumer as to discomfort the competition. Competitors respond and prices spiral down.

Guerrilla marketing goes some way to incorporate the conflict, or strategy, paradigm while diminishing the problems. We discuss that in the third part of this chapter. The "win/win" component is at the heart of the marketing concept. Good marketing causes markets to grow: consumers win, retailers win, your brand grows and so do the competitors'. Maybe they do not grow in volume but profits grow as well as ultimate cash flow.

Many have attributed economic failure in communist countries to the lack of competition. State monopolies undermined growth. This misses the point that the failure resulted from the absence of marketing. Competition to meet the demand curve is part of that but not the key part. Of far more importance is marketing's ability to shift the demand curve. We revert to this in looking at the origin of marketing (see chapter 13). For now, we need to recognize that the conflict paradigm is an essential, but dangerous, perception of marketing.

WHEN FLANKER BRANDS BECOME EXPENDABLE (KAMIKAZE)

As John Kay[3] reminded us, when one ice cream seller sets up on a beach, the ideal position is the centre of gravity, so to speak, of the potential customers, i.e. in the middle. When a second ice cream vendor comes along, the optimal spot is right next door. This is why the "positioning" of the second, "me-too," brand is often so close to the original.

The third vendor (brand) can pick any spot without it making much difference and thus will exploit this differentiation as much as possible. Following similar game theory, or war game theory, logic, a leading brand will sometimes introduce a flanker brand to protect it from the competition.

Smirnoff in the UK in the 1970s had clear brand leadership having beaten off Cossack. Vladivar emerged from Warrington, Cheshire, as the main competitor. It was cheaper and more fun. Their marketing was regional and their stunts provided columns of PR. Consumers were beginning to side with the underdog. IDV introduced Popov to match the Vladivar positioning and thereby reduce its differentiation. The price was the same, regionalization was also in the north-west and the most crackpot PR agency in the district was hired to out-zany Vladivar.

> **The damage is much greater for competitor brands and thereby gains equity for the main brand.**

Popov was a flanker brand and it was also expendable. It had no brand equity to start with and then borrowed, so far as possible, from the enemy. It could afford to attack Vladivar directly, and lose, because that helped Smirnoff gain larger ground. This is "kamikaze marketing." It is destructive to your own flankers but the damage is much greater for competitor brands and thereby gains equity for the main brand.

GUERRILLA MARKETING

Norman Dixon's priceless treatise on military disasters, *The Psychology of Military Incompetence*, applies almost as well to marketing. "Group-think," for example, was coined after the Bay of Pigs disaster. Any sensible outsider would have known that invasion was doomed and yet the intelligent military

---

[3] *Foundations of Corporate Success* (Oxford University Press, 1993).

staffers, up to and including the President of the United States, became so infected by the selective perceptions which fed on each other that they ended up believing the impossible. In milder forms, this explains why committees are, contrary to popular opinion, more likely to take radical, both great and disastrous, decisions than individuals.

Dixon defines successful warfare as delivering maximum energy to the right place at the right time. Both time and place should be as tightly targeted as possible. To do that, information has to be available, accurate, and precise. Thus there are only three components: energy (resources), positioning and information. One strength of the conflict paradigm is that much the same can be said of marketing. Little will be gained by dissipating resources over too wide an area or at the wrong time.

Matching terrain to competition and ensuring that resources are adequate for the terrain.

Critical is the concept of focus: concentrating energy on a narrow target. The sun may be a huge object, far more important than the whole earth but also a long distance away, and yet an itty bitty piece of glass can focus the rays of the sun onto a small spot to create fire, right here and now. This mixed metaphor is intended to throw light (sorry) on the global marketing problem: how do we use our inadequate (to marketers, and to the military, they are always inadequate) resources to increase our sales and profits both absolutely and relative to competition?

Guerrilla thinking is not only important for little companies, which have no choice but to think small, but also in the major multinationals. P&G, for example, now claims to be a guerrilla marketer. Mainstream marketing is too expensive on a global basis. This is *not* advocating "think small" as a generic formula. In Japan, thinking small is typically disastrous. What I am advocating is matching terrain to competition and ensuring that resources are adequate for the terrain. It follows that, since start ups are risky, you should maximize learning relative to investment by selecting terrain no bigger than you have to.

The term "guerrilla," as you know, arose when the Spanish people were fighting bush wars with Napoleon. The concept is two thousand years older. Classically, three stages are involved:

1. The ruling power perceives the insurrection as no serious threat.
2. Evasion. The guerrilla forces avoid major confrontation with the regular army whilst they build up their resources. Mao Tse Tung[4] distinguished

between active and passive defense. The strategic need at this stage is to gain strength for the ultimate "war of annihilation."

3. Counter-offensive. Now the guerrilla troops can be concentrated, firstly in mobile warfare, and then encircling and crushing their regular opponent.

Perhaps Mao's greatest contribution was to draw attention to, and then demonstrate, the advantages of defense and weakness in achieving ultimate victory. As he saw it, the "imperial powers" (i.e. the Europeans and Japanese) underestimated the positive benefits of defense and retreat. Macho-man wants to attack and sees defense as weakness only necessary until an attack can be mounted. Von Clausewitz recognized, intellectually, the advantages of retreat; he cites Tsar Alexander's in 1812.[5] Von Clausewitz showed why defense was essentially more often a winning strategy than offense. Even so, he clearly hankered after attack. Western marketers also think that is where the action lies. To the Chinese, brought up with Taoism and the concepts of harmony and balance, attack and defense are, so to speak, the yang and the yin of warfare demanding equal respect and understanding.

Mao's case for defense is sophisticated. So far from being bad for morale, being the "victims" of aggression can inspire and rally popular support. In Russia, the popularity of the Red Army in 1917 was due in part to the aggression of the White. Exactly the same can happen in marketing. Popular support for small brewers is increased by any aggressive tactics by the majors.

Let us take the three stages in turn:

Invisibility

When launching a new brand, the less seriously the competition takes it the better. While there are contra examples where the major brands' counter-moves drew added attention (and then sales) for the newcomer, the more frequent situation is that a new brand or company or product is too fragile to withstand attack. It is not difficult, nor expensive, for a major brand owner to mess up a competitor's test market to the point where it ceases to be a test.

> **The less resources that have to be diverted to staving off competition, the more can be given to stimulating consumer**

We know that 39 out of 40 new brands fail (or whatever). The vulnerabil-

[4] *Selected works of Mao Tse Tung*, vol. 1, chapter V (Peking, Foreign Languages Press, 1967).
[5] Von Clausewitz, *On War*, p. 396.

ity of a new born anything is high. The less resources that have to be diverted to staving off competition, the more can be given to stimulating consumer demand.

Evasion

The popular image of guerrilla tactics of ambushes and hit and run is only partially correct. The aim is not to inflict damage on the conventional forces but to gain supplies. Sophisticated players of this game believe it is important *not* to inflict casualties on the conventional forces for two reasons: the bigger the hit the larger the retaliation. Conventional soldiers have family and friends too. Guevara advised Castro to take good care of any prisoners (unlike Batista) as they would be more likely to join Castro one day if the prisoners were well treated, respected, and released to tell everyone about that. A guerrilla army has no time, place, or resources to keep prisoners of war.

It is critical for a guerrilla force to build relationships with the local community. They depend on them for cover and often for food. Most of all they need good information for themselves and bad information to go to their opponent. This will only happen if the local community favors the guerrilla forces. Hence Mao's affection for defense. If the local population prefer the guerrillas' formulation and think they are losing, and that local help will save the cause, the locals will rally round. Likewise for the local brand of beer or cheese or whatever.

The USA was convinced during the Cuban revolution that Castro's arms were coming from Russia. Actually they were coming from the USA, rather closer, thanks to the Batista forces. Likewise Mao's weaponry came from "the arsenals of London as well as of Hanyang, and, what is more, it is delivered to us by the enemy's transport corps. This is the sober truth, it is not a jest."[6]

Differentiating a brand gives it its own space and arouses competitors less.

The richer the enemy, the more the guerrillas can gain. Whether General Westmoreland had read Mao or Guevara before he went to Vietnam, I do not know. In the air, there was no contest but who won the battle for information? General Templar in Malaya in the 1950s had a much easier job than the Americans in Vietnam for two reasons: Malaya is a peninsula with a short

[6] *Selected works from Mao Tse Tung*, p. 249.

boundary with Thailand and while the insurgents were ethnic Chinese, the locals were Malay.

This evasion phase is equivalent in part to brand differentiation, cooperation with competitors, and alliances. Differentiating a brand gives it its own space and arouses competitors less. During this stage the brand should build its strength, harvesting whatever resources come its way.

Concentration

Whether it is in the small wins early or the pitched battles later, all writers point to the importance of focussing energy onto the point of contact so that, in that place and at that time, the enemy is outnumbered, encircled and suppressed. Failing that, at least ensure your positioning occupies "the high ground," whatever that may be in consumer terms. It may well be as simple as a higher price. As far as Mao was concerned, only now could resources be spent, only now could losses be justified by gains.

Mao's formula[7] for deciding on attack was: "we should in general secure at least two of the following conditions before we can consider the situation as being favorable to us and unfavorable to the enemy and before we can go over to the counter-offensive. These conditions are:

1. The population actively supports the Red Army.
2. The terrain is favorable for operations.
3. All the main forces of the Red Army are concentrated.
4. The enemy's weak spots have been located.
5. The enemy has been reduced to a tired and demoralized state.
6. The enemy has been induced to make mistakes."

Finally, we have macho time. The need for patience does not stop now, however, because this period too can last a long time. Mao experienced many years (it was confused by World War II) of mobile warfare before the final pitched battles with the Kuomintang in the late 40s, 20 long years after they started. The mentality I am describing here is some distance from the "how much market share can we gain for the next quarterly results" preoccupation of modern western business. In a world where brand names prevail for 100 years and more, reconciling short- and long-term interests will never be far down the agenda.

---

[7] *Selected works from Mao Tse Tung*, p. 215.

Memo to file

Subject: KAMIKAZE AND GUERRILLA MARKETING

- The conflict or warfare or strategy paradigm is immensely important but also flawed.

- On the positive side, it stimulates innovation, the market, management and sales people.

- Against that, marketing is not a zero sum game but should be win/win. Customer orientation is more important than competitor. The customer provides the profit and the competitor may, or may not, be a key factor in that. Finally, competition is expensive, if not downright wasteful.

- Kamikaze marketing is the rarely practised art of using a flanker brand to destroy a competitor. You lose your flanker but that may be a small price to pay for destroying a major threat to your main brand.

- Guerrilla marketing is the most useful manifestation of the conflict paradigm. Plenty of books, of varying quality, use the concept. Its strengths are: winning over the local population (consumers in the analogy) is the critical success factor and resources are explicitly guarded until they are effective (less waste), the need for differentiation, uses for information, the need for patience and then striking when there is sufficient advantage to win. In short, guerrilla marketing is apt.

12

THE EDUCATED LUNCH

Reserve time for random thinking

Key issue
- **Get away from roles and rituals for a free format focus on improvement, or a free lunch**

Call your company's marketing director at 2.45 and her secretary says "She's in a meeting." Is she really in a meeting or is this a well-trained secretary? You and I think she is still at lunch.

Lunch is, perhaps, the most important part of a marketing director's day. What may seem as R&R (rest and relaxation) is truly an escape from R&R (roles and rituals). Lunch is an opportunity to break formality and to float ideas. Lunch may be the one opportunity for genuine marketing the marketing director gets all day. Most marketing directors regret they have so little time to do any marketing.

> **Lunch may be the one opportunity for genuine marketing the marketing director gets all day.**

Lunch is the opportunity to teach, to be educated and to be a little bit crazy – all important aspects of marketing. The educated lunch is not about making decisions.

First let us consider the rituals:

- **On arrival at office:** shuffle the mail and paper work. Complain that the e-mail has not reduced the paper. Get someone to deal with it. Return phone calls, if you are that old fashioned. Anticipate what might be bugging the boss. Ask the sales people why sales are not higher.
- **Before lunch:** meetings.
- **After lunch:** meetings.

- **Last thing in the office:** sign mail. Return some calls from those you missed in the morning. They have gone home. Wonder why your calls were not returned. Do not answer the phone which rings as you walk out, because at that time of day it is never good news.

- **Evening:** read the papers that arrived while you were in meetings.

Meetings come in one of three forms: they are selling something to you, you are selling something to somebody else, or you are meeting to resolve why you have so many meetings. Note that they are all decision oriented. You do not escape until you have all agreed something, even if it is only to meet again. Better still, appoint a subgroup. Note also that committees are passé: if you are not a board, try "team" or "steering group." When decisions are not enough, meetings become "action oriented."

Meetings need to be short and to the point. Large meetings are good for information, coordination, and decision; small meetings are good for creativity and innovation. Some formats suit anything. Nevertheless meetings sustain, and are sustained by, rituals and roles. They develop regularities. They may be weekly or monthly, morning or afternoon; agendas become standardized. Those failing to attend are assigned tasks. This, another ritual, ensures they turn up next time. Those attending fulfill the roles they have been given or assume. Meetings become predictable. Predictable becomes boring.

The educated lunch is a necessary release from all that. Marketing needs the balance of order and disorder. The body may be weighed down by Entrecôte de Cardinal Richelieu and a bottle of Chambertin 1970 but the mind is liberated. Just one great idea makes it all worthwhile. If a green salad and a bottle of Aqua Libra produces a better result for you, then go mad and order a second bottle.

The educated lunch must be distinguished from the working lunch. This abomination is just a meeting continued over curling sandwiches. The slightly more upmarket variant provides salad, and allows you to drop mayonnaise on brand plans. There are other variants as well, romantic lunches (defined as those which you cannot even think of charging), the important lunch (serves middle-aged spread), old boy/girl lunches, we-must-meet-again-but-now-we-have-was-it-such-a-good-idea? lunches. None of these are designed to maximize the profit of the business. The educated lunch is serious in intent but light in tone. (There is also the educated breakfast or dinner for workaholics.)

An educated lunch may take place with the agency, colleagues, competitors (often the best), customers, suppliers, or anyone who can enjoy the escape but will also help you build your business. The first course may be a gossip or a moan about how business is terrible. The fish course is supposed to stimulate intellect. Some ridiculous notion should be proposed and challenged. Top it with a crazier one. Then you are ready for the meat and potatoes of thinking and learning. A good lunch provides the intellectual protein and starch you need to fuel new ideas.

Meetings are for rituals, roles, and vertical thinking. The educated lunch is a leveller; few should be there and the talking stick should pass to whomever has fun with new thinking. An unremarked property of the finest food and drink is that they provide the best employment for the mouth. The ears get liberated; so does that grey stuff between them.

Don't rush an educated lunch. You need the release. Phone the office and say your meeting is overrunning.

Memo to file

Subject: SUSTAINING THE MIND

- Attach this essay to your next expense claim.

13

MARKETING TODAY AND TOMORROW

An overview of how marketing is evolving

Key issues

● **Tell me again: what is "marketing"?** ● **The evolution of marketing thinking** ● **How helpful are economics? (Answer: not very.)** ● **The three basic paradigms of marketing: neo-classical, conflict and relational** ● **Different forms of marketing: business, direct, network, services, retail**

DEFINITIONS OF MARKETING

At its most general level, "marketing" is the presentation of a proposition in the way in which it is most likely to be accepted. Whether it is the packaging of a brand of cat food or the election manifesto of a political party, marketing is distinguished from other business activities by the way it takes the customer's point of view and looks back.

"Consumers" are the end users. In the long run, consumers are paramount but to reach them, any intermediate customers have to be satisfied first. Evangelists market churches, charities market appeals, even the police worry about marketing to the public. Whatever the category, marketing is the least painful way to achieve objectives.

As a definition of marketing, Kotler[1] suggests "a social and managerial process by which individuals and groups obtain what they need and want through creating, offering and exchanging products of value with others." Core concepts include *needs, wants, and demands; products; value cost and satisfaction; exchange, transactions, and relationships*. Note that he does not include "brand."

Barrett[2] simply sees marketing as "primarily concerned with the management of choice." The UK Chartered Institute of Marketing calls it "the management process responsible for identifying, anticipating and satisfying customer requirements profitably." Comparable US organizations define it similarly. The seeds of the heresies we review in category marketing (chapter 3) lie in failing to distinguish the different needs of immediate intermediary and ultimate customers. "Heresies" are beliefs which are nearly true, but not quite. Note too that this approach could be satisfied by taking a 1 percent introduction fee and advising the customer to buy from a competitor. Needs would be satisfied and profit made but that would not be what they mean. There is an unstated inference that marketing involves the customer preferring your product to the competitor's.

> **The brand, profit, cooperation, competition, and the different needs of the different types of customer are central to marketing.**

While on the subject of heresies, note two more. Some definitions of marketing verge on the altruistic: they are only there to help the consumer. Consumerists, however, believe marketers are only there to help themselves. This contrast illustrates perhaps the most important contribution of marketing to business thinking: outside in. Historically, businesses, like anyone else, thought of their own needs first. Marketers start with the end user and work back. The logic is that the business is more likely to profit from satisfying customer needs if it starts with a full understanding of those needs.

Marketing, as noted above, is important for not-for-profit institutions and also for generic, unbranded, products. Nevertheless for practical purposes, the *brand, profit, cooperation, competition, and the different needs of* the different types of customer *are central to marketing*.

Thus marketing is the brand owner's process of maximizing cooperation with customers, building their relationships at the expense of competitors', to achieve thereby both the brand owner's and customers' objectives. At its simplest, it is the arithmetic sum of the two heresies above: both needs must

[1] Philip Kotler, *Marketing Management* (Englewood Cliffs, NJ, Prentice-Hall, 1991), p.4.
[2] Gavin Barrett, *Forensic Marketing* (London, McGraw-Hill, 1994), p.1.

be satisfied, not just once but repeatedly. The objectives for most brands can be summarized as short-term profitability and brand equity.

THE EVOLUTION OF MARKETING THINKING

Marketing is complex and also dynamic. Three views of the evolution of modern marketing are:

1. The historical economic pattern from production to market orientation, from achieving volume to reducing costs, and finally to adding value.

2. Marketing has retained its close association with advertising since the turn of the century. As advertising was able to capitalize on mass media of increasing size and breadth of appeal, mass marketing followed and remains dominant for many sectors. Direct marketing methods use new technology to focus resources far more closely on target markets.

3. The economics tradition has influenced marketing theory, perhaps more than practice. We will review why this is just as well.

A Finance VP at Seagram once said, and he no doubt borrowed it too, that there are only three ways to raise the profits of a business: sell more, make it for less, and put the price up (see figure 13.1). That is an elegant essay on commercial evolution. Once upon a time, the problem was to make enough of whatever it was. The world was short of everything; if you could make it, you stood a good chance of selling it. But manufacturers got better and better. Soon everyone was making everything. Competition became tough.

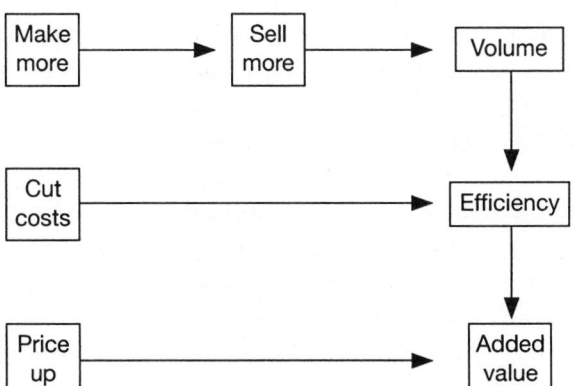

Fig 13.1   The evolution of profits and marketing

The market set lower selling prices. Profits went to those who could cut costs. Time and motion studies were born in the early years of the century. Black Model Ts rolled forth from assembly lines. Economies of scale encouraged growth and acquisition. Marginal costing allowed the big to grow bigger. As distribution improved and the world was perceived to shrink, production could be concentrated to serve the globe at lowest cost. Originally Ford erected plants to serve the needs of a county, then a region. Today each production unit takes its place within a global production network; one production structure supplies one world marketplace. The process continues but a new wave has been building up behind the first two: value.

When everyone has one of something, the only way out of the crowd is up. There comes some indefinable time when matching the neighbour's latest purchase is not enough: you have to go better. Raising the stakes in this particular social poker game requires others to play as well. In boom years, neighbours will indeed raise the stakes, but in a recession the analogy fails as it becomes fashionable to be cheap. Sooner or later, expenditure is back in style.

The evolution, therefore, is through production increases to cost cutting to added value, but not in a neat and orderly fashion. All three sources of profit continue to coexist, with the emphasis moving steadily to value, usually defined as quality divided by price. Improving quality requires both functional product improvements and psychological (image) enhancement, often through advertising, PR, or direct marketing.

> **The evolution, is through production increases to cost cutting to added value.**

Marketing is the management of these added values for consumers, as well as the indentification of costs that can be cut without detriment. Marketing deals with all aspects of increasing profits (sales volume, price and costs), but with adding value most of all. As the returns from volume and cost reduction diminish, future profits will come from added value being translated into higher prices.

Chapter 1 reviewed how modern marketing was created by the media's need to sell advertising space. The association between business and advertising has remained close. Some companies even have their advertising agencies write their marketing plans. Odd as this may seem today, there are advantages: objectivity, a deeper grounding of the advertising in the needs of the business, quality of thinking, and saving overheads.

Through the 1960s (and even now), marketing was seen as largely a matter of presentation, of adding glitz to whatever production wanted to put out.

Marketers were kept well away from the fundamental issues of product and consumer satisfaction.

The 1970s presented marketers with a number of rude shocks. Oil prices created a crash and a recession. Inflation played havoc with media costs. Years of successful cost efficiency had made the mass media moguls greedy. Consumers began to broaden their use of media away from the main TV channels and top daily papers. At the same time, demand and reader/viewership were down and costs were up.

There was no watershed. Agency life was uncomfortable for a while but the highs and lows of agency life are endemic. Nevertheless, the mid-1970s marked the start of the development of direct marketing using new technology in order to achieve better accuracy in targeting.

There is nothing new about direct marketing as a concept; mail order, now rechristened "catalogue marketing," had been around for generations. Telephone selling was available in the 1960s, albeit in primitive format. The most developed marketers were the direct mail companies themselves who could readily adapt their main medium. The difference lay in the database technology. The largest telephone selling (now called telemarketing) business in the world, is in Omaha, Nebraska, because the locals were familiar with large computer database technology developed for the HQ of US Strategic Air Command based there.

The first area for development was lists. These names and addresses were bought from societies, other traders, book clubs or anything to which people belonged. The value of a list depended on how current it was and how accurate the names and addresses and the spending power of those included were. The consequence for the consumer was, of course, junk mail.

Computer technology can now make direct marketing interactive through Internet, interactive television and telephone. The simplest system has the consumer press telephone touch tone keys in response to pre-recorded questions. More sophisticated systems recognize voice. These computerized speaking machines have the advantage of being available 24 hours a day and handling peak traffic with fewer delays. Direct marketing reduces the number of stages in the distribution process and offers the convenience of in-home selection and sending gifts without either visiting stores or the post office.

Telemarketing is reputed to have grown by 40 per cent per annum in the UK in the 1980s.

In databases today, lists are still the key. Once logged in, however, they can begin to track purchases and identify those who purchase regularly or recently and the price brackets, quantities, and types of products purchased.

With that data, the computer can predict more accurately than ever before those likely to buy in descending order of expected profit. With phone calls running at about $5 per call and direct mail not much less, the costs and benefits can be tracked with some precision.

Telemarketing is reputed to have grown by 40 percent per annum in the UK in the 1980s. Clearly this rate of increase will not continue but refinements to the databases and technology should maintain significant growth through the 1990s.

HOW HELPFUL ARE ECONOMICS?

Marketing and the "dismal science" are equally concerned with the marketplace and the laws of supply and demand. Few would quarrel with Adam Smith's perceptions of the need for balance nor with his demand for liberty to market in free markets. The parting of the ways came about in Cambridge, England around 1800. The debate was whether demand induced supply (the position of the great Rev. Thomas Robert Malthus) or whether supply created demand (Dr David Ricardo was in the blue corner). As any marketer knows, both can be true but Malthus is right more often. Unfortunately, Ricardo won the debate at that time. Bear in mind we were still in the age of production. Ever since, economic thinking has been dominated by supply considerations. From time to time, economists, notably Keynes, wake up to demand driving concepts, but the prevailing tradition, especially in Cambridge, is production-oriented. If costs can be reduced enough, for example, demand must follow.

Advertising is regarded with particular suspicion. It appears to add to cost and, worse, turns products into brands. Brand differentiation and loyalty causes them not to be wholly interchangeable with like products. They become mini-monopolies. Anathema. Economic models do not allow for the possibility that advertising changes consumer preferences: its role is seen to be information. Consumers, also assumed to be wholly rational, use advertising to reduce search time, and thus costs.

These assumptions are unreal. Consumers are indeed rational but they are emotional too. They can be influenced by advertising, albeit to no great extent. Depending on the product category, rationality or emotion may be more important. Consumers actually *like* brands to have individuality. Why should they want a world of dreary commodities just to make the algebra easier for economists?

Some of the problem lies in dogma. Economists recognize that markets are not "perfect," meaning no barriers, complete information, and interchange-able products. On the other hand, they would like them to be and persuade governments, when they can, to legislate in that direction. Competition in this perfect market is seen as the driver, or at least a necessary condition, for optimal economic progress. Cooperation, other than arm's length transac-tions, between market members is suspected of distorting competition. Adam Smith suggested "people of the same trade seldom meet together, even for merriment and diversion, but the conversation ends in a conspiracy against the public, or in some contrivance to raise prices."[3] Any form of monopoly, including the brand, is automatically bad.

The "perfect" market for marketers is not quite the reciprocal, but nearly so. Marketers are more ready to recognize that competition is important than economists are to recognize the virtues of cooperation. Marketers do not like full monopoly either but brands, brand loyalty, and continuing relationships are to be maximized. The economist's price–quality curve slopes from top left to bottom right, whereas the marketer tries to shift the curve towards the top right (see figure 13.2).

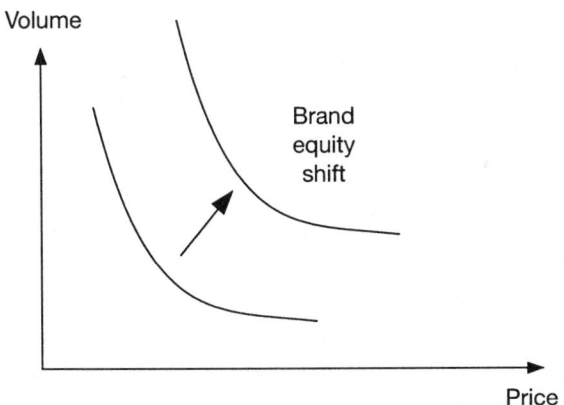

Fig 13.2   Marketing effort – price-quality curve

The extent to which that shift takes place is a measure of brand equity. The economist's curve correctly, most of the time, describes the commodity situation. The marketer is trying to move at right angles to this. The eco-nomic theory works fine where all the products are interchangeable and all consumers have perfect information. That is the very antithesis of marketing which seeks to differentiate brands, and thus the products, and to communi-cate only the more attractive features of each brand.

[3] Adam Smith, *Wealth of Nations*.

Professor Joan Robinson pointed out, back in the 1930s, that each brand is a mini-monopoly so far as its loyal consumers are concerned. So long as it does not forfeit their loyalty, they will continue to buy. Thus, for a strong brand, the demand curve is more likely to look like figure 13.3: demand is initially upward as price supports quality and then flat. Beyond a certain point, the consumer realizes that the brand is not playing fair, credibility departs, and sales volume plummets. While there is anecdotal evidence to support this view, it has not been adequately researched.

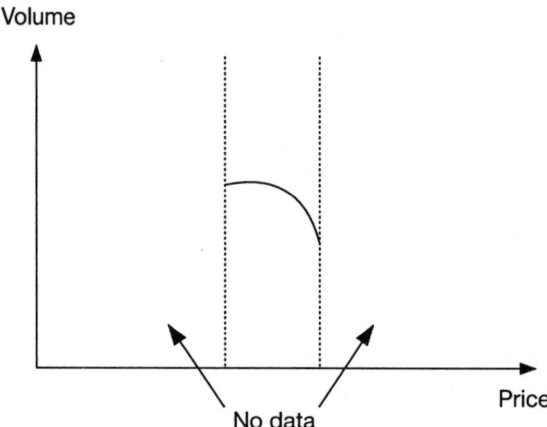

Fig 13.3   Marketing effort – demand curve

The consequence of all this is that the economist and the marketer are each attempting to drive towards an ideal world which is very nearly the opposite of the other's. Both recognize that the real world matches neither but the mind sets are incompatible. The economist, with a rational model, is closer to the world of the engineer. Analysis involves breaking chains into parts.

Conjoint analysis is now a popular research tool. It assumes that a brand is a bundle of attributes or utilities. The whole is the sum of the parts. By asking the consumer to make a series of choices, the relative importance of the util-ities can be identified, thus enabling advertising to focus on the most salient and the cost of the least valuable to be reduced. On the face of it, this is a powerful tool for raising volume (better advertising) and price (better per-ceived quality) and reducing costs all at the same time.

It is, in fact, rather a useful tool for certain categories, especially where quality can be ascertained by the consumer. On the other hand, it is flawed in two respects: consumer rationality and the whole being the sum of the parts.

The danger of such tools is that marketers become beguiled by the logic and start believing that consumers make decisions in some way like the model when they do not.

Marketers are well advised to have had an economics education just as linguists should have learned Latin. It is good training for the intellect and underlies so much modern business language. How else would you come to terms with cross-elasticity? On the other hand, the relevance of neo-classical, supply driven, economics to the modern world is more questionable.

Some economists recognize that. "Transaction cost economics," for example, rationalizes the problem (to the neo-classicists) that firms internalize transactions through vertical integration rather than rely on the (supposedly more efficient) marketplace. Rather than admit defeat, a new branch of economics has grown up. Similarly, the classical assumptions lead to the conclusion that a closed economic system will gradually wind down as resources are used up or become scarce. That, too, proves to be wrong. "Endogenous growth theory"[4] contrasts the increasing returns from knowledge with the diminishing returns expectations of classical economics. Rather than adopting ever more elaborate ways of justifying the unjustifiable, marketers should burn their economics textbooks.

> The economist and the marketer are each attempting to drive towards an ideal world which is very nearly the opposite of the other's.

THE THREE BASIC PARADIGMS OF MARKETING

The teaching of marketing came mostly from microeconomics and is summarized by the equation

$$\text{Sales} = f\{a_i P_i\}$$

where P_i (i= 1 to 4) is one of the Four Ps (product, price, place and promotion), and a_i (i= 1 to 4) are the weighting factors.

Obviously it is not that simple but the underlying concept is that by manipulating the components of the marketing mix (the Four Ps), the required level of sales can be achieved. This approach has a number of advantages. It is disciplined, quantitative and applies theory from other areas, notably psychology.

---

[4]   Gene M. Grossman and Elhanan Helpman, *Innovation and Growth in The Global Economy* (MIT Press, 1991).

The problems with it are:

- It is somewhat introverted, i.e. it focusses on the company's actions.
- It takes inadequate recognition of competition. The equation above may be shown as market share and the *relative* size of each action, e.g. share of voice for advertising, but the comment remains.
- The focus is on short-term transactions.

Dissatisfaction with this "neo-classical" paradigm led to a more strategic approach where the focus became the competition. The game was to establish "sustainable competitive advantage" (SCA) and lowest costs in order to price the enemy out of the water. This perspective deals with all three of the problems above but it is less easy to apply to the annual round of plans and budgets. The problems with this "conflict" paradigm are considered in chapter 11, "Kamikaze and Guerrilla Marketing." Most firms seek to include some elements of both perspectives in their planning processes.

Perhaps the 1960s to mid 1970s represented the high point of neo-classical thinking with the next 15 years dominated by the conflict model. Philip Kotler and Michael Porter (see appendix 2) are, respectively, their best-known representatives.

In essence, a competitor orientation looks the wrong way. Customers, not competitors, provide the business. Competition is wasteful but cooperation is profitable. Recognition has recently been growing that marketing is about value laden, long-term relationships. That is equally so in all forms of marketing: packaged goods, business, services, and retail. Mutual understanding, over time, allows the parties to the network to help each other to achieve their objectives. This paradigm is otherwise known as "Relationship Marketing" and is covered in chapter 25.

> **Nevertheless it is the third, relational, paradigm that will determine the future of marketing.**

All three paradigms are valid. We need econometrics to refine our spending calculations. Competition is an essential spur to consumers, retailers and brand owners alike. Nevertheless it is the third, relational, paradigm that will determine the future of marketing.

DIFFERENT FORMS OF MARKETING

Industrial or business to business marketing

This form of marketing deals only with direct customers as distinct from the consumers who eventually use the product manufactured by the customer. For practical purposes (purists will quibble) this equates with the trade marketing leg of consumer marketing. In order to streamline the marketing roles in consumer-oriented companies, trade or customer marketing is being increasingly split away into separate departments, leaving brand or product managers to concentrate on the consumer.

Business-related marketing represented 26 percent of all marketing in the UK in 1994[5] and its share is growing. Some respond to this opportunity by portraying it as a new speciality. Maybe.

Industrial marketers *do* have to worry about the "consumer." The industrial (or, synonymously, business to business) marketer should "look through" the customer's business to see what happens to the goods/services (hereafter just called

> **Business-related marketing represented 26 percent of all marketing in the UK in 1994.**

"goods") all the way to the consumer. Ultimately there is always a consumer, i.e. end user.

Advertising is less important and personal selling, usually in teams, more so. Branding is just as important though here it is the reputation of the supplier that is the added value component. The key components of positioning are the same.

Clearly it is more difficult to brand components of other companies' end products, though Intel chips, Philips screws, and Nutrasweet achieved that. On the other hand quality, selling, service, and logistics assume more importance. They are not different just more significant. Some believe industrial marketing is differentiated by the fact of multiple buyers and multiple sellers. The sales director calls on the buying director, region on region, area on area, and the marketing department of the selling company may deal direct with the marketing department of the buyer.

Different? For many packaged goods, the "consumer" is a family of separate individuals. In cereals, for example, the "consumer" is not as fickle as the statistics indicate. Different family members prefer different brands. The problems of multiple buyers still apply. Conversely, some business customers are effectively single buyers.

Hutt and Speh[6] authored one of the main textbooks in this area and concluded that industrial marketing, in general, is a matter of managing relationships, not optimizing individual transactions.

[5] Datamonitor, reported in *Marketing* (July 13, 1995).
[6] Michael D. Hutt and Thomas W. Speh, *Business Marketing Management* 3rd edn (New York, The Dryden Press, 1989.

Direct marketing

This links with telemarketing and database marketing (using information systems to target customers and consumers, retain history and follow up). Some forms include the immediate take-up of a TV, radio, or print advertisement. Cost benefits can be accurately assessed since the response to each individual advertisement can be measured. Direct marketing is also moving from its "transactional" roots to the relationship approach provided by modern databases.

The line between "direct" and traditional marketing is fuzzy, 19 percent of all UK TV advertising was "direct response," i.e. the ad included a phone number to call at once.[7]

Network marketing

Network marketing is the use of personal contacts to build both sales and informal organizational structures and is also called multilevel marketing to reflect the importance of the structural relationships. Examples include Amway, Tupperware and, more recently, air and water home filtering systems. In contrast, *networking*, or "internal marketing," also refers to the needs of marketing managers to build personal "selling" relationships within a large organization in order to get anything done.

Services marketing

The Economist's definition of services is "those fruits of economic activity which you cannot drop on your toe: banking to butchery, acting to accountancy."[8] It is not wholly correct as anyone who has handled an accountancy report should know. Today goods come banded with services and services with goods. A washing machine is not just a home laundry service but comes with a service guarantee. Tangible products and intangible services are so regularly banded together that their marketing can hardly be divorced. It may be easier in one case to differentiate and/or add value via service, in another via tangible product. Are Burger King consumers buying a tangible product (the burger) or the fast service? Clearly both. They could make better burgers at home and get faster service from an automat. The product and the service are wholly interdependent.

Part of the growth in services arises from the modern tendency of firms to

---

[7]   According to BT, *Marketing* (July 13, 1995).
[8]   "The Service Area in a Fog", *The Economist* (London, May 23, 1987).

outsource work they would once have done in house. Cleaning and canteens for a start. Another is to recognize the way technology is being brought to bear on service. ATMs are a way to recover your money without being insulted. Bank executives were surprised that people actually preferred to queue outside in the rain to avoid dealing with bank clerks. On the other hand, many people enjoy the warmth, human or otherwise, of a bank's ambience and relate well to particular clerks. Service offers variety; there is no one "right" service for all any more than there is a right-for-everyone product.

> **Charging customers a premium for using their own time, energies, and skills, and at the same time providing customer satisfaction, is an advanced form of marketing.**

The most significant factor is that the customer is typically part of the service delivery process. Perhaps the greatest boost to productivity this century, if not in all time, has not been transport or computers or automation but "self-service." In chapter 4, on "Distribution Channels," we considered the impact of the consumer's changing use of time.

Self-service became a brilliant invention once marketers recognized that it did not have to be matched with an offsetting discount. Charging customers a premium for using their own time, energies, and skills, and at the same time providing customer satisfaction, is an advanced form of marketing. The essence is to make it fun. Australian pubs sell the raw materials for barbecues and the customers do the cooking. Handel's Messiah at the Albert Hall in London attracts a huge DIY choir, paying full concert prices for their seats.

Retail marketing

The single largest service industry is retail – ignoring government as a "service industry" and taking "finance, insurance, and real estate" as being substantially retail – and retail branding is growing in importance. The Gap may once have been a price situation but today it sets its own style. In most European countries,[9] retail is the first or second largest sector for advertising.

Retail marketing is both different from packaged goods and the same. It is the same in the need for branding (differentiation, quality, consistency), packaging (the store), and the rest of the four Ps (product, price, location, and promotion). Retail marketers also need to satisfy both the consumer and the immediate "customer," in this case the individual store manager who may well be a franchisee.

---

[9] *European Marketing & Media Pocket Book* (Henley on Thames, NTC Publications, 1994).

The differences mostly relate to staffing and the attention to detail in the physical store – more complex than packaging. Retailers are fond of saying that the three secrets of retailing are location, location, and location. As demographics shift around town, maintaining the right portfolio of outlets is more than a specialized business.

> **Retail marketers also need to satisfy both the consumer and the immediate "customer."**

Even so, staffing is the bigger problem. If the "brand" is the set of people the consumers meet, how can consistency be achieved? Especially in this age of empowerment. Uniforms help, a bit. Training has grown in importance and most stores take half an hour a week on topical issues in addition to special programs. My bank told me off for phoning during one of their customer care sessions. British Airways continues to invest heavily in charm training.

The aim is to build a personal relationship between each member of "boundary staff" (i.e. those who meet the customers) and the brand. In the traditional Mom and Pop or small chain, that personal relationship existed between the owner and the employees. They did not work for the store; they worked for the person. In the modern retail group, the CEO's personality may not be known to the store staff, or even his or her name. In any case, they come and go. Today Laura Ashley is a myth, and maybe she was when she was alive. The important thing is that every member of staff should know what "Laura Ashley" represents.

Ben Schneider at the University of Maryland has worked on this issue. The idea that contented boundary staff lead to contented customers is largely a myth; the correlation is thin. On the other hand, where boundary staff have a clear idea of their brand's positioning, and recognize and are rewarded for customer satisfaction, the staff's perceptions of customer satisfaction, and that of the customers themselves, are very closely correlated (i.e. >0.7, since you were asking).

Integrated marketing

Finally, "integrated marketing" highlights the interdependency of marketing actions. Advertising, packaging PR, pricing and the other mix elements should not be considered separately but together. This glimpse of a cardinal principle of marketing is usually a pitch from an agency that is not pre-eminent in any one field. But the agency is right. So listen.

Memo to File

Subject: MARKETING TODAY AND TOMORROW

- Marketing is the art of using the customer and consumer points of view to achieve your objectives with least time and resources. For a brand that means maximizing short-term profit *and* brand equity.

- The three profit growth fundamentals approximate to the evolution of business priorities: Volume → Efficiency → Added value.

  Marketing contributes to all three but especially the last.

- Economics provide a valuable training discipline but its assumptions are incompatible with marketing.

- The three fundamental paradigms of marketing are the neo-classical (microeconomics), conflict (strategy) and relational (cooperation). All are valid but the trend in marketing thinking is from the earlier to the latter.

- All the specialist forms of marketing illustrated the same trend: understand the brand's personality and then manage its relationships with all its customers, especially the end user, in order to satisfy, preferably exceed, the objectives of the customers and the brand.

14

NOVATION

New brands, products and renewals

Key issues
- Marketing as "organized rational innovation." What does it take? ● Change cultures and champions ● The agenda for innovation: the New Money Machine ● Setting priorities

---

NOVATION IS CENTRAL TO MARKETING

"New, improved" is a tired old cliché which alerts consumer suspicions. Nevertheless our jaded palates demand both refreshment and ever-increasing quality. "Novation" also means the substitution of one obligation for another. A likable attitude to the consumer. Even so, for most of this chapter we will use the more customary "innovation." Consumers like what they have but also crave changes. Changes spell opportunity. Ken Simmonds, one of London Business School's luminaries, describes marketing as "organized rational innovation" and calls that the eighth paradigm of marketing. The previous seven illustrate how each commentator defines marketing to suit that commentator's own training and experience. What we see is as much a comment on our spectacles as on what is really there. Economists see marketing as microeconomics, social scientists as interpersonal exchanges, architects as structures, militarists as commercial conflict or warfare. See the marketplace how you will, the perception of marketing as novation lies deeper.

Whenever someone uncovers a new technique for making money, imitation becomes a stampede. That technique soon stops making money for new players. Thus there are no rules in marketing because the rules themselves have to be innovated. Marketers have to persuade their colleagues to change and then persuade customers and consumers to accept those changes. The combination of more affluence, more choice of brands, media, and retailers requires more innovation to stand out from the throng; it spoils consumers for choice. Today, innovation matters more but produces less. The challenge is on.

Brands differentiation requires constant refreshment. Mars introduced the Mars Ice Cream. Tide averages a new variant every year since the brand was introduced in the 1930s. Otherwise premiums disappear and

> **Innovation is more than creativity; it is the commercial realization of creativity.**

brands become commodities. Domestic light bulbs were once heavily advertised brands. Remember Osram? Today few care, or could name, which bulbs they buy.

Innovation is more than creativity; it is the commercial realization of creativity. Deservedly or not, Britain is seen as creative but not innovative. Too many analysts[1] have crawled over the reasons for Britain's declining share of world trade to detain us here beyond the thought that the failure successfully to innovate and to market are one and the same. Innovation requires an enthusiasm for change and an enthusiasm for teamwork; creativity can be purchased but innovation is down to you.

CHANGE CULTURES AND CHAMPIONS

The London 159 bus route was created in 1906 to run from North West London to the far South. Generations of management fiddled with the route but 80 years later it was still attempting to traverse about 12 miles of traffic congestion from the western fringes of Hampstead to Thornton Heath. Only 159 bus drivers were able to find both extremities and not all of them. The average speed of London traffic has been unchanged, at 11 m.p.h, since horseless carriages were first introduced. That, you might think, would have given bus managers some inkling of the interval at which buses should be released from each depot. Despite this experience, waiting for a 159 gave a good impression of what eternity must be like. Following the reorganization of London Transport into smaller areas, decision making moved closer to the garages. In 1992, the route was divided into two: the 159 would go from Streatham into the centre and return; a new 139 service would go from

---

[1] See, for example, John Stopford and Costas Markides "From Ugly Ducklings to Elegant Swans," *Business Strategy Review* (1995) vol. 6, no. 2. Their research confirmed the centrality of strategic innovation and found the obstacles to be human short sightedness and unwillingness to articulate the purpose of the firm in other than financial terms.

Hampstead, overlap with the 159 to give extra buses where they were most needed, and then return. The reluctance of the natives of Hampstead to visit Streatham was, in any case, matched by Streatham's disinterest in Hampstead. Splitting the route was a simple idea and an instant success. It was too radical for the previous regime which had no culture of change.

Some believe that any major alteration requires to be triggered by crisis, real or imaginary. All change is pain; it needs a bigger pain to make it acceptable. It is true that an organization set in its ways will need some major stimulus to adapt. On the other hand, modern companies are making change a way of life.

Change can be categorized by the scale of its impact:

- **Seismic shift** following acquisition or a new CEO or a disaster or all three. The only seismic shift that concerns this book is changing a business to a market orientation, if it does not have one already. That is more an issue of leadership than marketing. Talking culture change does not bring it about. On the other hand, a CEO who gets into the market place, looks at marketing measures, asks market questions and bases bonuses on market place results (brand equity) will rapidly induce a market orientation.

- **Major shift** such as entry to a new product category, line of business, type of customer, or country. Different organizations successfully adapt in different ways. One classic is the use of "champions," pioneered by the 3M Corporation. These are senior managers with the muscle and know-how to crash the concept through the organizational barriers of inertia and negativism. The system only works when the manager develops a personal commitment and even an evangelical enthusiasm for the change. The manager needs to know the extent of the difficulties but understand how relationships can be managed to give the result. Sometimes the champion is the CEO but there is a limit to the number of such causes any one manager, or the organization as a whole, can, or should, handle. The application of this principle to radical new brand or product development is considered in "Ugly Duckling."

- **Minor improvements** are what the Japanese call "*kaizen*" or continuous improvement. All employees make constant small improvements to their areas of business. The positive attitude to change becomes endemic. Total quality management shares with marketing the concept of seeing things from the customer and/or consumer viewpoint and then *measuring* the improvement from changes. The concept of empowerment is grand but implementation can be a nightmare. An "improvement" by the sales person can be a step backwards for accounts. *Kaizen* needs teamwork to be effective.

If you wonder what brand managers actually do, we have just got to the nub. Seismic change has to be managed from the top as does the creation of a culture which allows *kaizen* to flourish. Within whatever corporate culture exists, marketers can seek out and inspire novation. Their speciality lies in bringing all those minor improvements made, in a large company, by very many people into harmony. Just occasionally, they get a shot at a major change, a brand launch, a line extension, or whatever. That may not seem heroic but it is how Agincourt was won.

> **Within whatever corporate culture exists, marketers can seek out and inspire novation.**

Marketing is "organized rational innovation" and it is the brand manager who does the organizing and makes sure that the constant stream of innovations are rational. The culture of the organization needs to be developed to encourage continuous improvement.

THE NEW MONEY MACHINE

The historical evolution of marketing was volume, followed by costs, followed by price. In the beginning was volume: if you could make it, you could sell it. As production increased, the focus switched to costs: you had to make it for less. Quality was always an issue but as production skills improved again, the opportunities for cost reduction began to achieve diminishing returns. The post-60s developments looked increasingly for values that could be added to give consumers more than utilitarian satisfaction and justify more than utilitarian prices.

> **Volumes and costs need to line up before you make a profit.**

Marketing draws profits from all three of these commercial fundamentals: volume, cost reduction, and added value.

The New Money Machine applies this principle to marketing planning. It is based on the one-armed bandit, not inappropriately some will think. Added values are the cherries. Even one will pay out and if you can get a whole line, the payout is handsome. Volumes and costs need to line up before you make a profit. Here's how it works:

1. Convene a meeting of top management in some oasis to review the organization's, and therefore their, future. The objective is to identify innovations, establish their credibility, costs, and potential benefits. You may

regard what follows as practical or just an agenda. The need is to free thinking from the shackles of convention.

2. Review the five-year plan, brainstorm, let syndicates loose, or do whatever you usually do to get the motivation and creative energies surging.

3. Recognize that new money can come, acquisitions apart, *only* from one of the three kinds of change outlined above. If it is seismic, it is the CEO's job; major change needs a champion and minor change is for everyone with the brand manager, or equivalent, coordinating. Shifts are not necessarily positive; they can be expansion or contraction, plus or minus.

4. Major shifts can be territories, customers/channels of distribution, product categories, production and distribution techniques or facilities, competition entering, leaving, or alliances. The game is to align individuals with sources of new money. Peer pressure does not create champions but it can force reluctant initiators to think about which are the most likely, or least unlikely, sources. As commitment to their opinions grows, so does belief and from this champions emerge.

5. The appeal of one-armed bandits lies largely in the satisfaction of pulling the lever. When electric models were first introduced, the hand level was replaced by a button. No fun. The hand lever, which provides the illusion of control, had to be replaced. The New Money Machine is the same. The champion gets to pull the lever. Whether the champion gets coins clattering into the cup below depends a lot on luck. Sophisticated machines allow good progress to be held in one quarter while another pull rotates the rest of the fruit. If volume looks right, hold it and rotate price and costs.

The game can be played with coins and a machine or metaphorically. Childish? Of course. It is a contrivance. It is no more than a toy, as all planning devices are, to tease out possible actions that would not otherwise come to light. An agenda for innovation should simulate the real world and encourage managers to *own* those innovations they believe in. Everyone plays and no one gets hurt. The objective is to liberate thinking, to make anything seem possible because then perhaps it is.

The required attitude is exemplified by this story. Art Fry[2] sang in the choir on Sundays. The paper he used to mark the beginning of each hymn fell out

---

[2] Based on: Carol Kennedy, "Planning Global Strategies for 3M," *Long Range Planning* (1988) vol. 21, no. 1.

and he did not like to turn down the corners of the pages. Where he worked, the glue factory had a product which had failed but it did give a weak paper to paper to paper adhesive. It solved his problem so well that a few weeks later he took some samples into the marketing department. He knew they, as the best marketers in the business, would recognize an opportunity when they saw it. They didn't. Art is not someone who gives up easily. He made up pads, sent them to colleagues around the offices and waited for the enthusiasm to reach the marketers. The pads were an immediate success but the marketers were unmoved. Eventually Art got them to make a small market test – in a small mid-west town where they recycled the few incoming letters that came in. Marketers know how to run market tests.

By now he was pestering the chief executive who was persuaded to send pads to his opposite numbers, the CEOs of the Fortune 500 companies. They loved them too – where could they buy them?

Of course this is the story of Post-It notes in 3M. Art Fry is a hero; the name of the marketing VP is in decent obscurity. It is a tale of perseverance but the more interesting part of the story is that the Marketing VP was right. The new product did not meet the needs of the market that the VP was tasked to service. Wrong paradigm.

SETTING PRIORITIES

The meeting should have provided a set of innovations, what is involved, the costs, and benefits. Conventional wisdom now requires the setting of priorities. This may not be a good idea. Good, fired up champions will ignore them anyway. Art would have done. Priorities may be set under the wrong paradigm. Strategic innovation needs to change the business definition.

Avoid priority setting for the sake of tidiness or rationality.

Speed to market has become an imperative as competition hots up. The leisurely days of endless research are gone. Setting priorities can provide reasons for delay; it is easier to put things back than forward.

On the other hand, internal combat can do wonders to test the strength of champions and improve their products. If no one will fight for them, you have the wrong innovations, the wrong managers, or both.

Clearly managers need to have their own priorities. When these compete for resources, the need for priority setting arrives. In other words, avoid priority setting for the sake of tidiness or rationality. Use it gladiatorially to strengthen the change concepts and the champions. Nothing should delay getting the concepts to the consumer for only the consumer should be allowed to choose.

Back in the office, many enthusiasms will wither and die. Those that do not will need nurture, encouragement, limited funding, testing. That process is not just building individual new ideas into profits but also building the organization's change culture. Novation should not just be allowed but expected, from everyone everywhere.

Memo to file

Subject: NOVATION

- Innovation is the life blood of marketing. Creative ideas are valuable but the greater part is harnessing them to profitable productive change. Brand management needs to ensure it is organized and rational.

- Wisdom before the event requires participation within a culture of change. Get your team together to review a full agenda for innovation.

- Major changes need evangelism. Establish champions and give them internal workouts.

- Leave priority setting to the marketplace.

15

ORGANIZATION STRUCTURE AND ENTROPY

Bureaucratization can kill marketing. So how should you organize?

Key issues

● **Marketing organization structure and size** ● **Downsizing, delayering and outsourcing** ● **Disorder is a natural condition which increases faster than organizational size**

ORGANIZATION STRUCTURE AND SIZE

Few organizations in the 1990s escaped being re-engineered, downsized, and delayered. This chapter supports the smaller is better principle though some firms have taken it too far. Having consultants do the outsourced work at twice the cost makes little sense. Nor does the removal of the opportunity for marketers to learn as they move up the ranks. Encourage small mistakes or they will make big ones. Finding the right balance includes:

● **A clear distinction between "boundary spanning" functions and internal ones.** Success is created at the border of a business. A sale is only a sale when an outsider buys something. Corporate swindlers such as Robert Maxwell survive from year to year through representing internal sales as external. As a rule of thumb, a company should be more relaxed about taking on another boundary spanner than another analyst. The first one should directly improve market relationships, as well as some internal functions. The internalist adds costs for sure and to relationships indirectly at best. Unfortunately, it is the internalists who get to make the cost cutting recommendations, frequently on using external consultants. If they looked at the consultants' own organizations, they would find some of the highest boundary spanner/internalist ratios in business. And the lowest internal reporting requirements.

- **Eliminate work before people.** Proof that this has not been done shows how busy modern marketers are. Brand assistants have been removed but not the work they did. Preoccupation with immediate detail, rather than the big issues facing the brand, is probably the main cause of the poor press marketers have had, e.g. McKinsey.[1] Much, perhaps most, internal paperwork can be jettisoned if only the top people were not too burdened with paper to attend to it. Ask "who needs this paper?" and you will find that everyone assumes someone *else* wants it. Have a paper (OK electronic too) moratorium for a month. Whoever then has to *ask* for a report to be compiled is then the guilty party. In the perfect world, you should only have to produce information for yourself and share it with others if they want to see it too. Brand managers do need to see brand equity measures; top management merely needs to look over their shoulder.

> If there is a specialist marketing function at all, it needs to be small enough to welcome teamwork with the other functions.

- **Clear focus on what customer relationships and parts of the mix are key.** Organizational learning of the key aspects is why these need to be in-house. The rest can be externally supplied.

- **Marketing is too important to be left to marketers.** If there is a specialist marketing function at all, it needs to be small enough to welcome teamwork with the other functions and strong enough to convert other functions to marketing thinking. Cross-functional brand planning is an important finding from the McKinsey and other studies.

- **Specialization.** The marketing as relationships concept recognizes that time is more important than money. Boundary spanners have to specialize in one type of relationship, and, within that, individual personal relationships, to maintain sanity. Chairmen deal with shareholders, sales with immediate customers, marketing with consumers and so on. The extent to which this specialization requires internal support, e.g. sales by trade marketing, is open to question but not to generalization.

---

[1] John Brady and Ian Davis "Marketing's Mid-life Crisis," (1993) and Michael George, Anthony Freeling and David Court "Reinventing the Marketing Organization," (1994) both in *The McKinsey Quarterly*, no. 2 and no. 4 respectively.

DISORDER IS A NATURAL CONDITION

"Entropy" is the natural state of disorder; physicists study it. Universities are its natural habitat. The rest of us take it for granted. Entropy is the condition of my desk, most organizations, their customers' businesses, and their consumers' minds. Why do people expect things to be tidy? Why do they spend so much time cleaning up? (Joan Rivers used to say she hated house-work; you clean up and next year you have to start all over again.) Where did this passion for tidiness come from?

Undoubtedly some order is necessary to get things done; enough, but not too much. In marketing, there is no evidence that the most analytic, structured, orderly marketing plans produce the best profits.

The right balance between order and disorder in any household or business is too subjective to discuss here except in one respect: what implication does entropy have for the structure of large businesses? The success of a large business depends on how it is divided into units, how well each works, and how they work together. The repercussions of entropy can be serious.

Business activities can be represented as flows of information. People costs can be modelled by charting information flows. For example, an eight person business unit has 28 two way information flows (figure 15.1) but two units of four people, with a liaison dyad, has only 13 (figure 15.2). A 16 person unit would have 80 connections compared to 28 in four linked units of four people each. The arithmetic of scale is apparent: the number of connections rise much faster than the number of persons in a unit. Thus this arithmetic underlies the need for departments within units within companies within groups.

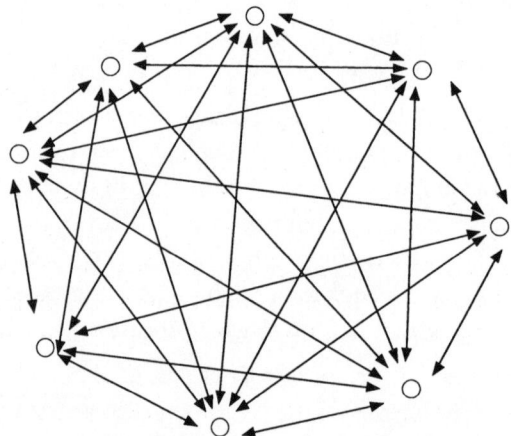

Fig 15.1   Communication flows – eight person unit

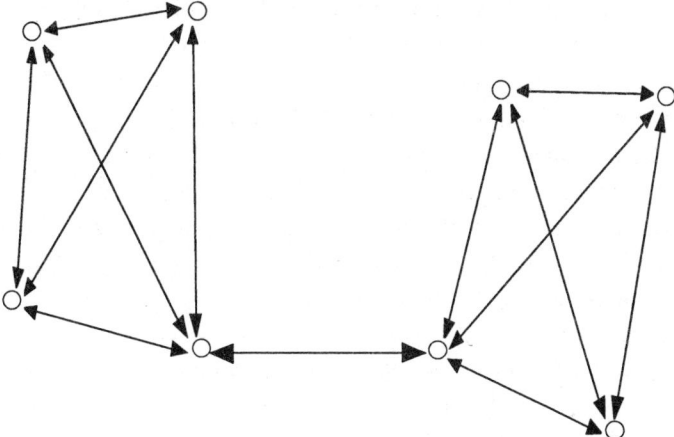

Fig 15.2   Communication flows – two x four person units

When structuring a large organization, managers should be seeking to optimize the placement of internal borders to minimize the needed number of connections. Other things being equal, the laws of physics tell us that smaller is better than bigger.

The second law of thermodynamics says that the entropy of an isolated system always increases. Furthermore, when two systems join together, the combined entropy is greater than the sum of their individual entropies. Businesspeople recognize that the shambles inherent in any two businesses is much worse when you put them together. A system left to its own devices runs down, but merging two such systems is worse. The bringing together of the UK regional railway companies in 1948 was a fine example of combined entropy.

Entropy has been overlooked when explaining why acquisitions fail and why large organizations fall apart. The armed forces, on the other hand, are all too familiar with the experience that the larger the numbers involved in an exercise, the more cosmic the bungle is likely to be. Don't blame the generals for defeats; entropy is usually to blame. Armies used to get larger and larger because fire-power correlated with manpower. Today, armed forces use technology to keep payrolls down. Marketers may one day achieve the same but the headcount benefits of IT to marketing are still some way off.

Tidiness decays because disorder is natural. The larger the organization the more help nature gets to ensure disorder proliferates.

Success in any field depends on focus, good internal communications and organization. Teamwork depends on trust and other human factors but also on sheer numbers. Some say the perfect committee size is three, with two off sick. Others that 100 or 200 or 500 is the perfect number of people in a business unit. How should a 100,000 people organization be structured?

Entropy is minimized by having the largest possible number of strategic business units (SBUs). An SBU is a unit of the business that is self sufficient and could operate without the parent company (something a lot of SBUs dream about). That implies that each SBU must be commercially and economically viable. An SBU is a marketing organization with the resources and authority to achieve its objectives. In reality, the distinction cannot be precise. Some functions can be delegated to SBUs but some have to be shared at group level. Even so, the concept is robust enough to be used to structure organizations not only in all large businesses, but also in the armed forces, and in health and education.

> **Entropy is minimized by having the largest possible number of strategic business units.**

What we have not yet allowed for is that these SBUs are themselves particles, so to speak, in the group's space. The more SBUs there are, the more entropy will exist at this level. In other words, the teamwork within each SBU is terrific but the SBUs are getting on so badly between themselves that the group is falling apart. Bird's Eye used to have a meat division, a fish division, and a vegetable division. What kind of problems would they have had in launching a paella? Any system of order suppresses thought. Maybe regular reorganization is part of the solution, but then such preoccupations become part of the problem.

If market researchers are allowed to add two awareness numbers to create a mythical measure called "total awareness," we can do the same with entropy. The "total entropy" of a large organization is therefore the sum of the entropies *within* each SBU plus the entropy *between* SBUs. They can be visualized as being akin to the information flows in figures 15.1 and 15.2. Minimize total entropy and your organization is well structured. What could be simpler?

Memo to file

Subject: ORGANIZATION STRUCTURE AND ENTROPY

- In any reorganization, consider the optimal boundary spanners/internalists ratio. Maximize organizational learning capability and teamwork.

- Entropy, the state of disorder, is natural. Focus your efforts on putting order only where it matters for results.

- A large business should organize itself into the number of SBUs that minimizes "total entropy," provided no SBU is smaller than can be economically justified.

- Each SBU should be a marketing organization with whatever it takes to grow success.

16

POSITIONING – MARKETING'S MARTIAL ART

The brand's choice of fighting ground is crucial to its success

---

Key issues
- **Differentiation and preference: the brand's fundamentals**
- **Making space for the brand – choosing the competition**
- **Defining the consumer ● Perceptual maps ● Defining the distribution channels ● Using Asian lessons in strategy**
- **The positioning statement**

We will talk about brand positioning as a marketing activity in the virtual reality of the consumer's mind. "Virtual" because we cannot really read a consumer's mind and because all consumers differ. This virtual reality can also be seen as a battleground where brands compete for space and domination. In this chapter we draw heavily on these mental and military metaphors in drawing up the brand's "positioning statement." This sets out where the brand stands relative to its intended audience, competitors and distributors. The marketing process differentiates that location and makes it as attractive as possible.

BRAND DIFFERENTIATION AND PREFERENCE

The value of a brand is created by the consumer in his/her own mind. Constant rediscovery of this old concept is witness to its vitality. Positioning is the art of dominating, relative to competitors, that territory. Fanciful? Difficult certainly. Quite apart from the multitude of consumers, each different, just one mindset, even if it could be so accurately determined, changes with mood, experience, and competing needs.

"Positioning" is variously defined but Ries and Trout who popularized the word[1] in the 1980s are clear about the between the ears approach. To them, "positioning" is encapsulated by a very few words that distinguish this brand from any other, the more narrowly the better. Philadelphia, for example, is "the best cream cheese." The brand should position

> **A brand is a brand primarily because it is different to other brands and secondly because it is, in some way, superior.**

itself in the most favorable slot in the consumer mind. If it is already occupied, the competitive brand should be "repositioned" by your activity. Rather a tall order.

To avoid confusion with the wider "positioning statement" which includes other definitions, e.g. target consumer, this short distinguishing phrase may be called "the consumer proposition."

Some marketers believe that positioning is not a matter of imagery but of substantive product characteristics. Cars with larger engines are positioned apart from those with lower horse power. Real product advantages are always preferable to images. In practice, marketers need all the help they can get, i.e. both.

A brand is a brand primarily because it is different to other brands and secondly because it is, in some way, superior. These two stages are the raison d'être of any brand. Any brand building activity must be based upon them. Differentiation is primary because it cannot be better without first being different. Before both, the consumer's present, and likely future, preferences have to be thoroughly understood, and then the extent to which other brands meet them. If you light upon an important consumer need which no other brand meets, you are lucky indeed.

Häagen Dazs arrived on the US market because other ice creams were getting cheaper and lower in calories. The opportunity arose to position an ice cream as luxurious (expensive) and high in calories (indulgent).

Over time, even the most accurate positioning, immaculately executed, will become less correct as the consumer drifts from its acceptance. Repositioning is one of those occasional exercises, once every five years, say, to return alignment.

---

[1] Al Ries and Jack Trout *Positioning: The battle for your Mind*, (New York, McGraw-Hill, 1986).

MAKING SPACE FOR THE BRAND – CHOOSING THE COMPETITION

Positioning has militaristic overtones. Attacks should be launched from a more favorable position. You should take the high ground, provided you can defend it. Otherwise you will be exposed. The military, or conflict, paradigm is reviewed more fully in chapter 11, "Kamikaze and Guerrilla Marketing," but it interweaves here.

Positioning is related to strength: unless you are strong enough to take on the brand leader(s), it is better to find a niche to build the brand's strength before embarking on a wider campaign. The ice cream vendors on the beach have been mentioned elsewhere. The first vendor should take the centre and the second should go alongside *but only if the second is, near enough, as strong as the first*. If the comparison is invidious, the second vendor will do better at some distance.

As for Häagen Dazs, the ideal case allows the brand to get close to consumer ideals and, at the same time, a long way from the competition. More usually, the big brands have got there before you. At this point, you should choose your competition with care. By and large, you should choose whichever of the top three or four is the weakest. Avoid macho instincts to tackle the brand leader unless you are already number two or the brand leader is weakening fast.

In any case, make the brand's own space in order to develop its own personality.

THE CONSUMER

Whether you should begin with the target competitor or consumer, is open to debate. Marketing fundamentalists claim you should always begin with the consumer but as positioning is essentially a *strategy* matter, the competitive perspective is relevant. In practice, one consideration leads immediately to the other and the sequence matters little.

What does matter is that weak brands should define the consumer segment, i.e. the target market, they most wish to gain. The narrower the focus, the better. Identifying the competitor helps identify the target consumer and vice versa. Again the target consumers should be those most likely to switch *and* the most valuable. Light users may be valuable if they are trend setters. Positioning should usually be up wind of the ultimate objective. Let the sound of the sizzle attract the steak hunters.

Chapter 27 deals with "Surgical Segmentation" but the concept is simple enough. Any group that can be separately identified and reached, and whose consumers are more like each other than consumers outside the group, is a "segment." There are three conditions here which are not easily met in practice. We tend to assume, for example, that all 21–25-year-old males in manual labour drink beer. This group would be termed a segment. It is easily identified and reached but it is not, in fact, so homogeneous. Some young men prefer wine; some are teetotallers.

> **The target consumers should be those most likely to switch *and* the most valuable.**

Nevertheless, positioning needs a clear stereotype of the target consumer. The more the marketer can identify exactly who the target consumer is, the more likely the target's needs, and the positionings of competitor brands, can be clarified. Some brand managers find likenesses in magazines and pin them on their walls. At least that was who they said they were. A single picture can tell the copywriter more than a page of analysis even if the market researcher does want it in numbers.

PERCEPTUAL MAPS

Better to be fixated by the consumer's relationship with your brand than with competition. Intensity of focus may reveal what others miss. Excessive concern with competition is distracting and enfeebling. If the consumer-brand relationship is strong enough, there is nothing to worry about. In any case, there may not be much to be done about other relationships. All you can fix is your own. Iago may have ruined Othello's relationship with Desdemona but he did not do himself much good. The consumer and the brand are two personalities that the marketer, as matchmaker, is trying to get to entangle with one another. Presenting the best features of the brand tends to work better than knocking copy. We need to know who and where the competitors are, usually to stay out of their way, not to compete. Before we do anything we need a map.

Mapping the consumers' minds may sound millennial, the maths a bit advanced, but the concept is straightforward: decompose consumers' wants into attributes and then assess how well each brand delivers each attribute.

In 1970, the UK target vodka consumer wanted first purity or cleanliness of spirit, then potency, and then a whole list of attributes with diminishing enthusiasm. "Smoothness" is one of the most demanded characteristics of spirit drinks. Vodka was able to go further and offer alcohol with almost no impurities. On the face of it, purity and smoothness were the strongest potential claims. Potency was interesting because vodka was perceived to be stronger than other spirits such as whisky, gin, or rum whereas, in reality, it was 6.5 percent weaker.

Having established what the attributes are, the consumer can tell you how each brand rates on that scale. The sheer variety of attributes is where the mathematics come in. The most important to the consumer may not be actionable to the marketer because all brands rate the same. You can either consider the most actionable and forget the rest or you can apply factor or cluster analysis to reduce the number of attributes to understandable size. Better still, draw the positions on maps. Using purity and potency as two dimensions for example, the 1970 vodka market could have been mapped as in figure 16.1.

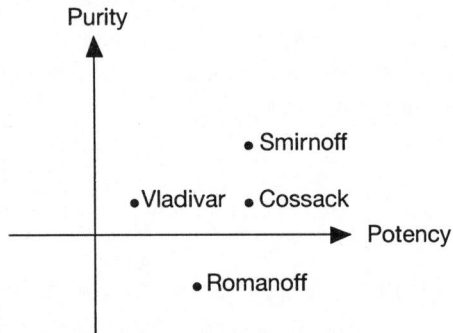

Fig 16.1   Vodha perceptual map (1970)

We now have a map of where the brands lie. We also know where the ideal position is though there may be conflicts, e.g. wanting the most expensive brand at the cheapest price. In addition to marking the positions, the map can indicate the strength of each brand. The perfect positioning is the point on the map representing the ideal from the target consumer's point of view which is also furthest away from the competition, especially the strong competition.

Even if you like this technique, and quite a few marketers do not, perfect positioning rarely exists. The usual choice is between over-competitive positions and those empty spaces ("Bermuda Triangles") that are empty for good reason. All previous brands that have attempted that positioning sank without trace. Neither will really do but by reviewing the map a least bad position can be identified where there is a chance of brand differentiation in ways attractive to the consumer.

Perceptual maps are rather useful models for internal discussion but they should not be taken too seriously. A brand is more than a sum of attributes, or "utilities" to an economist. This type of analysis is subject to cognitive bias and the elimination of the very life force the marketer is seeking to understand. It is not unlike dissecting an animal on the laboratory bench and complaining that the animal is dead when the parts are finally put back together.

> **A least bad position can be identified where there is a chance of brand differentiation in ways attractive to the consumer.**

An alternative is to use associations by "projecting"[2] brands onto some totally different species, animals for example. In 1992, a professional UK organization was reviewing its strategy. First it had to determine its positioning. Every member of the steering group had a different slant on what the organization should be. They were asked to project the characteristics of their professional organization by identifying which religion it was most like. Some said Church of England because it was traditional, broad church, and, perhaps, undemanding. Others said Methodist as they were looking for a stronger network and missionary zeal. Buddhist, Quaker, Greek Orthodox, Judaism, and others claimed places for various reasons. The exercise was not intended to be definitive but a way of expressing the desired characteristics of their own group indirectly. It certainly exposed the conflicting expectations the members of the steering group had for their organization. The steering group collapsed shortly after and the organization lumbers on without clear direction.

Whatever methodology is used, the outcome needs to be a clear picture of how the brand and its competitors relate to consumers' wishes, how they are differentiated, and where the preferences lie.

DEFINING THE DISTRIBUTION CHANNELS

One more set of players need to be targeted before the war games can commence: the most important distribution channel(s). This may have been set by consumer and competition. If the consumers are the female counterparts of male world travelling executives and the competition are the leading perfume makers, we are into duty free shopping.

[2] Dennis W. Rook "Researching Consumer Fantasy," *Research In Consumer Behavior*, vol. 3, (1988) pp247–70.
Sidney J. Levy "Dreams, Fairy Tales, Animals and Cars," *Psychology & Marketing*, vol. 2, no. 2, (1985) pp.67–81.

Duty free is a good example of the distribution medium being the message. Few airports can claim any longer to be luxury experiences but the glamor lingers. Conversely, the perfume brand owners fought, in the early 1990s, to keep their products out of cut price chemists because of concerns not so much with price as with the damage the association with grotty shops would have on their brand equities.

In principle the whole channel should be considered but in practice the immediate customer is usually the prime concern. As with the consumer, the brand/customer relationship has to be understood from both sides. Identifying what the brand needs from the trade is easy enough, but why should the trade provide it? Their shelves are already full; consumers are already satisfied.

> **Duty free is a good example of the distribution medium being the message.**

The questions are the same whether you are establishing the immediate customer's perspective or the consumer's: what is different about this brand? What is better, i.e. why should I carry it? The salesforce will have had years of answering these questions and should do so now. If the inside team do not like the salesforce's answers, some painful re-evaluation is needed.

Distribution is only one part of the marketing mix, albeit one the marketer may overlook (it being the sales team's job). Of course, the brand's positioning is determined by the rest of the mix but the reverse is more important: the positioning determines the mix. We have now arrived at the fun, the point at which positioning becomes a martial art. You know where the combatants are. Will you attack, defend, or hide?

USING ASIAN LESSONS IN STRATEGY

The players in this virtual reality game are the distribution channels represented by the immediate customer, the competitors, and your brand. The battleground (pace Ries and Trout again[3]) is the consumer's mind and you want to win. You have fewer resources than you think you need. Your budget has been reduced even from the puny amount you requested. Life was ever thus.

There are no rules in marketing because rules, once established, would cease to provide competitive advantage. Worse still, consumers would be bored and irritated by repetition. Innovation is the life blood of marketing. Worse again would be to reduce millennia of sophisticated strategic thinking

---

[3] Al Ries and Jack Trout, *Marketing Warfare*, (New York, McGraw–Hill, 1986).

to a few simplistic phrases. So let us do just that by extracting some lessons from Asian writers on strategy from Sun Zi to Mao Zedong (see chapter 11 "Kamikaze and Guerrilla Marketing"):

- Only go where the competitor is if you will crush him. If he is bigger than you are, go some place else.

- Gain strength by cooperating with competitors in the short term. Helping them at their own expense reduces the apparent threat and builds your resources for the day you can strike decisively.

  Only go where the competitor is if you will crush him.

- Joint ventures are a valuable source of learning about your partner of today who may well be your enemy of tomorrow.

- If the competitor is big and trampling out new territory, he is probably making nice places for you. It may be worth following at a discreet distance.

- If competitors are fighting each other, leave them to it. Resist the temptation to join in.

- Find out which way the wind is blowing. Stay upwind of consumers and downwind of competitors.

- Do not do for consumers what they can do for themselves. For example, if your product is pale in colour, do not waste money telling them what they can see for themselves.

- Do not make your plan obvious. If you do not know what you are doing either, it may even help.

- When the fantasizing is all done, positioning must be realistic. A brand can only be, and should only try to be, what it is. A facade cannot be defended for long. Positioning is making the best of what a brand is, not trying to make it into something else.

How did the positioning exercise work for Smirnoff in 1970? Purity was the key attribute but it was decided not to go for it. Other vodkas, mostly Cossack at that time, did the same research and tended to major on purity. Consumers knew vodka was relatively pure anyway. They also knew that Smirnoff was more expensive and therefore, by inference, better. The perception that vodka was stronger than it really was, was the key fact. So was Russianness. There were associations with large, husky men in furs and spurs downing glasses in one and throwing them into fire places while blondes fainted. The label showed clearly that Smirnoff was made in England.

Many knew that it came from Harlow, Essex. They preferred to enjoy the myth. Potency was where Smirnoff positioned itself. Over the decade, sales grew from about 300,000 cases a year to over 2 million.

THE POSITIONING STATEMENT

Just as there are many variations on the positioning theme, so each writer has a pet format for a positioning statement. This is just one:

Brand description: A paragraph to explain what the brand and its component products are is useful even where, especially where, the team know all that.

Consumer proposition: A *very* brief distinguishing phrase, e.g. "The Cream of Manchester" for Boddington's beer. The phrase may be the tagline on the advertising but often is not. It is a strategic statement, not copywriting artistry. Keeping a proposition focussed requires *sacrifice*. A brand that is all things to all people is nothing to anyone. The smaller and weaker a brand is, the narrower the focus, and the more the consequential sacrifice. Narrow focus is good practice for large brands too but very large, much extended brands like Mitsubishi can sustain a broader proposition. Brand extension usually requires the proposition to become more abstract, i.e. less product related, but not necessarily less precise. Virgin can no longer maintain a product proposition across entertainment, airlines, cola, financial services, and vodka but the brand personality, a.k.a. Richard Branson, is singular.

Partner consumer: Hitherto the phrase "target consumer' has been used in line with convention. One of the themes of this book, however, is that the consumer and the brand (owner) are partners, that both benefit from the exchange. The word "target" is appropriate enough for the competitor one hopes to outwit, but is hardly friendly to the user. The partner consumer can be expressed in demographic or psychographic terms but my preference is for a simple pen picture, e.g. young, unmarried bricklayer with a Kamasaki motor cycle.

Target competitor: This is typically answered with a list of all the other brands in the category and thereby loses all meaning. Target *the* brand from which you aim to take most business. Or two brands if you plan to go in two directions at once.

Differentiation: Why, and how, is your brand different from the rest of the category/the target competitor.

Preference: Why is your brand *better*?

Pricing strategy: Which of the pricing strategy alternatives (skimming, penetration, etc.) do you follow/plan to follow? Will you be above, below, or at parity with the target competitor?

Target channel: Which customer group, apart from the end consumer, matters most?

Trade factors: Apart from the differentiation, preference, and pricing factors above, why should the trade carry your brand?

Positioning statements are usually designed by committee, and look it. The consumer proposition is a page long when it should be a sentence. Everyone has their particular proposition in there somewhere. The positioning statement of an international brand will typically have elements contributed from the most powerful national businesses. This United Nations approach is not all bad; the national businesses can continue to build on their success. Unfortunately it consolidates the walls between countries and their ability to learn from one another. Brand strategies will differ; advertising and promotions will not be transferable.

The better route is painful. David Ogilvy originated the idea that a brand should be interrogated until it confessed its true essence. To do that across all countries' experience is better as there is more to draw upon, but also more sacrifices, usually of sacred cows, to be made. The process should define a precise proposition, and a precise target consumer. Defining the same target competitor and trade channels across all markets may well not be feasible. You may be the number two brand in each market with different market leaders. Ultimately each case has to be decided on the circumstances. The counsel here is simply that marketing thrust will be improved by greater precision and that requires greater sacrifice.

Memo to file

Subject: POSITIONING

- Positioning is the art of establishing the brand in the minds of the target consumer most advantageously relative to competition. Positioning uses both real and image attributes.

- That requires total understanding of the stereotypical partner consumer, your own brand and the relationship between them. Do not try to make your brand into what it is not, or what the consumer finds incredible. A durable relationship requires realism.

- Understand competitor positionings but do not be mesmerized by them.

- Use your brand's weakness to take advantage of competitive strengths. Note Asian strategic arts. Only compete when you will win without excessive cost. The rest of the time, cooperate or stay clear.

- Ensure your brand has a current positioning statement updated as part of the annual planning process.

- Positioning = precision = sacrifice.

17

PRODUCT SATISFACTION

Whether goods or services, the product should bring the customer back for more

---

Key issues

● Product differentiation and advantage ● Does quality really matter? ● The Reverse Salami Principle – how to stop quality degradation ● Consistency versus product improvement ● *Kaizen* and line extension ● Product or brand life cycles ● What is different for durables?

PRODUCT DIFFERENTIATION

There is much confusion between the terms b*rand* and *product*. Which is the hero and which the afterthought? As we considered under "Brand Equity" (see chapter 2), the product may be aimed at other businesses or private consumers, and it may be physical goods or intangible services or, usually, both. We adopted the "holistic" view that

Brand = Product + Packaging + Added values

The product consists of all those utilitarian attributes that rational consumers get for their money. They include technical and economic benefits: with a car, for example, benefits include fuel economy and space for passengers and freight. "Product" here excludes those more ephemeral qualities of brand personality, consumer perceptions, and psychosocial benefits which add value to the product from the consumer's point of view. Packaging is simply the external skin of the product that the buyer sees; in the case of a service, packaging refers to the appearance of sales staff, paper, shop fascias, or whatever the user encounters.

Vodka, the product, is pure ethyl alcohol (C_2O_5OH) mixed with water(H_2O). It is, in the practical sense, useful for removing stains from ties but not much else. Virtually all of those lovely qualities that create demand and satisfaction are in the mind; to proclaim the chemical formulae to be reality and dismiss the intangible attributes as irrelevant fantasy would be like throwing a diamond ring out with the potato peelings.

> **To gain advantage, you first have to distinguish the product from the competition.**

Stephen King, one of the most perceptive UK writers on brands and advertising, summarized the difference between brand and product as follows:

- A product is something made in a factory; a brand is something bought by a customer.
- A product can be copied by a competitor; a brand is unique.
- A product can be quickly outdated; a successful brand is timeless.

Nevertheless, product and packaging differences do matter. It may seem eccentric to have to mention that, but previous generations of marketers became so absorbed with images that reality was left behind. For UK High Street banks, "marketing" meant advertising, promotions, and anything but the product itself. Yet marketing essentially requires consumer satisfaction with the product. Some say that is not enough; the marketer should aim to *delight* the consumer. Any substantive advantage a physical product or a service can gain over the competition will help sales now and long after competition has caught up in real terms. Product advantage lingers in consumer memory.

Thus, when this book suggests

Marketing = Branding

   = Product differentiation + Advantage + Packaging + Intangibles

it is product advantage itself that is critical, i.e. quality from the consumer's point of view. Improving packaging and the intangible, added values, aspects of branding, while important, are secondary. To gain advantage, however, you first have to distinguish the product from the competition: if the consumer sees them as all the same, there is nothing to build on. Thus vodkas rely on subtle flavors or countries of origin or raw materials to differentiate themselves from one another even though they are all $C_2O_5OH + H_2O$. Having made that separation the brand owners can then seek to demonstrate why Finland or Russia or potatoes provide better vodka.

Smirnoff is put through nine columns of activated charcoal and emerges cleaner and purer. No other vodka follows that process. The difference is subtle and immensely uninteresting to the modern consumer. When Smirnoff was first introduced, however, the difference mattered. Proving the quality then, still supports the brand today.

Procter and Gamble has traditionally insisted on verifiable product advantage before any new product is launched. The "white box test" compares the products, in research, without the benefits of packaging and added values. That is an admirable spur to R&D and marketers alike. Large or small, these advantages give the salespeople a difference worth talking about and reassurance to the rational part of customer judgement. Whatever our true reason for buying, we like to be able to justify our choice.

Rosser Reeves coined the expression Unique Selling Proposition (USP) in the 1930s. One of the founders of the Ted Bates advertising agency, Reeves was dedicated to the idea that the product must have a difference, preferably a verifiable advantage, and it should be used consistently in all advertising. For him, the medium was not the message. Marketing trends took that idea in and out of fashion but Reeves was fundamentally right. Sales forces the world over have reason to be grateful for his championing such a primitive thought: give us something we can tell our customers. "USP" has fallen out of use, which means it will return, in favour of "Product Differentiation."

DOES QUALITY REALLY MATTER?

Emerson is supposed to have first said that a better mousetrap would bring the world to the maker's door. Elbert Hubbard claimed he was, in fact, the maker of that better dictum and who ever heard of him? There's the rub. Publicity creates markets, not products. Awareness drives demand through packaging, advertising, and promotion. Low cost production, mass marketing, and economies of scale fuel the competitive pricing that creates high market share; profits will follow. Or so some think.

There developed a conventional wisdom that the market leader would also be the most profitable. The second brand would be profitable enough but there were few, if any, prizes for the unplaced horses. Examples can justify this judgement. Academic research is ambiguous; market share may or may not be a predictor of relative profitability. You can rely on research like that. Brand leaders are indeed more likely to be profitable than the laggards but the relationship is weak.

Much of this research came from the PIMS database in Cambridge, Mass. The initial conclusions were that share drives long-term profits. Clearly it does not drive short-term profits as steep price discounts send share up and profits down. Closer

Both share and profits were correlated with quality as perceived by the customer.

examination[1] showed that both share and profits were correlated with quality as perceived by the customer. Plausible that: if consumers think the product is better they will both buy it more often and be prepared to pay a higher price.

In the 19th century, quality was known to be important; new wealth had created a demand for better rather than more. Quality could be measured in terms of weight, thickness, strength, and/or delicacy. In this pre-Einstein age, quality was self evident and absolute. Finer fabrics were measurably finer. Quality could thus be defined numerically. Men in white coats could inspect production to guarantee satisfactory standards were set. Tolerance of the substandard was not a 19th century virtue.

Enter the marketers. From their point of view, the product could be anything the consumers, and in the meanwhile the customers, wanted. If they preferred lighter saucepans, give them lighter saucepans whatever the quality inspectors may say. What consumers will pay more for, is better. Quality also became relative, not absolute. It was good to be better than the competition but there was no need to be *much* better.

Measurement moved from the production line to the marketplace. Since consumers' opinions are unreliable, researchers devised all kinds of methods for establishing perceived quality preferences: blind and double blind trials, inviting consumers to price the alternatives, trading off one feature for another (or "conjoint analysis," which has a better ring).

This turned out to be a less than precise science. Some of the best examples lie in the beer industry. In the UK, Watneys caught the marketing virus in the late 60s. Draught bitter had recently progressed from what reactionaries now call real beer to pasteurized liquid with the fizz injected from cylinders supplied by British Oxygen. Wooden barrels gave way to metal kegs. The beer reached the consumer in unchanged condition and wastage was dramatically reduced. Flowers had led the way. Watneys hastened to catch

[1] Bradley T. Gale, *Managing Consumer Value*, (New York,The Free Press, 1994).

up with "Red Barrel." With hindsight, it was unwise to draw attention to what proved to be a negative feature but brewers believed at the time that consumers should prefer it.

The previous management generation might have listened to their publicans, but the modern marketers knew better. Marketing was about scientific measurement. While relationships and communications with the publicans deteriorated for other reasons, Watneys conducted still more independent research. Red Barrel could be improved, according to taste tests, with a sweeter, cheaper, lower proof beer to be called "Watneys Red," abbreviated just to "Red." The image makers were turned loose. Footprints appeared all over town leading to signs saying "Red is Coming." London's premier nightclub was hired for the launch to the sales force. The Chairman donned red socks for the occasion. Senior sales managers had a premonition of the disaster to follow.

The more discerning, i.e. more loquacious, bitter drinkers in the pub were already mocking Red Barrel ("Why is Watneys like making love in a punt? It is … near water."). Red proved their point. In a focus group, maybe, they could not tell the difference, but with their buddies in the pub they certainly could. The word of mouth is more powerful than the best advertising; and as it turned out, the advertising compounded the problem with a slickness and jokiness that further detracted from the seriousness of the beer. That traditional English bitter is serious while lager is a matter for levity may be a generalization too far, but it seemed to be true then.

A similar story happened in the USA. Budweiser and Schlitz had struggled neck and neck since prohibition days. In the mid-70s, Budweiser was ahead but not by much. Both had between 15 and 20 per cent of the market. Today, Budweiser and its associated beers have half the total domestic beer market. Schlitz has virtually disappeared. Unlike Watneys, Schlitz had no retail estate to give it a second chance. When it lost its name for quality, the opposition was tougher, and the mistakes may have been worse. But the parallel with Watneys was strong. Schlitz found ways to reduce the maturing time for beer and to change the formulation. Both saved money and the consumer, in research, could not tell the difference. In reality, they started talking. August Busch, by contrast, was seen to make a fetish of his conserva-

> **The consumer's mind, once made up about quality, is hard to shift.**

tive, demanding adherence to old values and standards. Whether he really does, or not, is beside the point. That is what the consumer believes and, more importantly, wants to believe. By the time the Schlitz company returned the beer to its original quality and standards, it was too late.

The consumer's mind, once made up about quality, is hard to shift. Examples are not limited to beer. All over the world, marketers were conducting usage and attitude studies on their brands and being satisfied by the quality results and by the changes they were making.

THE REVERSE SALAMI PRINCIPLE

Both beer examples illustrate the "Salami Principle." This well-known American metaphor refers to the practice of taking such thin slices off the sausage that the sausage each time appears unchanged. Eventually there is no sausage left and yet measurement proved that it was unchanged. Marketing moved the focus for determining quality from the production line to the marketplace. That was good. Unfortunately marketing's techniques were not up to the job of measuring quality once it arrived. The salami slices are often too thin.

The marketplace abounds with examples. Did you notice when Mars Bars shrank in size? At first consumers either did not notice or thought their impression was false. Chocolate bars get smaller and police officers get younger. Sooner or later they do notice, sales fall, and the wunderkind passing through marketing that week launches a new improved giant sized chocolate bar for the same price.

> **Those who truly believe in quality do not degrade their products.**

Rescue action may work or not. Dog food may have non-meat additives until the dog stops eating it and the owner loses confidence in the brand for good. The dog's reaction may not happen until the fifth or sixth product degradation. The dogs that were used by the brand owner to test each step of the process could not tell the difference.

Those who truly believe in quality do not degrade their products. Those who, for cost or profit reasons, are coaxed into the salami machine should always check the next stage against the original and competitive products, not the already sliced one.

Many have commented on the irony that the prophet who gave the quality mission to the Japanese only did so because he was without honor in his own land, the USA. Deming had this consistent thread: *quality can be measured*. How to measure it, as we have seen, calls for care and imagination; it is the path to continuous, consistent improvement, which the Japanese call *kaizen*. It can also be seen as reverse salami: the quality slices are being put back on. Each piece is still small; both consumer and producer should benefit. When

Deming arrived in Japan shortly after World War II, he found willingness to learn, space limitations requiring better rather than more, and recognition that increasing incomes would also lead to demand for premium goods.

There is one Japanese characteristic, however, that was crucial to success and has been less documented. They will think this impolite but the word "arrogance" is used in admiration. Arrogance is admirable because it works. Research on consumers' preferences are affected in three ways:

1. Japanese marketers assume, without asking, that a Japanese consumer will want the best. Only the best deserve the best.

2. Because of the much greater sharing of culture and values, the marketer has a better idea of the consumer's point of view before asking. The market is more homogeneous, at least in the cities.

3. If Japanese consumers think it is the best, so will everyone else in the world, once they understand.

Such self confidence pays. It means that the Japanese producer is better able to anticipate what the consumer will find valuable and believes, rightly or wrongly, that once the domestic market buys it, so will the rest of the world. The 19th century English behaved similarly in consumer technological products, they have been proved more right than wrong.

What came out of the great quality success stories is a blind faith, which then proves to be right. Can this be marketing? People driven by messianic fervour tend not to stop for a little conjoint analysis. Can such apparent disregard for consideration of the consumer be commercial? Speculative it is and yet quality-oriented marketers may be achieving a critical identification with consumer values. Forget market research carried out by a bunch of cranks on consumers who do not know what they are talking about.

A famous and successful magazine publisher was once asked how he managed to launch title after title with so few failures. His research team must be excellent. It turned out that he had no team and no research. He was a compulsive watcher of television; and that told him all he needed to know about consumer interests.

"Would I like it better?" is a perfectly reasonable question to ask. Then make it and market it at a higher price than the competition. If it sells and resells, the chances are that it is indeed seen as better. As we have discussed elsewhere, price and perceptions of quality are bound up with one another. A consumer will give a higher priced article the benefit of the doubt on quality until proven otherwise. Such proof can come in any number of ways; beer drinkers in the pub, newspaper or magazine reviews, poor usage experience, appearance in discount stores or coupons, and inappropriate marketing are some of them. But beware, the combination of high price and damaged reputation can be lethal.

A consumer will give a higher priced article the benefit of the doubt on quality until proven otherwise.

On the other hand, high price supported by perceived quality spells high profits. They reinforce one another. Quality does not necessarily cost more; getting rid of inspectors, rejects, wastage, and attributes not valued by consumers may even reduce costs. All you have to do is to see things through the eyes of the consumer.

CONSISTENCY VERSUS PRODUCT IMPROVEMENT

The story is told of the newly appointed Managing Director of a famous Scotch whisky company travelling the Atlantic by sea in the early 60s. He was delighted to hear a wealthy American call loudly for his brand in the bar each evening. By day four, he felt he had to introduce himself to his enthusiastic consumer. "Why is this your favorite whisky?" "It isn't," came the reply, "I'm just fascinated by the way every bottle is different."

Customers like that are even fewer than variable whiskies. A brand name is a mnemonic for a bundle of expected attributes. In this rushed age, the consumer does not have time to stop and think. The name bubbles up to consciousness, and it is assumed the product will be the same as last time. And it had better be.

For the worldwide marketer this can be a problem. Over the years, products and packaging may have been adapted to local market preferences. Now, global marketing has arrived. Whether consumers really worry about their favorite brand tasting different in one market to another is unclear; management does. The drive is on to standardize and upgrade packaging, to improve consistency.

Suppose we are marketing air freshener. All the products began from the same base but since then France has a different range of perfumes, Germany has modified the packaging, the UK has found a cheaper formulation to keep costs down, and Italy has changed the release cap. These were all improvements to meet consumer demand. The countries may all be in Europe but, as every international marketer knows, they are completely different. In any case, these changes have now been made; to change again will be inconsistent.

This is the everyday reality of international marketing and the key perception here is the dynamic of product improvement, i.e. convergence to future consistency as distinct from standardization today. Whatever local management may say, it is unlikely that the improvements are mutually incompatible. Even if they are, it is even more unlikely that there are not other improvements that would be attractive to all or some consumers in each country.

Local management can use local differences as a barrier to sharing improvement or the catalyst for it. Do they wish to learn or to protect? Brand management can demonstrate vitality or reach for the embalming fluid.

> **Leave the existing product in the best shape you can and introduce the improved product alongside it.**

The last section recommends *kaizen*, the relentless search for small, incremental improvements. Applying the Reverse Salami Principle means constantly making changes. These are also "consistent" because they are individually imperceptible to consumers who, when they do eventually become aware of them, will be pleasantly surprised.

Where quality improvement has to be perceptible, consider line extension as an alternative. In other words, leave the existing product in the best shape you can and introduce the improved product alongside it – possibly at a higher price though that needs separate consideration. If there is a real, substantive improvement, flaunt it. There are a number of reasons for this:

- If you cannot conceal it, do not try.
- An improvement for some consumers is not necessarily an improvement for all. It is worth distinguishing "monotone attributes" where an improvement for one consumer is an improvement for all (e.g. energy consumption or fuel usage savings) and "non-monotone attributes" which are matters of choice (e.g. the color of the wine).
- If you are creating a new part of the market, try to own it.
- A product with monotone attribute improvement is likely to become the standard bearer for the brand: more differentiated, more product advantage. The old product may serve a useful role as the flanker: keeping the competition occupied.

In other words, substantive product improvement, by you or the competition, lies at the root of the "life cycle" concept.

PRODUCT OR BRAND LIFE CYCLES

The brand or product life cycle theory goes like this: where there is life, there is death. It is the natural order. Since brands and products are created, so must they die. They are better managed by acknowledging the stage they are at: middle-aged brands should not wear jeans. Marketers should maximize profits by observing the natural cycle (see figure 17.1).

Such strategies are likely to be self-fulfilling. As soon as a downturn is interpreted as a life cycle decline, the brand is prepared for the mortuary. Applying embalming fluid ensures it gets there. The theory is compounded by the analysis of consumers into separate segments of innovators, early adopters, early majority, late majority, and laggards. As brands or products move from niche to mass markets, the theory goes, the innovators become bored and switch. By the time the laggards are catching on, the early adopters have left too. The life cycle, a form of fashion, inevitably follows its natural course.

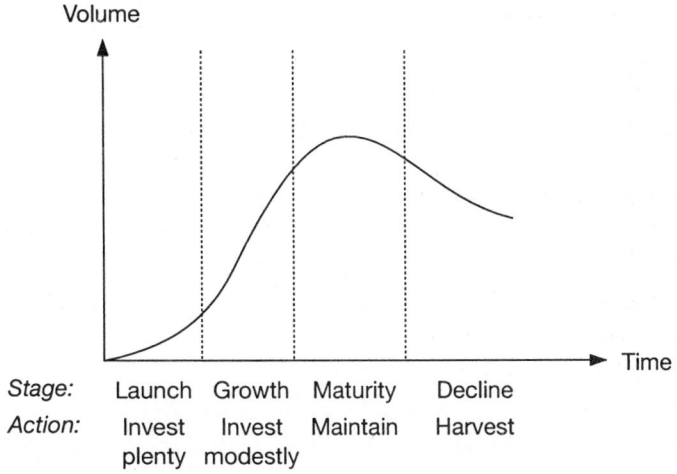

Stage:	Launch	Growth	Maturity	Decline
Action:	Invest plenty	Invest modestly	Maintain	Harvest

Fig 17.1   Product life cycle

The life cycle theory, for repeat purchase goods and services, is piffle. Brands can survive for ever by changing the products under their umbrellas. Brands of soap have become detergents and then biological detergents leading to concentrates. The life cycle concept works better for products than brands, just as the theory that the world is flat works well for most practical purposes. At the same time, it is profoundly misleading.

Brands and products survive until something better takes their place. The process needs to be understood in terms of competition, not the inherent life forces, whatever they may be, of the brand or product. The life cycle of salt appears to be quite a long one. It will continue into infinity until someone comes up with something that delivers the benefits of salt plus. This has nothing to do with the life cycle of salt but the appearance of competition.

To believe in the life cycle is to cause it to happen. It is not unusual for brands to reach a plateau before rising again, but the life cycle chartist will see a plateau as prelude to decline. Baileys Irish Cream had a dramatically fast climb in most countries between 1974 and 1980. Cynics forecast, using the same natural metaphors, that mushroom growth would lead to equally fast decline. When sales leveled off, the tea trolleys were taking round tranquilisers. With hindsight it was obvious that consumers were trying the new products that had followed Baileys but, finding them less palatable, returning. Sales continued upwards and the life cycle was forgotten. If any of those follower products really had been better, then maybe the life cycle would have "proved" itself again.

Inaccurate as it may be, the life cycle metaphor for consumables does help us with line extensions. Consider how Tide has thrived. It was invented in the mid-1930s with the claim "Wash-Day Miracle." In the next 50 years it has had about 70 measurable product improvements and is now available as Regular, Tide Free, and with bleach, all in regular, compact powder and liquid formats. These line extensions provide improvements for some users, or usages, which are not improvements for others.

Thus the longevity of brands arises from the vitality with which they are managed. Product improvements both for the existing portfolio of products and for extensions sustain and develop them from generation of consumers to generation.

WHAT IS DIFFERENT FOR DURABLES?

Much of this book focusses on brands the consumer continuously buys. Consumption leaves space for another. Life cycles do have meaning for durables or other products which are used until they wear out. Once a consumer has an oven it will be a long time before it is replaced, unless a much better one comes along.

The diffusion of innovation, i.e. the spread of new products, follows, for durables, a pattern akin to the life cycle diagram on page 193 (see figure 17.2).

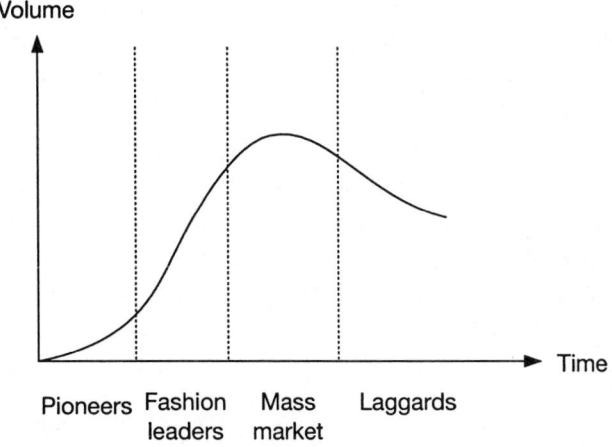

Fig 17.2   Diffusion of innovation – durables

Whatever the point at which the new product plateaus out, the plateau will remain until a substantial technological breakthrough appears: color TV to follow monochrome; digital text, high definition, bar-coded video setting each follow one another. Marketers of durables do indeed need to track where their product, not the brand, is on the life cycle and adapt policies accordingly.

Consistency and change bring equal dangers. This chapter discusses how both can be served. Japanese high tech companies manage to do it. Can you?

Memo to file

Subject: PRODUCT SATISFACTION

- Differentiate or die. Secure verifiable product advantage where you can. Even when competition catches up, the perception should linger.

- Perceived quality is the strongest indicator of future profitability. As part of that, consistency matters too. Variations from market to market need a strong rationale.

- Use the Reverse Salami Principle *kaizen* to turn product degradation on its head. Continuous small improvement should converge market-to-market differences toward common excellence. Delight your consumers when they discover what you have done.

- If the improvement is real and substantive, flaunt it, probably in a line extension. Line extensions upwards (more quality, higher price) build brand equity.

- Brands do not have life cycles unless you embalm them. Vigorous management with product improvements cause them to live for ever.

- Products only die when they are mismanaged or the marketplace gets a better offer.

- Life cycle concepts are more useful for durables. Understand the diffusion of innovation and adapt policies to where products stand.

18

PACKAGING FOR THE PARTY

First impressions are just the beginning of what the pack can do for the brand

---

Key issues

● Functions of packaging ● First impressions of the brand set up the brand's equity ● Refreshing the make-up. Packaging should be improved little and often. No one should notice and yet it should always be at the leading edge ● Retailing. The fascia and the whole in-store experience are the "packaging" of the retail brand. Similar considerations apply to other service brands

---

FUNCTIONS OF PACKAGING

In this self-service age, packaging is too important to be considered an afterthought: for first purchases, the packaging is the most immediate feature of the brand. Some go so far as to propose that the package be designed before the product; if the package must communicate to the buyer what lies inside, then why not to the producers also? While that may be extreme, there are cases where the package made the brand. Long Life, for example, was the first UK canned beer. The package dictated both the necessary qualities of the product and the way it was marketed. Deodorants likewise developed from the spray can. However, technical packaging advantage evaporates even more quickly than product advantage because packaging suppliers immediately widen their market to their other customers.

Perhaps the humble tea bag best illustrates how packaging can add value:

● It eliminated the need for the tea pot. Direct to mug or cup, it simplified tea service as well as washing up.

● It facilitated use of cheaper raw materials (smaller leaf).

● No measuring by the consumer is needed.

Initially, the tea bag was more important than its content. Only when it became universal did marketing attention revert to product quality. More recently, round tea bags again captivated the consumer.

The trend to added value, better quality without necessarily more volume, applies to packaging as well as product. Packaging has to carry the product in every sense. The paper label of yesterday will not do for the consumer of tomorrow. With fragmented media, there is no certainty the consumer will have seen whatever advertising is current; with a major fmcg launch, usually only about 20 percent of first-time purchasers have any awareness

> **The package may well be the only communication about the brand and the product the consumer will receive.**

of advertising. The package may well be the only communication about the brand and the product the consumer will receive.

Packaging includes these roles:

● Advertise the brand and the product. The positive effect that packaging can have on brand equity occupies most of this chapter.

● Keep the product in shape and in good condition. It must withstand transportation and handling. Open dating now indicates for how long quality will be maintained.

● Stack well and make optimal use of retail space.

● Be easy to read. There are increasing pressures to make packaging easy to read for the elderly or the sight impaired.

● Tamper-resistance. Modern terrorists and blackmailers have heightened consumer awareness of the need for seals.

● Safety. Medicines and products deemed dangerous are now so difficult to open that only under-age children seem to know how.

● Convenience. Carrying handles, size of units (e.g. tea bags), applicators such as a spreader on the nozzle.

● Use. Subject to safety, they should be easy to open and serve as storage until they are used up – sometimes for years. Flexible wrapping may be wonderful in all other respects until one comes to open it. After squirting yourself with the content, it spills out when you put it down.

- Mandatory requirements include legal and technical, words and numbers, and bar codes.

FIRST IMPRESSIONS

Packaging, for many brands, is the most important form of advertising. Perfume bottles typically cost far more than the perfume because they provide the most potent sign of quality. Packaging thus identifies the brand (differentiation), conveys quality (product advantage), and promotes the added values as well as providing the functional benefits above.

Branding must be overt, and yet sometimes discreet as well. Colors must reflect the brand as it has always been, and yet be modern and fashionable. The package must communicate prestige and value for money. It has to shout "buy me" from the shelf but then merge gently into the decor when you get it home.

Pity package designers. They can expect haphazard and conflicting instructions. The packaging has to do all that advertising does, without the media to do it, and then meet all the functional needs too.

The place to start is with the identical brief that the advertising agency had, or will have. The positioning statement and the objectives that make up brand equity measurement provide at least an agenda for discussion. Some companies have internal design managers; others have formal design specification formats. All the same creative briefing principles apply: lay out the *marketing* problem and do not try to help the professional solve the problem. Are the "mandatories" really mandatory or just conventions to be broken? Must the pack be a can? Must it be cylindrical? When the briefing is in place, the limits to creativity need to be probed. Good designers shock complaisant clients. The color of the client's neck is an index of creativity. However, this should be the most enjoyable part of the process for the marketer. If the company's production experts are not showing signs of alarm, maybe you have the wrong designer.

A well-known whisky maker rounded up the usual designer suspects, around 1990, to pitch for their new up-market line extension based on a black theme. Ideas were tabled, all elegant and refined. The choice was going to be difficult. The final designer shuffled in looking his usual scruffy self.

Those who did not know him wondered if he had mistaken the boardroom for a hostel. Their more enlightened colleagues knew him to be dressed in the latest grunge fashion, no expense spared. He had no artwork case, no artwork, and not even an overhead transparency. From a pocket he produced a white snooker ball. "This is how I see your present product," he said. "And," producing the black, "this is the new one." He got the business.

When the feathers have unruffled, the designer should leave with a written brief. The objectives and the limitations should leave no room for doubt and all the company's relevant functions, e.g. purchasing, production, distribution, and sales, should sign them off.

> **Packaging sets up brand equity before all else.**

Of course all the functional issues matter, but first impressions come first. Packaging sets up brand equity before all else. Think of it as dressing for a drinks party or dressing for an interview: your choice determines what strangers will think of you. Being true to your own personality is not a license for self-indulgence. Their opinion matters, not yours.

Each brand has a personality and the package, or dress, largely determines whether the consumer wants to get to know the brand better or not. The consumer in the supermarket is in a hurry. It is a crowded room. If that first impression is not right, they will not wait for a second.

REFRESHING THE MAKE-UP

Just as last year's clothes may seem just a little outmoded, so does last year's packaging. It should be constantly updated: if not every year, at least every other year. Otherwise, sooner or later the brand will need a major facelift which will confuse loyal users and passing acquaintances alike. If you notice when make-up has been refreshed, then it must have slipped too far.

Repackaging can invigorate tired products. It can motivate sales forces and customers. It can upstage the competition. All it takes is imagination, vision, and enough of a budget to hire top talent and execute a solution without scrimping. That looks wonderful on paper, but top talent and no scrimping is a formula for spending more money than is available. Vision and imagination, at least, are free. The conventional wisdom is that packaging changes should be small and frequent rather than large and occasional. There are always exceptions. If your brand has a severe image problem, a more drastic solution is required.

Maintenance is not expensive if it is regular and well done. Otherwise it simply becomes essential. A rare outburst of tact withholds the name of the brand to which this conversation refers:

"Brand X is in severe need of repackaging."

"I agree."

"When will it be done?"

"When we can afford it."

"When will that be?"

"When sales pick up."

The budgetary issue should be an irrelevance: good repackaging earns its keep.

The role of packaging in revitalizing products is more likely to grow than lessen, especially as the other Ps of the marketing mix achieve diminishing returns. There are limits to how much better some products can get, and to how much their price can be increased. Promotions beyond a point become counterproductive. Advertising has so many media, so many impressions, so much regulation, so much inflation that its value has been eroded. Packaging has one supreme advantage as a communicator: if consumers are near enough to read it, they are near enough to buy it. A pack in the hand is worth two on the shelf.

RETAILING AND SERVICE "PACKAGING"

A narrow view of packaging for retail brands is the container for private label to which all the previous comments apply equally. If designing for packaged goods is complex, the wrapping for the retail brand

Benetton is more identified by a store than by its sweaters.

is really the store front and the whole in-store look the retailer offers the buyer. If packaging is of only passing interest to the fmcg marketer, and it should not be, the opposite is true for the retail marketer.

From time to time, "burger wars" break out between McDonald's, Burger King and competing chains. Product attention focusses on size, price, quality, and cooking method of the burger, the buns, and the rest of the menu. Otherwise attention is on the rest of the brand experience, i.e. visiting the restaurant or take-away.

The packaged goods marketer has to worry about the shelf on which the brand will sit. The retail marketer is equally concerned with environment, being here the High Street or shopping centre or airport terminal. No one design can fit all and yet the brand must speak consistently to the consumer.

Its personality and sense of style must attract under all circumstances. Benetton is more identified by a store than by its sweaters or even its advertising.

Retail "package," i.e. store, designs, at any point in time, will differ due to:

- Making the best of the immediate environment,
- Space available,
- Local planning restrictions,
- Character of local clientele,
- How long ago the store was constructed or last refurbished.

Building and developing brand equity, with consistent personality and style, through those hurdles, accounts for the rapid maturity of retail marketers. Refurbishing premises to bring them up to date is not cheap. Cycles vary, of course, but the update frequency for packaged goods is possible only for the basic latest design, i.e. that applied to new stores or refurbishments. Other stores may be five or six years behind.

Thus the costs of store fashioning compete for funds with advertising. Some chains cannot afford both and the choice is tough to make. Chains with appeal based more on their functional and psychological aspects will find sales turnover a poor measure. Brand equity is more reliable, even if the effects are slow to show.

Memo to file

Subject: PACKAGING FOR THE PARTY

- Packaging can directly impact the functional, psychological, and economic aspects of brand equity. Consider the opportunities for each separately.

- Nevertheless, the overall design look of the package is primary. First impressions come first.

- Refresh the brand's make-up little and often, perhaps every year. If the consumer notices the change, you left it too long.

- Fascias and store design are advertising, maybe the only advertising you can afford. Track the impact on brand equity.

- Dress your brand for the party to ensure the consumer will ask it to dance.

19

PRICING IN GRANDMOTHER'S FOOTSTEPS

The price premium is the litmus test of marketing: getting it right

> ### *Key issues*
> ● Price is the litmus test of marketing. Not just key to profit, but also brand strength ● Price entry strategies: skimming, penetration, retaliating first ● Basic controls to see the whole picture ● International pricing. The "grey market" (arbitrage) undermines brand positioning ● Classic pricing trouble spots ● Invisible pricing

THE LITMUS TEST

Pricing can be simple or incomprehensible or both. Many professionals just follow the brand leader or, as brand leader, move prices up whenever the competition is likely to follow. Too superficial to win Oscars from economists, this policy still makes money. At the other extreme lie sophisticated computer simulations of industry–customer relationships. In between lie the serpentine contortions businesses bring to pricing and discounting. Houdini was an apprentice pricing manager before he decided to go straight.

Without special offers, price wars, coupons, and the myriad devices for giving consumers their money back, bargains would not seem like bargains nor shopping so complex. Many famous grocery brands in the USA today never sell except on offer. Consumers can live by deals alone. Even if consumers inadvertently buy at full price, retailers will still claim the discount from the brand owner if they can get away with it.

Any marketer who initiates money-off schemes, without thinking through the consequences, is crazy. Many such schemes are crazy, period. There are signs that marketers, customers, and consumers are tiring of them. Tactical discounting and promotions will retain their roles in the marketer's toolkit because craziness in moderation is good. But such methods should be secondary to the main business of building brands.

Pricing is central to marketing in many ways. It communicates positioning to consumer and customer alike and therefore must reinforce the competitive stance the marketer wishes to adopt. A premium price signifies quality, which is why it backfires if the quality is not there. A premium also signifies brand strength, differentiation, and consumer preference.

> **A premium also signifies brand strength, differentiation, and consumer preference.**

Price is conventionally seen as a trade with volume: the higher the price, the lower the volume. This is not always the case. The method, frequency, and timing of price changes can produce different volume results for any given ultimate price change. Some dispute this and believe that price elasticity is constant; the same price change will have the same volume result however you get there. In particular circumstances, a price increase will stimulate *more* volume if it draws consumer attention to the higher quality.

What are we trying to achieve with pricing? The consumer should be able to buy at a price which maximizes the brand owner's profit over time and is consistent with the positioning of the brand. Consistency is an ingredient of brand loyalty. Both are questions of habit. Consumers will purchase day to day goods habitually, so long as inconsistent brand behavior does not disrupt that habit. Rapid changes of pricing unsettle the consumer. When the current spate of "deals" recedes, loyalty will be rocked for the opposite reason: the consumer has come to expect regular price dips and surges on certain brands and will be unsettled when they cease.

This is not to suggest that strong brands should not run price-offs. Harrods, the upmarket London store, has had sales in January and July for ever. Not to do so would be inconsistent. Sales serve to introduce new consumers to the store, provide a reason to advertise on television, offload less successful merchandise, experiment with new lines, and increase the bustle in slack months. These sales increase loyalty and brand equity.

Nothing, not even volume, translates to the bottom line as quickly as price. Figure 19.1 shows a classic price volume relationship and the consequential profits and losses. To choose price point A appears to maximize profit: something like this appears in any textbook, but beware. Such analysis is simplistic.

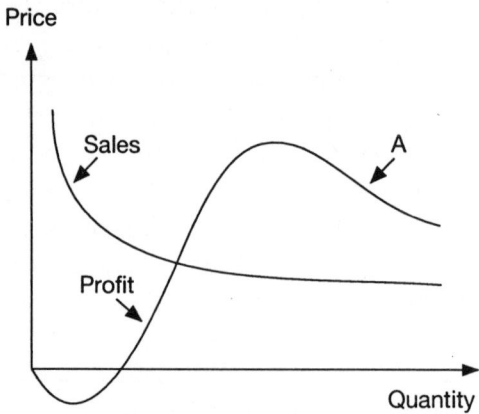

Fig 19.1   Prices, profits, and volumes

For a start, it ignores the downstream effects as the brand moves through the distribution channel: how will each customer choose to pass prices on to the next until the eventual consumer price is reached? It ignores discounting and tactical offers which shift sales from period to period. How will that affect the calculation? How will competitors react? If different competitors have different price structures in different markets, how can one match them all and yet prevent products leaching from the intended market to others? How will consumer repeat purchases be affected? How will prices affect long-term brand image? How will short-term pricing affect the ability to price up in the future?

Such analysis also ignores the impact of inflation which, to some extent, carries pricing along in its own stream. Pricing strategies for no, low, medium, and hyper-inflation environments will be totally different. In some ways, medium inflation provides the easiest cover for marketers: overpricing can be corrected by pausing a while.

The analysis also omits price segmentation, perhaps the biggest area for profits growth in the next decade. The ability to price differentially to each cluster of consumers allows the profit to be maximized separately for each segment which, mathematically, automatically maximizes total profit.

Price cannot be considered as a single number but as a chain of links each of which can stretch. Each link is the price at which one intermediary sells to the next on the way to the consumer. When each segment has a different set of prices, each brand has as many price chains. Every chain is intertwined with those of competing brands. All are floating along in multicurrency estuaries moving with the tides of inflation. If that is clear, you will not have any more trouble with pricing. Forget simplistic price volume charts, mug up on the microbiology of DNA and go for the Nobel prize on the meaning of price.

Pricing in the real world has more variables than the mind can consider at once. We are rightly suspicious of computer systems that claim to do so. Still more of neo-classical economics and elasticities. As a result, very few sophisticated models are in use. Most people keep as many variables constant as they can (i.e. match competition) in order to control those few that do move. Even so, the effects are not always those which were intended. In a large company different managers may be changing different variables without full understanding of what others are doing.

Price is the litmus test of successful marketing because it is directly linked to the short- and long-term profitability of the brand. It shows strength or weakness, confidence or timidity, control or confusion. Price is the biggest component of brand equity. If you want a single number indicator for brand equity (dangerous), sustainable relative average consumer price is perhaps the best.

PRICE ENTRY STRATEGIES

Strategically, pricing should interpret the positioning of the brand on the customers' shelves and in the minds of consumers. There are two main options if the brand is the first to market and a further two for later entrants:

- "Skimming" is a high entry price with an accordingly wide margin per case which can be used to build the market. Luxury goods will do this. As new competitors enter and the market grows, margins and price are reduced. So long as market leadership is retained, profit should grow with the market.

- "Penetration" is the opposite. Either because consumers are reluctant to try the product or because time is critical, the price entry point is low. Competitors are dissuaded from joining and consumer trial is encouraged. Once the market is stable, the brand leader can inch prices up (see below) and recover the investment.

- "Retaliating first" applies less to the first than to a later entrant whose target is clear. For example a major player may wait to see how a start up venture does in a new area and then come blasting in if it looks good. They aim to take the new market in one strike. It is not nice but it is business. Conversely, the identified target may be expected to respond to your entry: get your retaliation in first.

- "Follow my leader" is used by later entrants who elect to differentiate themselves in ways other than price. When Croft Original was introduced to the UK market, it matched the brand leader's consumer price and continued to do so until it, in turn, became brand leader.

Some marketers compromise. That may be right but it lacks conviction, especially for the first entrant. Whether you are bold or a compromiser, ensure that the price and the brand positioning are consistent. A few more words on the first three of these strategies:

> **Whether you are bold or a compromiser, ensure that the price and the brand positioning are consistent.**

Skimming

There is much to be said for feeling your way down to the correct price from above. In times of inflation this can be achieved more subtly by allowing the market to catch up. In the same way it may be better to increase the scale of production as manufacturing skills improve. Establishing as much premium as the brand will bear is helpful to brand equity. Competitors are less likely to react to the higher prices and lower volumes. Investment may be less and profits more immediate. Indeed everything is rosy save two snags. Depending on the product category, immediate volume may be critical. So may competitor reaction.

High fashion products, such as the hula hoop, will sell all they will ever sell within the first year. The production process may have high economies of scale; the marginal costs of production may be low but the fixed costs high. Going for large early volumes in this event is less risky. Retailers may simply block entry to anything that does not offer a fast enough rate of sale (velocity).

The British have a history of producing fine inventions, jet planes for example, in a niche way only to have foreign competition scoop the market with greater volume at lower prices.

Penetration

The need for fast sales growth can be akin to riding a wave – miss it and you have missed out. Catch it and provide the critical levels of distribution necessary for advertising to be cost effective. One of the key differences between the wine and spirit industry and branded foods has been a propensity for premium priced entry for drinks and penetration strategies for foods. This is partly a difference in the amount of "heritage" needed to persuade consumers to accept the brand. Heritage is more important for drinks and takes time to build.

Foods, on the other hand, need rapid distribution. To get that, retailers need to be assured that heavy advertising is part of the package. Penetration pricing encourages trial.

Most of all it discourages new competitors. If the margins are lower and shelves are full, the gap for a latecomer is less.

Retaliating First

The microcomputer industry is strewn with examples of the established companies struggling with down-pricing as new competitors invade. Apple had development problems with Mac which delayed the launch and increased the costs. New entrants were forcing down competitive prices at the same time. It was a double whammy. A decreasing price spiral is very hard to stop. Ultimately enough companies go bust or leave the business for profitability to be restored. There is no magic to stopping the spiral; the objective has to be to stop the spiral beginning.

Continuous technical development, as in electronics, is more difficult to manage than known change points such as deregulation, reduction in tariffs or increasing quotas, major new entrants, or the expiry of patents.

Especially when there is reason to expect strong, lower-priced competition, the strategy should be to take the hit immediately *before* it becomes necessary. This builds customer and consumer loyalty and makes the competitor's lot more difficult. It is not an easy decision. The short-term profits will certainly be lower than the previous plan figure. They may even be lower than they would be, initially, if no action was taken. Nevertheless the likelihood is that the profit decrease will prove less over the medium term than would otherwise be the case.

You will probably not believe it. Quite right; the theory cannot be proved with examples. Every case is different. Any company facing such a situation should recognize it has a major problem on its hands and turn, for once, to quantitative methods. These decisions are rare. Management will not get a second shot; rewinding the video will not play it again. The appropriate degree of sophistication will vary but the need is to play out, or model, the possible repercussions of the alternative strategies. Designing full market simulation models may take more time and money than is available. The basic PC spreadsheet and data packages provide enough software to create simple "what if" projections within a few hours. All this can do is aid judgement, true, but aiding judgement before critical pricing decisions is the time to do it.

An alternative or additional move is to introduce a price flanking brand in parallel with the one under threat. The purpose of this is simply to keep the competitor busy enough with the flanker to keep the heat away from the breadwinner. So long as the flanker does not lose serious money, you are ahead.

BASIC CONTROLS: WHO REALLY SETS PRICES?

In the cool carpeted offices of Megabrand Global, all these pricing variables are modeled electronically. Sensors in the marketplace instantly pick up changes in competitor, customer, and consumer pricing and behavior. Price elasticity is the measure developed by economists to relate incremental changes in price with their effects on volume. See the Glossary for a formal definition of "elasticity" ("price elasticity" and "cross elasticity" – one brand's price and volume movement affects another's). For the reasons above, you only need to know these terms in order to fend off the technicians. Megabrand's computer uses such things to calculate sales responses to fore-cast marketing activity, marginal costs arising from different volumes. Market share gains are being balanced against profits for the short and long term. All the myriad complexities of pricing can be reconciled by informa-tion technology. Paperless presentations flash directly to screens, committees decide, and the sales force have something exciting to tell their customers.

All that is possible, but for most (all?) companies, it is fantasy. That modeling is getting closer to reality is not denied. Nor is the value of running these models to com-pare with old fashioned instincts. Just be sure your model is built from experience, not economic theory. Otherwise you will turn your brand into a commodity.

Loss of control of pricing is not only due to the growing strength of retailers but the complexity of multinational business structures.

Megabrand, in practice, prices according to the instincts of the dominant managers. This is probably just as well: they got to be dominant because they have been trained in the business and they have been right enough to com-mand respect. With the focus on profit accountability, pricing responsibility has had to be delegated. Can sales be responsible for deals failing if they cannot deal? The growing power of retailers shifted control of marketing budgets to sales management, perhaps more than top management realize.

One of the major drinks multinationals found that their managers had nearly a hundred different ways of giving money to customers in the main EU countries alone. Just to discover this took a year because so many words for "discount" do not translate; or so the local managers claimed. Pricing autonomy is held dearly and is protected by obfuscation.

In the US foods business, price discounting ("promotions") typically required 15–40 percent of the brand budget in the early 70s. Twenty years on, it rose to as high as 80 percent, though that may be diminishing again. Retailers terrorize suppliers with delisting, "slotting fees" (they buy spaces on the shelves), and de-slotting fees (to pay the cost of taking your brand off the shelves/retailer's computer). A constant stream of tactical discounts is necessary to maintain visibility, velocity (rate of sale), and competitive edge. With profit margins as low as 1 or 2 percent, retailers insist that such tactics are necessary for survival. They may weaken the brands on which retailers ultimately survive but they need blood money now.

Loss of control of pricing is not only due to the growing strength of retailers but the complexity of multinational business structures. Accounting systems, in large organizations, may not always be capturing the full picture. The marketing budgets are clear enough but how many companies net discounts off from sales before recording turnover in value terms? In an age where price lists are entered for fiction prizes, what really is the price? There are volume discounts, drop size allowances, dealer loaders, bonuses, inventory equalization offsets, merchandising support, annual rebates, loyalty bonuses, prompt payment, or cash with order allowances. In a large organization, each department wants to influence customer behavior to make that department's operation more efficient. Over time one arrangement piles on another until few (in some companies, no one) can understand what is happening in total, still less the effect on profit.

> **Discover who is making the pricing (discount) decisions and ensure that they are accountable for them.**

Large organizations should not try to determine what *should* happen, instead they should find out what *is* happening:

- Forget sophisticated (in practice simplistic) computer models that claim to determine price.

- Instead, set up a sophisticated system to log actual prices through each channel down to each consumer segment.

- Discover who is making the pricing (discount) decisions and ensure that they are accountable for them. Sales will stick marketing with the bill if they can get away with it. Of course, if marketing is truly making the decision, then they should be accountable.

● If you have the technical IT resources, start collecting the data in a form that will model the outcomes of those pricing decisions so that the relevant managers can better learn from experience.

INTERNATIONAL PRICING

The aim today is to recover control over pricing without losing the flexibility of local dealing. Nowhere is this truer than in Europe post-1992. Retailers can buy in the EU country of their choice. They can join together to exchange buying information or buy jointly. Brussels, in trying to maximize prices for the farmer whilst minimizing consumer prices, has to squeeze everything in between. A blind eye will therefore be turned to the growing strength of retailers. Who cares about retail competition if the consumer is getting a better deal?

German supermarkets are an education in retailer power. As 1992, which supposedly was the date for a truly open common market, approached, marketers realized that their whole European profitability might be dictated by a handful of supermarket groups. Unless firm action was taken, every retailer in Europe would be buying on the lowest terms. For many categories, these were the prices in Germany where the strength of supermarkets, a post 1920s horror of inflation, a cultural view that only the cheapest was good enough, and tough buying, had together held prices down despite the opportunity provided by, or perhaps because of, the strong D-Mark. European directors would put prices up and German sales managers would hasten round to the back door with a bag of cash, taken from the marketing budget, to offset it.

Brand marketers today are seeking to recover the initiative from retailers and, sometimes, from other parts of their own organizations. This is not an issue for small companies with little competitive freedom nor many managers in the loop. But any multinational today should think it has problems reconciling local and global/regional pricing and profit responsibilities, problems with sharing information and competitive intelligence.

As mentioned above, the problem is wider than Europe. The simplest way to segment consumers is by country. By charging each segment the optimal price, total profitability is maximized even though country to country price variations can be considerable. In the last twenty years, modern telecommunications have created an arbitrage ("grey" or "parallel") market. A customer in country A (low price) can over-purchase on the understanding that an arbitrage operator will re-sell the surplus to country B at a profit to them both. By taking the goods out of A, the customer, e.g. a supermarket, is safe from flooding its own market. At the same time, it may purchase goods from the same arbitrageur if the terms are better than those from the official marketer in country A.

The consumer is happy (lower prices for the same goods), and so are the retailers, arbitrageurs, and regulatory authorities (the free market works). The brand owner and the local marketer are less happy; the segmentation strategy has been disrupted along with the positioning of the brand which is now not just lower but *inconsistently* priced. If the product

> **By charging each segment the optimal price, total profitability is maximized**

was mass marketed in country B where it had long been available, but was new to A, where it needed larger margins to allow it to build, the arbitrage activity may prevent the brand ever taking off. Thus the consumer's apparent short-term interest may not match the long term.

Regulatory authorities know that distributors have legitimate interests to protect. There is a quagmire of nods, winks, and permissions that maintain a reasonable balance between brand owners, distributors, retailers, and consumers. Many failed to see the logic in denying cut-price chemists access to well-known perfume brands. Yet to do so would undermine the psychological benefits in the brands themselves. For once the psychological benefits prevailed over the logical. US legislation, which tends to be protectionist whatever the proclaimed free trade philosophy, prevents, at least in theory, goods made overseas by subsidiaries of US companies being grey marketed into the US if the parent objects.

Regulation is an unreliable support; sometimes it is hostile. Better is to use Professor Hermann Simon's "price corridor." The concept here is that exact matching of prices within, say, the EU is impossible, at least so long as currencies are not aligned. On the other hand, there is a corridor within which price variation is beneficial, limited segmentation is possible, and the mount of arbitrage is tolerable. The width levels of variation is a purely pragmatic matter: where does arbitrage offset the benefits of variation? Prices outside these bounds need to be brought inside but they do not need to be equalized. Figure 19.2 illustrates the concept.

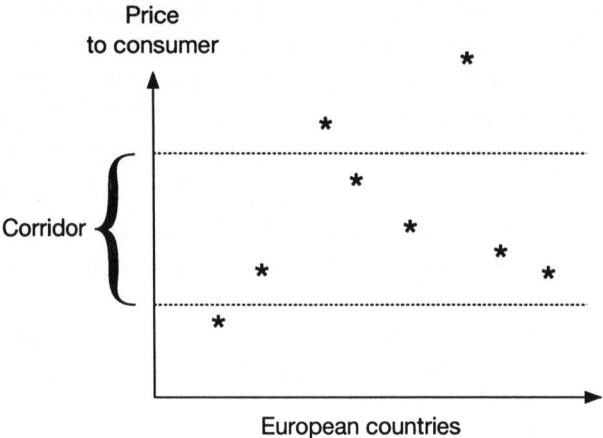

Fig 19.2   Price corridor

What is optimal for the brand across all countries, is suboptimal for some, if not all, distributors in individual countries. Chapter 7, "Global Marketing," addresses this difficulty.

CLASSIC TROUBLE SPOTS

Computers have not solved any problems. They have just quickened the pace. Competition sees tactical pricing as a game of poker and raises the ante that much faster. Reaction times are so quick that they can hit the street almost when you do. The coupon craze in the US alcoholic drinks business was an example. Product managers discovered that you could give $1 off the next purchase and economically drive up today's sales. Most coupons were not cashed. Those that were built brand loyalty, or at least the next sale. Furthermore, you could give lower prices to those concerned with price and not waste money on the price insensitive consumers. Salespeople liked them because they built a relationship with the retailers.

Competitors joined in. Most brands began to have coupons; the stakes in alcoholic drinks rose from $1 to $2 to $5 or more a bottle. At one point, coupon value equalled the price of the bottle; wine was being given away free. Off licence stores looked like Fifth Avenue after a ticker tape parade. As fast as salespeople put their coupons on top of their competitors', consumers threw them on the ground. Worse still, they began to cash them. Almost as quickly as they appeared, coupons in the US alcoholic drinks business began to disappear.

Giving money away is crazy because the competition need little encouragement to do it too. Everyone loses money and it cheapens the brand in the eyes of the consumer. Marketing should be the business of adding value, not subtracting it. Some idiots still believe you can lose money on every case but make it up on volume. For the sane, tactical dealing and discounting is an important but dangerous tool to be used with discretion.

> **Tactical dealing and discounting is an important but dangerous tool to be used with discretion.**

Although small steps and following competitors may generally be wise, the marketer also needs to know when to be bold.

The classic trouble spots are:

- Not seeing the whole pricing picture: individual managers doing what seems right in their own small market. They may not have the necessary experience, know the knock on effects, allow for competitive response, or have enough regard for the longer term.

- Reacting to price competition, e.g. private label, by joining them. This will commoditize your market. Brands have to differentiate and add value. Nescafé improved quality and *raised* price and advertising. Burger King, in 1994, substantially increased the size of their burger rather than cut price.

- Paradoxically, if price and quality are really out of line, as was the case for Marlboro in 1993, then you should cut hard and conspicuously to ensure the consumer gets the message that the problem has been rectified. These two situations are tough to distinguish. Sometimes you have to retreat to live to fight another day. Marlboro cut price hard and then enhanced their marketing efforts. Other firms, faced by now smaller margins, might have then cut marketing back too. Marlboro were right. Once their position was recovered, Grandmother's Footstep-sized price increases began again. Everyone remembers the cut; few noticed the increases.

- As a general rule, it is a mistake to cut price to mess up the market entry of a competitor which, this being marketing, makes it a good thing to do, albeit rarely. A price skimming strategy is, however, based on just that: enter high and cut just before each new competitor enters. If you are going to do this, be hard and pre-emptive. Too much is better than too little.

- Actual pricing out of control, i.e. out of line with the brand positioning. Typically, the sales and marketing functions are not in harmony. The approach to rectifying this depends on the culture of the business.

INVISIBLE PRICING

As a general rule (and there are no general rules), pricing strategy should be confident, strong and invisible. Complete invisibility is impossible. The word is directional: the lower the profile the better. Use inflation as a cover to avoid the attention of consumers and minimize that from immediate customers. If you think competitors will follow, ensure they know your moves in good time. If not, draw their attention to someone else.

"Grandmother's Footsteps" is a game played by children in schoolyards around the world, albeit by many names. "Grandmother" faces the wall away from the other children who have to cross the yard to touch "her." They have to move when she is not looking. If she sees anyone move, that child goes back to the far wall. Consumers prefer price decreases to increases. That statement of the obvious leads to the strategy of visible cuts and invisible hikes: Grandmother's Footsteps.

Should pricing be decided by market research? Ask customers and consumers how they will react to price alternatives? Save your money. Consumers do not like price increases and they do not necessarily want large decreases either. If market researchers ask hypothetical questions, they will get dumb answers. Rational consumers will prefer to pay less for the same quality rather than more but this is not just a matter of rationality. It is a matter of behavior: what consumers say they will do when only the cognitive part of the mind is in gear, and what they really do, are different. Brands are there to provide consistency. In an age where change is constant, consistency is attractive.

There are many techniques for changing prices discreetly without the greater error of misleading customers and consumers. UK banks had a bad press in 1991. One of their mistakes was to vary their charges, already complex and excessive in the eyes of their customers, without adequate notice. Somehow price changes have to slip in above the threshold of awareness but below the threshold where customers or consumers change attitudes, still less behavior.

One advantage of following competition is the camouflage they provide. Let them take the heat and then just follow. Such is the privilege of brand leadership. The strategy depends on the brand leader pursuing a progressive pricing policy.

In the sixties, the Distillers Company (DCL) rarely moved prices at all. Chancellors of the Exchequer in the UK did their best to fill the vacuum with duty increases. The strategy was to take advantage of the economies of scale that should have been open to their market share which was in excess of 50 percent and squeeze the smaller competitors. Ultimately the competition, primarily Bells in Scotland, took the lead in price and then in share. Bells were canny. They ceased to match discounts slowly but progressively. They matched prices for one sector (pubs and on-premise consumption) while appearing to be more valuable where net prices were

> **The strategy of visible cuts and invisible hikes: Grandmother's Footsteps.**

more obvious: the supermarkets. The DCL's policy backfired; they lost the profits that were open to them, the reputation for quality, and brand leadership.

Invisibility may be provided by seasonality. Many businesses will raise prices just after the peak trading period where both customers and consumers have had their fill and are in no mood to purchase anyway.

Another window for the invisible price adjuster is just prior to the holiday season when again minds are not so set on the trench warfare of negotiating. Have you ever wondered why actual wars typically begin in August? Or just before dawn? The return from the annual holiday is the true beginning of the new year. Invigorated, ready for anything, a price change might be just what is needed to set off changed buying patterns. Put up your prices before the holiday; cut them, if you must, after.

Perhaps pricing is more than a children's game of Grandmother's Footsteps but the model is closer than that of the economic, rational adult. It is a game which competitors, customers, and consumers all play in ways that can broadly be predicted if time is taken to work it through. Some probabilities can be ascribed to each scenario. Judgement can be assisted. Computers should be increasingly used to simulate the market, competitor responses and answer the "what if" questions. They will not use the simplistic equations of the past but track customer and consumer responses as they really happen in the marketplace. In the meantime, paradigm shifts apart, companies will not go far astray by walking in Grandmother's Footsteps.

Memo to file

Subject: PRICING

- Pricing is the litmus test of marketing skills: only the product is more important.

- Follow-my-leader is generally a low risk policy.

- For market entry decide between skimming, penetration, retaliating first and follow my leader. Ensure it fits the brand positioning. Then go for it.

- Pricing, deals, discounts, special offers need to be under control in the sense that the key decision makers out in the real world need to see and understand the whole picture. If your finance and IT people cannot deliver that today, ask them when they can.

- Control is essential not just for the profit of today or tomorrow but to deal with the increasing power of retailers and the trend towards regionalization/globalization.

- Most of the time, play Grandmother's Footsteps: invisible hikes, spectacular cuts when you must.

- Do not start a price spiral unless you are sure you will win when all the reactions are in.

20

PUBLIC RELATIONS ARE PRIVATE AFFAIRS

Sometimes the Cinderella of the marketing mix. Fitting the shoe

---

Key issues
- **Active PR. Making friends with the media** ● **Passive PR. Making opportunity out of crisis** ● **PR may be light on money but it is heavy on time – sponsorship, for example** ● **Hubris and trade media**

ACTIVE PR

Why buy advertising when editorial space is free? Moët et Chandon powered their domination of champagne in Europe through public relations, with only rare excursions into advertising; but for most brands, most of the time, it is a side show.

Journalists have space to fill with news, not puffery. Marketers brands are a constant source of fascination to themselves but not to anyone else. Champagne consorts naturally with interesting occasions. High tech products have intrinsic direct interest. For the majority, the manufacture of the news necessary to gain space is more expensive, and especially more time consuming, than media advertising.

Management needs to take a hard look to see if their brand is likely to be a PR promotable item, either directly or through association. Since they may not be familiar with what PR can do, a couple of speculative pitches from PR agencies should clear the fog, especially if the advertising agency follows right along with why they should have the money instead. These really are alternatives. Few brands are large enough to afford mainstream PR and advertising. In most of this chapter we will assume that you have chosen the active option; you will build brand equity using the PR lever.

The next section considers the alternative, passive, strategy: maintaining good relations but only using the medium when you have to, in a crisis for instance. No brand should attempt to cold shoulder the media altogether. Communicating with its consumers is a brand's bread and butter. The chapter concludes with trade media where slightly different guidelines apply. Ostensibly trade media are there to communicate with retailers or other business channel intermediaries. In reality, they are read more avidly by your competitors.

If active PR is your strategy, here are some basics:

- Press releases are a waste of time except when really important hard news has to be circulated fast and visibly, such as an acquisition. In the subtle world of trying to gain free space for marketing messages, press releases can be discounted.

- You need very good relations with a very few, top level journalists. Unless you have them, hire an agency that has. Hiring the agency will be difficult as they will all claim personally to have shared a word-processor with every editor and TV producer worth knowing. Those networks will mostly be true. In China, everyone is connected with Li Peng. Choosing the agency is discussed in chapter 31.

- Much of the best PR is happenstance. Organized companies are able to maximize advantage from such serendipity. The USA wine industry, assailed by anti-alcohol propaganda, refrained, or more precisely, was restrained from singing the praises of its products. Sales slipped sharply between 1989 and 1991. Then the program *60 Minutes*, watched by over 20 million, broadcast the "French Paradox" which stated that the high fat content of the French diet was not a killer when accompanied by copious red wine. American sales of Cabernet Sauvignon jumped 45 percent, sliding to a steady 25 percent increase after two months. The wine makers ensured that the other 200 million Americans heard about the French Paradox. For the media, this was news indeed.

- Make your journalistic contacts true partners and *listen* to them. They are skilled communicators by training and can represent what consumers think of your brand as well as many focus groups. If they think an angle is fun, it probably is.

- The journalist's interest in exclusive stories lies at the heart of the mixed relationship between marketers and the media. Few stories are big enough to warrant general coverage. The skimpy story is the best you have and a friendly niche is its only chance.

See the journalist as a partner. Disasters apart, journalists need human interest. Readers do not want to know about Gold Blend, the instant coffee brand, but they are interested in the Gold Blend couple in the long-running TV commercials romance. UK sales rose 40 percent as a result of interest in the first five-year sequence of 12 episodes and 13 percent from the second. The campaign travelled to the USA and, in 1995, to France where romance was supposedly replaced by the realism of divorce. Most viewers hope they will get together again.

> **You need very good relations with a very few, top level journalists.**

When the fictitious J. R. Hartley used Yellow Pages to trace a copy of his out of print book on fly fishing, everyone started going into bookshops and asking for it. Almost in self defense, the publishers had to provide one. I saw the book being purchased by serious fishermen on the West Coast, USA. Nature imitates good advertising.

Mutual trust begins with acceptance that "off the record" means what it says. If it is not actually said, then anything goes. The vast majority of journalists respect the convention meticulously, but only if the magic words are spoken. Within a relationship (marketing, once again, is the business of managing relationships), discreet bargaining is possible. The journalist wants a usable story; the marketer wants the brand name spelt right. In one sense the marketer does not care what is said so long as the story fits the heritage of the brand.

Moët et Chandon spent time chasing winning occasions, especially motor racing, with free magnums. The occasions themselves were irrelevant to the brand but the photographs communicated celebration and success.

PASSIVE PR

Even if they are not looked for, PR opportunities will come along. Sometimes good, more often bad. Plenty has been written about crisis management but it all adds up to preparedness. Any top PR operation, inside or out, maintains high level relationships with media and top management, drills them in handling awkward situations, and knows where to find them at any time. If you want to know where your spouse is, phone the PR department.

There are three levels of response: being unprepared, responding adequately, and turning it into an opportunity to promote the company. Shell poorly handled the summer 1995 oil platform. You will recall that everyone, save Greenpeace, had agreed it should be sunk in deep water in the Atlantic. Greenpeace claimed, wrongly but emotionally, that it should be broken up on land. Shell was preoccupied by a management reshuffle going on at the time and claimed there was no crisis. Consumers in continental Europe stopped buying Shell, the German government and Shell affiliates ratted on Shell UK who, in turn, ratted on the UK government. A victory for Greenpeace and a lesson in how not to handle a crisis.

Johnson and Johnson turned the tampering with their brand leader analgesic Tylenol from a disaster to a triumph. Prompt product recall convinced Americans that Tylenol represented safety. Intel, faced by IBM-reported problems with the Pentium chip, first reacted badly by denying there was a problem and then recovered just in time with effective customer guarantees. British Midland turned their motorway crash disaster into an opportunity through the immediacy and compassion shown by their chief executive. Both the awareness of, and attitudes to, British Midland were greater after the event. Perrier reacted promptly enough but never did fully recover because the problem (benzene in the water) struck at the heart of the Perrier proposition.

This may be the one and only time your brand has the world's attention.

These examples illustrate some principles:

- No one can identify what the crisis will be. If you could, you would fix it. The all purpose crisis team of top executives should be available at any time. Even if you do not have a PR agency on normal retainer, consider having one, for a nominal fee unless there is a crisis, as part of the team.
- Never deny that a crisis is a crisis. If the media think it is, it is.
- People understand that some time, albeit not much, is needed to establish the facts.
- This may be the one and only time your brand has the world's attention. Quite apart from the crisis itself, how do you want your brand to be seen in that 15 minutes of fame?
- Don't dither – decide. If you have opposition, Greenpeace for example, study their modus operandi. It is your brand versus their brand. Maybe you can both win.
- Do not feel impelled to answer the questions, just give out the messages you want heard. But be sure the messages are adequate.

Much of this applies when the crisis is benign but it is tougher to get the same sense of urgency. Some companies are blessed with top management naturally gifted in PR. Some of their best friends really are the media. For the rest, even with a passive PR strategy, consider retaining an agency just to review the brand's equity with you once a year and to be available when the crisis breaks. Moments of fame are rare; use them wisely.

LIGHT ON MONEY BUT HEAVY ON TIME

Balancing the time and money costs against likely benefits, deciding on outside or internal PR help or neither or both, will all come down to judgement of the unmeasurable. The key decision is whether PR becomes an important part of the mix. In the passive option, then some fairly basic training on do's and don'ts will equip some of the senior secretaries with all the company needs to get key messages out and deal with incoming questions. All journalists mostly need is to hear "I do not know I will get back to you," followed by a sensible answer within 24 hours. Curiously, many companies do not manage to do so.

Getting close enough to journalists for mutual partnership will take more from the diary than any top management should have to spare. This is really the problem. If PR will form the central part of the mix, an in-house team may be needed. Politicians are all trained in PR to a greater or lesser extent but those with departments to run leave the day to day PR management to a small team who wheel them in for briefings and photo opportunities. Time is the essence.

Sponsorship is an example. The prize money for Jose Cuervo's beach volleyball activities in the USA was initially low, but as enthusiasm built up, the marketing team could have spent the entire year doing nothing else. You risk moving from the marketer's world to the life of the sponsored activity. In the case of beach volleyball, this was not unattractive.

Do you suspect that a company that announces a new golf sponsorship has a CEO that plays golf? That certainly used to be true. It may still be, but enough sensitivity surrounds such use of corporate power to conceal the extent.

Let us assume you have decided to make PR a major part of your agency program and are reviewing a shortlist of PR professionals. Some firms now specialize wholly in particular forms of sponsorship. When they get to specific proposals, expect to hear about this great "event" which will carry the brand name, interest the media, be a hospitality opportunity for your best customers, and introduce you to famous and/or beautiful people.

Events can be just a Pavlovian PR response. They are tangible, finite, and chargeable. Food and drink flows. PR people barely need to eat at home; they must have the lowest supermarket bills of any in their socioeconomic group. Events are portable too: if one client turns this great idea down, it just goes back in the tool bag for the next.

Bright creative events are indeed valuable but they are not essential. They mostly deserve the cynicism they attract. Apart from the usual cost/benefit issues, the key questions are the same as for advertising:

- Does the event build brand equity? What will it do for awareness and attitudes?

- Does it fit with positioning and brand personality?

- What media coverage will it get? If an event does not get significant TV coverage, should you bother? This is what it is all about. Specialists measure frequency and reach of impressions from TV (and other media). Converting that to the equivalent of advertising is next to impossible. How many fleeting impressions of a Jose Cuervo banner is equivalent to a pack shot in an ad?

- How long will it take to be effective? Some of the best events run for 25 years before the full value shows up. The Hennessy Cognac Gold Cup was a case in point. Even the finest steeplechase events have less in prize money than flat racing (good) and the event was in November, timed to match peak sales. TV coverage was excellent. Even so, the build in awareness was very slow. If you take on an event, what are you getting into?

A CEO is entitled to some perks. A CEO who really hates boxing will not, whatever the marketing rationale, sponsor boxing. At the same time the selection of an event is likely to be a long-term decision, longer than any CEO should expect to remain in office.

The time line can, perhaps, be shortened by sponsoring an existing event. The Ever Ready Derby, however, is still "The Derby" and the Seagram Grand National is still the "Grand National." Two of the most successful sponsorships in the USA seem to indicate that creating a new event from the essence of the brand is the way to go.

The Jose Cuervo beach volleyball competition was perfect for the little known Tequila brand. It was wild and West Coast. It was young and fun. It was amateur and "no rules" – of course there are rules but the sport is informal. Importantly it was televisual. Over 15 years it built the brand, and the category, to a major place in the US drinks repertoire. The Margarita is the most popular US cocktail. Advertising played only a small role during this time.

The Pillsbury Bake Off has run for twice as long and now offers a prize of $1,000,000 or more. Amateur cooks from all over the USA send in their own recipes for cakes or other baked goods. Finalists compete in New York. For a business which has been adding value to flour based

> **Creating a new event from the essence of the brand is the way to go.**

products for over a century, the fit is perfect. Winning recipes usually join the Pillsbury portfolio of baked goods. This in turn stimulates more interest and entries.

While the "have event, will travel" approach should indeed be ridiculed, these examples show how matching the event to the brand positioning and selling opportunity is positive. When the NatWest Bank decided to sponsor cricket the fit was good. Where else could bank managers have the uninterrupted attention of their major customers for hours at a time?

If the event truly fits the brand positioning, brand equity benefits build and build.

HUBRIS AND TRADE MEDIA

Hubris is the feeling of satisfaction that you know at least some of the answers. The ancient Greeks believed that hubris was followed by nemesis. In other words, it is expensive. Perhaps the most famous example was the appearance of Gerald Ratner at the Albert Hall in 1991. An unguarded speech, which had previously amused many smaller groups with its candor, hit the front pages of the tabloids. He used a word tailored to their headlines: crap. It only applied to one item in his extensive range of jewellery products, but one was enough. Lack of respect for your own products and customers is rank bad marketing.

We cannot disentangle how much of the fall of Ratner was due to the four letter word and how much to overextending the business, high gearing, recession, or the general decline in the jewellery market. But after the Albert Hall, the value of the company fell 95 percent. Ratner's slogan, "the lowest prices in town," applied to the shares as they hit 21.5p after 389p. Within three months, Ratner was ousted from the chairmanship.

Hubris rarely meets nemesis so spectacularly. More routine but less dramatic examples can be found in the columns of the trade press, where product marketers are hyping their seasonal offerings. The motivation for the hubris is clear and it is good: we need the maximum publicity for our brand and its promotion. We must be positive and confident. Customers should know we have found the formula that will give retailers riches beyond the dreams of the Safeway. The trade press is a cost-efficient way to reach customers. Editors need material to fill the gaps between the advertisements, so let's tell them what we're doing so successfully. Everyone is happy.

The trade press is a cost-efficient way to reach customers.

Happiest of all will be the competitors who will read all about it and react accordingly. Ultimately all communications to customers get back to the competition but exposing your plans in the trade press ensures that such information is timely and reliable. But surely marketers are not so gullible? Surely the trade press is being craftily manipulated to provide disinformation for the competition? Aren't messages being planted to confuse competitors?

Sophisticated marketers have long since brought trade PR under full control. Some of the big names, Mars and P&G for example, rarely talk to trade press at all. This saves time and keeps marketers focussed on the main event. The availability of trade press for competitive signaling is important, but the opportunity for disinformation is limited. Few of us are clever enough to mislead competitors without disinforming customers at the same time.

Brand managers will see public conferences and trade media as channels for the good news about their brands. They happily trumpet forthcoming promotions and advertising and their budgets, albeit exaggerated just a bit. Why? When they took ad space, they got matching editorial coverage as part of the package. I know it should not happen but it does. When the category was being reviewed their brand could not be omitted. This mild form of blackmail sells a lot of trade media space. This editorial space needs news of some kind and forthcoming attractions are all they have.

Most of the time it does no harm. It may even impress customers and competitors alike. But before slipping into the old routine for another year, senior management should think about what they really want from this medium. If they did, then signalling would rate higher than it does.

Memo to file

Subject: PUBLIC RELATIONS ARE PRIVATE AFFAIRS

- Assess whether PR rates a serious part of the brand's marketing program. If it does, use the time and objectivity of professionals.

- Make friends with a few, carefully selected, media people with shared interests.

- Even with a passive PR strategy, have an agency tell you hard truths about the brand's image as part of the brand equity review and make them part of the crisis team.

- Be ruthless in the choice of sponsorship events. Create just one event that comes from the essence of the brand, that communicates personality, that maximizes TV coverage. Be patient and ration the time it gets.

- Take the trade press seriously. Resist hubris and use it for signalling.

21

PROMOTIONS, COUPONS AND GIVEAWAYS

The basic workhorses of marketing programs

> ### *Key issues*
> ● Temporary price reductions, trade or price promotions, are largely a waste of money ● The equivalent, "value promotion," in extra product is not quite the same but it is convenient to take them together ● Coupons are indirect price reductions, usually from the next purchase, and include vouchers, stamps, loyalty collector schemes, and their electronic equivalent such as Air Miles ● Sampling is too often forgotten by those into more sophisticated promotional concepts ● Other promotions range from trade fairs, to gifts, to competitions and prize draws, to exhibitions, merchandising and displays, to mystery shoppers, to events and to the opportunity to trade in old models ● Measurement of promotions' effectiveness is critical to corporate learning.

Promotions apply to the immediate customer and all stages of the distribution chain to the final consumer. This chapter is mostly concerned with the final consumer but, for simplicity, the word "customer" will be used generically, except where the distinction is important.

Promotions are temporary incentives and/or attention getters designed to increase sales or, less commonly, just brand equity. Like advertising, they may raise brand awareness and favorable attitudes even where they have no impact on sales. Coupons, for example, are designed to improve *future* sales. The concept is that users of other brands will switch to yours which, once sampled, will seduce them into eternal loyalty. The ability of promotion to prompt trial is a key attraction. Existing consumers should buy more quantity and/or more frequently to take advantage of the offer and consequentially use more either because they are prompted when going to the store cupboard or because they do not run short. Promotions are intended to *reinforce* brand habits of existing users.

PRICE PROMOTIONS – WASTE OF RESOURCES?

Prior to the 1980s, advertising was the largest part of the typical fmcg budget. As short-term pressures and the strength of retailers grew, price promotion took more and more of the marketing budget, replacing advertising as the largest component. In chapter 1, it was estimated that only 46 percent of advertising, after the launch stage, was worth while. Depressing? One of the same sources[1] claims that only 16 percent of trade price promotions are profitable. The figures for consumer price promotions are probably even worse.

If price promotions are such a waste of money, why do marketers go on doing them? The simple truth is that they are fun to start and the devil to stop. The first to introduce price promotions does well, then everyone joins in and everyone loses money. On the other hand, the first to stop loses more money than the others and risks being squeezed out of the game. Serious marketers wish they had never started. Price promotions are no more, and no less, addictive than cocaine.

> **The first to introduce price promotions does well, then everyone joins in and everyone loses money.**

Price promotions can increase sales in only three ways: growing the category, switching (brand share) and purchase acceleration (bringing forward

[1] Magid M. Abraham and Leonard M. Lodish "Getting the Most Out of Advertising and Promotion," *Harvard Business Review*, (May–June 1990).

the purchase). Price promotion can indeed benefit total category sales through bringing down prices and added visibility through displays and other marketing activity. Once the first mover has had the advantage and the others have retaliated, brand share is not typically impacted by promotions; they cancel each other out.

Purchase acceleration can be divided into two types:

1. shifting purchase but not consumption, i.e. no net effect.
2. increasing consumption, i.e. total category sales.

Demetrios Vakratsas[2] studied the US ketchup market and found that 30 percent of purchases were on price promotion but 60 percent of households accelerate their purchases to take advantage of promotions. This means that the *light* users of ketchup are influenced by price promotions much more than heavy users (60 vs. 30). Purchase acceleration was not affected by how much inventory they had in their cupboards, though research in Europe did not find that (smaller cupboards?).

In 1991/92, Procter and Gamble, Kraft, Alpo (a brand leader for dog food) and a few other brand companies in the USA announced they would terminate price promotions and bring in an "every-day low price"(EDLP). Retailers were furious. Most brand companies decided to wait and see. The economics were, and are, sound. Figure 21.1 shows a real example of price spikes down being matched by volume spikes up. These spikes do not just cost the manufacturer the price off; they introduce irregularities into raw material buying, production, and distribution. It would be cheaper and better to have a smoother flow. Worse still, special trade prices are offered patchily across the country with the result that retailers overpurchase to get to the next level of price off and then sell the surplus elsewhere. As a result, an arbitrage operation is set up, the brand owner does not know where the goods are going, and inventories expand in the areas being served by the arbitrageurs.

The EDLP effort had mixed results. Competitors were quicker to see short- than long-term advantages. Retailers saw it as a threat to their net margins which are as low as 3 percent in US grocery and largely funded by price promotions. Electronic point of sale (EPOS) tills exposed how much the retailer was supposed to pass on to the consumer but used cut-off dates to keep the change.

EPOS made it possible, for the first time, to be precise about the price at which brands were sold. Retailers, or Nielsen or other agencies, would estab-

[2] Unpublished doctoral dissertation, University of Texas, Dallas: *Effects of Deals on Purchase Acceleration*, 1994.

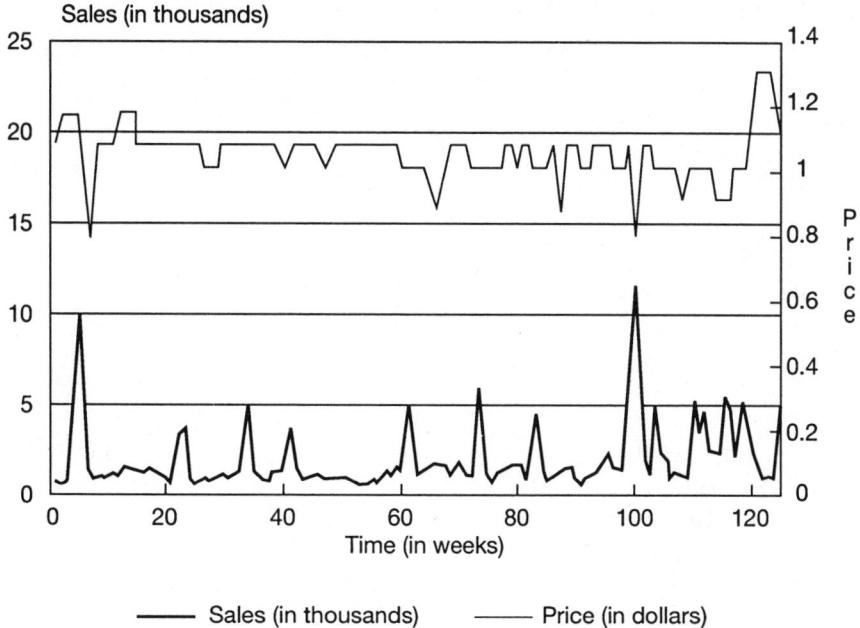

Fig 21.1   Real sales pattern – actual weekly sales and price of an fmcg

lish sales by counting stock and adjusting purchases by the stock differences from period to period. Shelf prices were noted but, when they changed, they could not be matched with sales. Since the sales turnover was known by product category, some allowance could be made for "shrinkage," that element of stock that disappears through breakages, pilferage, shoplifting, or inexplicable reasons.

Now EPOS allows the brand owner to compare the amount of product discounted *to* the retailer with the amount of product discounted *by* the retailer. Estimates vary, but it appears that the consumer is receiving only 25 to 50 percent of the funding provided by the brand owner.

In an age of retailer power, tightening controls to eliminate price promotions, or ensure they are passed on, will not be easy. Today retailers demand, and obtain, stocking, or "slotting" or listing, fees for adding a new line from a supplier,and then the same again for taking it off the computer when sales decline. Once brand owners start to use point of sale data to reduce retailer benefits, will they still get the data?

Since 1993, ECR (efficient consumer response) has been introduced to the US grocery trade as a more sophisticated approach to the problem. We review this and similar Quick Response within chapter 4, "Distribution Channels."

Within the price promotional swamp, five motivations can be discerned:

1. **Whoever begins a new cycle has a short-term advantage.** Customers take more product, more facings are available on shelf, market share expands. Some of the gains may be permanent. It is important to note the cyclical nature. Once everyone stops in the name of insanity, there is a lull. Then it starts again.

2. **Retailers love them.** They make the retailer competitive against competitors, the store becomes lively, and the increase in sales of the promoted brand will more than offset losses from others. The retailer's sales and profits will increase both immediately and long term as customers attracted by deals return. Only part of the promotional money from the brand owner will be passed on to the consumer; the balance will go straight into the retailer's own pocket. We will see why in a moment.

3. **The sales force loves them.** A regular calendar of promotions provide continuous topics to discuss, visible displays to achieve, and largesse to dispense. Talking of novel promotions is easier than finding anything new to say about the brand.

4. **Short termism.** The brand manager has targets to make by a fixed date. Loading the dealers moves profit from next period into the current one. In some organizations, failing to meet this year's target means you will not be around for the next one.

5. **The competition is promoting.** Brands that do not compete have a way of disappearing from shelves. Once the cycle has begun, it is difficult not at least to match what others are offering. If your company has established a pattern of such offers, how do you explain to the consumer why you are stopping? The retailer will not be concerned unless yours is the dominant brand. Your slot will be taken by someone else and you may not get it back.

In short, game theory is the technique you need. In the prisoner's dilemma, you will recall, the optimal solution requires the two prisoners to agree and honor that agreement. The one that reneges gets off scot free but if they both renege, they both suffer the worst of all outcomes. Price promotions are played without the opportunity to agree except most indirectly. We will revert to cost benefit calculations in the final section of this chapter.

You will have noticed that the consumer does not appear on this list. Surely money off purchases is what the consumer wants? Marketing is serving consumer needs and promotions are just that. Some go further and see marketing as a 3D activity: display, discount, and dominate. Particularly in a recession, this notion has its attractions. Creating bustle in the stores at least contributes cash flow; and the importance of winter and summer sales to retailers has long been established. The semi-continuous sales now available may be expensive, but bustle provides the opportunity for hustle. When you walk into a marketplace, are you attracted by the busy stall or the unattended one?

> **Price promotions do not build brands.**

Price promotions run by retailers from their own resources are at once good and important both for them and the consumer. A market philosophy depends on individuals freely deciding how their money should be used. Why then the hostility to those promotions being funded by brand owners?

It comes down to a recognition of roles. Retailers rarely add value to anyone else's brand. Their role is to move stock quickly and efficiently to the consumer. To some extent they create demand, but they owe no allegiance to any particular brand.

The brand owner, however, has to differentiate that brand from competitor brands, provide reasons to buy, and, as a by-product, create demand for the category as a whole. Building a brand is expensive. Any funds for the retailer's role are taken from brand building. The loss of brand equity may be slow to appear. The diversion from long-term brand building to short-term volume gains can be justified when the net effect is positive. The evidence is otherwise. Price promotions do not build brands.

The area is contentious. Some brand owners argue that the growth of power in the hands of a few retailers will ultimately strangle new brand development and competition. What seems providential for consumers in the short term may be less attractive later.

Three more factors disturb brand marketers:

1. **A brand is a brand because it supplies consistency to the consumer.** Confidence is a key ingredient. What effect does constantly changing price have on the consumer? Is loyalty impacted? If brands A and B are on offer on alternate weeks, does that prompt consumers to alternate between A and B and ultimately move to the cheapest? In the UK, retailer own brand groceries have increased steadily to 30 percent of the market.

2. **Discounting reduces the perception of quality.** As quality is in the eye of the consumer, you can say that price promotions actually reduce quality. That will damage any brand that includes quality in its positioning.

3. **The consumer is being trained to purchase only on promotion**, as the US ketchup data bears out (60 percent of households do this).

How can you kick the price promotion addiction? The first step is to recognize that it is bad. The second is to recognize that only very strong companies can step alone out of the competitive spiral. Collusion to stop price promotions is illegal in most western countries. Some will think that illegality is reason enough not to collude; others will be deterred by the difficulty of enforcing illegitimate deals. What happens more frequently is an intensive campaign of competitive signalling. Competitive signalling can take many forms. One company

> **Only very strong companies can step alone out of the competitive spiral.**

after another draws attention to the negative attributes of excessive price promotions, very possibly in the trade press, or academics write sponsored papers. The signs of this activity were apparent just around the peak of price promotions in the early 1990s.

Once the climate is adjusted, small moves can be made by small players or bigger moves by the larger ones. If they are followed, the problem is solved, for the moment.

VALUE PROMOTIONS

"Value promotions" are additional product in place of, or sometimes in addition to, lower prices. They have the following advantages over price promotions :

1. **Consumers like them** – 10 percent more coffee in a pack is more tangible than a 10 percent discount from a price they do not remember and may not believe.

2. **The different packs can be tracked through the distributive chain.** The consumer gets what the retailer gets.

3. **The cost to the brand owner is less** especially when, as in a recession, he has spare product on his inventories.

Similar comments apply to threefers (three for the price of two), twofers (two for the price of one) and BOGOs (buy one, get one free). Production like them less (special packaging) though they can off-load surplus. Value promotions have gained in favor over price promotions of which they are a less virulent form.

COUPONS AND LOYALTY SCHEMES

The common objective of these types of promotion is to get the consumer back. Sometimes (regularly in the USA) coupons are distributed to promote trial. Bonus miles may similarly tempt new members of a frequent flyer program. In principle, X cents off the next purchase is similar to collecting stamps from petrol stations or air mile credits from airlines. The denomination of a coupon, or whatever, is linked not only to the profit margins of the brand and the urgency of the need to get consumers back, but also to redemption rates. You can afford to be generous if people rarely cash them in. Clearly there is a delicate balancing act; the higher the value the more are cashed unless the collection rules are as complex as Japanese import facilitation. That in turn tends not to add to consumer satisfaction.

> **You can afford to be generous if people rarely cash them in.**

As with other promotional forms, whoever first introduces the scheme has the advantage until the rest join in. Thus such schemes move through any industry in waves. When ideas run dry, the cycle starts again.

In the UK, 8,110,000,000 coupons were distributed in 1991, more than double those in 1984 but redemptions increased only 65 percent. You might imagine that recession would encourage redemption but the *percentage* redeemed has almost halved from just over 10 percent to just over 5 percent.

Coupons legally discriminate between consumers who are more or less price sensitive. The more affluent, typically, cannot be bothered to cut out or keep the coupons and produce them at the head of the check-out queue. The less affluent, especially those with large families who can be co-opted to the collecting process, find them valuable. Thus the manufacturer is discounting only to those to whom it matters.

Coupons are expensive to administer and wasteful. At least 25 percent are 'misredeemed' (i.e. cashed without meeting the conditions). That costs the UK coupon industry £28m a year. Jolly good thing too. They disfigure packaging and newsprint. Fortunately, they show signs of disappearing.

Electronic forms of credit collection, from frequent flyer programs, have the huge advantages of not littering the premises, being easier to control and taking a step toward relationship marketing which is really how they should be seen. There is a difference between giving money away anonymously and personalizing the brand consumer connectivity. The first is poor marketing, even though you have to do it for competitive reasons, and the latter *may* be great – see chapter 25, "Relationship Marketing."

When retailers themselves practice a marketing format they have watched manufacturers develop, there are grounds for taking it seriously. In 1995 the UK supermarket giant Tesco made enough progress with its loyalty card for its chief competitor, Sainsbury, to join in. As with all other such schemes in the past, e.g. Green Shield stamps, most others will join too and, ultimately, the idea will fade away. Timing is all.

QUANTITY DISCOUNTS

Here we are dealing just with the immediate customer. On the surface, quantity discounts have the same money-off characteristics as price promotions. Again, most of the benefit will stay with the retailer. By bunching purchases, the retailer can obtain the same temporary advantages. If you really do have to give more away, this approach has some advantages:

- **The cost falls where it should**. The 1980s witnessed an unholy alliance between powerful retailers and supplier sales management to raid the brand budget for their purposes, not the brand's. Price promotions typically do nothing for brand equity yet internal accounting systems charge them against the marketing budget. The customer is bigger than the sales manager, who in turn is bigger than the brand manager. Guess who buys the drinks? Many sales managements are either volume-oriented or measured on profit contribution *before* marketing (AMP or A&SP) expenditure. Thus anything they can get from that source is a free ride. Much better is to recognize price-offs as discounts and charge them to sales.

- **They can be structured to smooth product flow and minimize costs** for the supplier. If an order costs £100 to process and deliver, irrespective of the size of the order, it makes sense to discount £100 on the larger quantities. The sales manager will have some complex arithmetic to show that the maximum allowance should be £200, or double any other number you think of. This is not only an incentive to move the order quantity from the customer's optimal point to the supplier's, it is an important difference from price promotions. Those introduce inefficient peaks and troughs into the supply logistics, whereas quantity discounts are designed to iron them out.

- **Assortment**. By taking groups of products together, many permutations can be achieved to persuade buyers to take more of the items they want less. This is a fine area for computer analysis.

- **Quantity discounts encourage the retailer to consolidate buying** with the fewest suppliers. The reason the sales manager gives to justify the higher discounts will be to exclude competitors.

● **Some legislation frowns on discounting policies which discriminate** between customers except for quantity purposes. Quantity discounts may be one of the few ways of legal discrimination. Within careful choice of break points and assortments, profits can be maximized.

The extent that these factors affect customer loyalty varies massively. For many companies, quantity discounts will remain an important part of the marketing mix. Once again, consistency is a key ingredient, but discounts should be reviewed annually at the same time as any monthly or yearly rebate scheme. Similar considerations apply to arrangements such as including loyalty bonuses based on the

> **For many companies, quantity discounts will remain an important part of the marketing mix.**

share of business a customer gives any one supplier. The mathematical complexities and the money involved well justify testing options through a small PC based model.

Quantity discounts are not accounted under "promotions," nor should they be. They have been included in this chapter to suggest that price promotions should be converted into quantity discounts and excluded from brand marketing budgets.

SAMPLING NEW CONSUMERS

Not only new brands need new consumers; every brand needs them to stay alive. However successful a brand may be there are always new consumers to be tapped. Consumers, on the other hand, are not desperate for new brands. A supermarket already carries thousands of lines, far more than any one consumer will ever need. Progressively greater varieties of retailer offer still more brands.

Marketing is full of paradox: offering a price promotion is bad for brand equity and taking 100 percent off the price of a sample is fine. It is really the difference between cheap and generous. A price promotion, typically, does not add to the relationship between brand and consumer. A gift, however, is another matter.

Unfortunately sampling is usually expensive, and if it is to be well done, especially so. Yet to skimp on sampling may be like giving a gift without the wrapping. If it is coupled with a price promotion, as many retailers insist, it is like giving a gift with the price still on. A current sampling vogue is free software. Whether this is expensive or cheap for the supplier, depends on how you cost it. Picking up a program through Internet is virtually costless. The concept is that the users have high utility costs in getting their minds around the new system. Free software off-sets that. Once the user has committed to the new software, they will happily buy upgrades. And in the 1990s software business, upgrades are fast and furious.

> **Most promotional activity associated with sampling can be quantified.**

Most promotional activity associated with sampling can be quantified. Demonstrators can sample the brand to consumers in store. Samples or vouchers or coupons can be direct mailed. There are fairs, on-street sampling, products given away with established brands, gifts in hotel rooms or at charity functions. The list is endless. They can all be tried on a small scale; the costs and conversion rates can be measured.

Less easy to measure is the style, the way the sampling relates to the brand's positioning or personality. To be offered a new variety of cheddar cheese by a demonstrator in a supermarket is one thing. But what about caviar?

Sampling, just as any other form of promotion, should reinforce positioning. It should be consistent, price premiumness and advertising, for example. Ensuring that marketing truly is integrated, in this sense, is a main reason for the annual plan.

A brand that is tired of sampling is tired of life. Many a brand manager overlooks sampling because it is rather basic and their brand is mature. The promotions houses visit with far more sophisticated ideas. Sampling will seem expensive compared to other ways of gaining new consumers. They may mean you cannot afford much but it does not mean you cannot afford any. If it helps you feel better about the cost, consider it market research and make sure the demonstrators tell you how consumers reacted to the product.

NON-PRICE PROMOTIONS

There are no firm figures of non-price promotion (NPP) expenditure in the UK, but in 1987 it was thought to be about 25 percent of display advertising expenditure, or in other words, £1,000m.

In reality NPP may include some price ingredients. NPP are in effect three-dimensional advertisements. Their function is to convey the brand's positioning and reasons to buy through a different medium. At least, that is the theory of integrated marketing.

Besides consistency, we are looking for relevancy, stand-out, topicality, fashion, originality and adding brand values. Relevancy is how well the promotion supports the product; stand-out secures attention; topicality gets the day (Mother's Day, for example) right and also the year.

NPPs should be fun. They are an opportunity for the brand and its consumer to share common values in an extended way. Branded T-shirts, match boxes, umbrellas, diaries, ties, playing cards and pens have been around for fifty years. Ash trays are not politically correct just now but in a year or two? The fun is in the medium, or in what is done with it.

Other promotions range from trade fairs, to gifts, to competitions and prize draws, to exhibitions, merchandising and displays, to mystery shoppers, to events, and to the opportunity to trade in old models. Some have synergistic benefits. Mystery shop-

> **Their function is to convey the brand's positioning and reasons to buy through a different medium.**

ping, for example, typically involves an employee or agent acting as a regular consumer at the retail store and handing over a cash prize if the assistant gives the "right" answers. Thus mystery shopping can simultaneously double as market research and quality control. In the durables business, from cars to washing machines, selling a new model requires some help for the consumer's disposal of the old one. When the market is tight, second hand cars are not easy to sell. Disposing of a large and heavy washing machine or refrigerator is not easy either. Thus the marketers of durables will run promotions on the disposal end of the equation because price generosity on the old machine does not detract from brand equity, or any informal pricing agreements, on the new one.

The purpose of all NPP is, in addition to increasing sales velocity, to add value to the brand as distinct from promotions which detract from brand equity. It should leave the consumer with a warm feeling of involvement with the brand.

MEASUREMENT

Pre- and post-evaluation of promotions is essential to discover how to improve in future. Yet many marketers do neither. At least formally. Of course marketers know why they agree to one promotion rather than another. Afterwards they have some feelings, which they may or may not share, about success or otherwise. Typically they are too busy with the next promotion to have time to commit any reports to writing. In any case, what use would such bureaucracy serve? The most likely outcome would be that accountants and other ignorant/interfering people would ask questions about past promotions and then they would have even less time for the new. The important thing about the past is that it is past. We should invest our time in building profits for the future.

Contrary to claims from IT enthusiasts, it is rarely possible to know if a promotion is truly a success or not. To do so, you must know what would otherwise have happened both during the time of the promotion and subsequently. You must know how customers and competitors would have behaved if the promotion had never taken place. This, the "baseline," is impossible to determine. When you are being sold the success of a past or future promotion, take a hard look at the baseline being assumed. What you can do, however, is to measure promotions against the prior expectations for it.

> **What you can do, however, is to measure promotions against the prior expectations for it.**

Those who do not study promotions, will be condemned to make the same mistakes. In other words, every time history repeats itself, according to Anon., the price goes up. Chapter 23 on "Pragmatic Planning" deals with learning and the need to put some objectivity between the activities and the marketing manager. Ownership of promotional ideas gets in the way of both pre- and post-evaluation by the owner. Companies deal with this in a number of ways: promotional decisions may be made by a team to include, at least, marketing, sales, and finance. Michel Roux, who was largely responsible for the success of Absolut vodka in the USA, routinely invited advertising space sales people to bring promotional ideas when they came to sell their media. Since few other such senior marketers would see them at all and space sales people are bright, highly paid, and seen in all the best bars, they were both motivated and able to represent what leading edge consumers would find most attractive. Importantly, Michel and his team could be objective in their selection of the promotional ideas to run.

A further means of achieving objectivity is to avoid falling in love with a new idea and running it nationwide. First test it on a small scale. Some ideas are too big to do this and if it is a *really* great idea, competitors may copy it. Many companies market research their promotions as an alternative means of achieving objectivity. As chapter 26, "Research is always Incomplete" will conclude, sceptics doubt the reliability of this form of research but it may be better than nothing.

Post-promotion evaluation is hard to do objectively if the intentions were not committed to paper before the event. Pre-promotion expectations need be no more than one side of a page:

- What the promotion is, where and when it will run. Is it a test or based on a previous test?
- Target market etc. compared to the positioning statement. If this is not a clone match, why is the promotion off strategy?
- Impact on the three basic consumer benefits: functional, psychological, and economic.
- Impact on sales, profit, and brand equity.

Then post-evaluation should also be no more than a page:

- Results compared to expectations for sales, profit and brand equity. Where hard numbers are not available, subjective guesses, or feelings, are fine. The numbers are less important than thinking about the issues.
- How the promotional execution varied from the original expectation.
- Lessons for the future.

If Abraham and Lodish are right that 84 percent of trade (price) promotions are unsuccessful, great pressure is put on promotions evaluators. They can hardly admit to a similar number failing and expect to stay in employment. The art of making discounted cash flows (DCF) provide the answer you want, lies in the residual value, i.e. the capital value so far out in time that no one worries about it. Not many people know this. Likewise, the art of making promotions look good lies in the baseline. Figure 21.1, on page 229 showed the sales spikes. The non-spiky line looks like a baseline? Many marketers use that. Then, of course, all the spikes are extra and due to the promotion. If the promotion was not run, then a competitor would have taken that slot, and the spike, or so the marketer claims.

That may well be so. On the other hand, if consumers are accelerating their purchases without any increase in consumption, and if they are loyal, then the baseline would be at the *average* level. The apparent promotional advantage of the spikes is more than offset by the rest of the time because volume is unchanged but peak sales are at discounted prices.

The truth usually lies between these extremes which simply indicate the need for care when deciding where the baseline falls and the period for which the promotion is evaluated. In particular, it is wrong to compare a promotional with a non-promotional period. You should look at a full cycle, say a quarter or a year, with and without the promotion(s) in order to eliminate short-term, acceleration, effects.

And in order to do that, you have to factor in the likely competitor reactions. As indicated above, to do this scientifically requires the mathematical flights of game theory. In practice, the marketing team need to think about just four boxes of a matrix, as shown in figure 21.2:

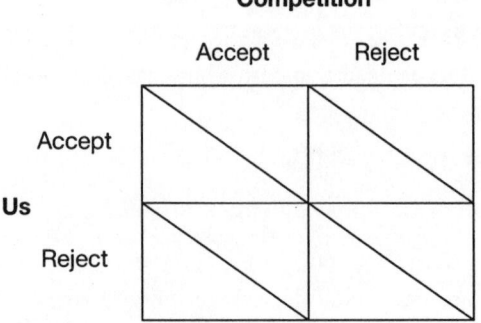

Fig 21.2   Promotions dilemma

CONCLUSION

Promotions cover a wide field of ingenuity. Marketers would do well to reduce the concentration on price and focus on sizzling activities which add value. Promotions can be seen as advertising in another medium but there is more flexibility. Marketers who would be embarrassed to copy advertising, think little of borrowing promotions from other categories and territories. Promotions are susceptible to testing and quantitative assessment. Expect to be shocked by the lack of thoroughness in testing and performance measurement.

Promotions are the second largest part of the classic marketing mix. Well handled, they will build brands at the same time as throwing off short-term profits.

Memo to file

Subject: PROMOTIONS, COUPONS AND GIVEAWAYS

- Use the brand's money to build the brand's, not the customer's, business. If price competition is too intense, it may be time for some competitive signalling.

- Account for price promotions as if they were quantity discounts, i.e. put them back to sales, where they belong.

- Other "value promotions" (extra product) are the lesser peril.

- However, do not throw out the pearl of sampling with the oyster of price promotion. How else are you going to increase business?

- Coupons and loyalty schemes meet two different objectives: indirect price reductions and repeat business/brand loyalty. Do not prejudice the latter by the former.

- Non-price promotions can be a creative form of advertising through different media. Treat them that way. The medium reinforcing the message is a double win.

- Check out the objectivity not only of the promotions themselves but also of how they are tested and how well performance is measured against expectations. Without this feedback, learning will be reduced.

- Think of a promotion as three-dimensional advertising. Does it communicate the brand's values? Is it new or secondhand? Creative or mundane? Effective or effete?

- If you have to choose between promotions which benefit either the short or the long term, reject them both. The best promotions build brand equity *and* short-term profits.

22

PERSONAL SELLING

The origin of all marketing even if technology is reducing the numbers

---

Key issues
- Role of personal selling within the marketing mix ● Cost effectiveness: sales, customer feedback, and competitive intelligence ● Managing relationships is a personal business. Trade marketing. Managing the sales force ● Selling as partnership

---

Pity the poor customer. Ever since Tom Peters told companies to get closer to their customers, they have been crowded by suppliers. Their sales forces were doing that all along. Personal selling was the poor relation of advertising when marketing was seen as image building. Today, sales people carry that title but the importance of the function has re-emerged.

THE ROLE OF THE SALES EXECUTIVE

Personal selling was the earliest form of marketing and will be the last for a simple reason: no business can log a profit until it makes a sale. Whoever does it and however it is done, only a sale can trigger the profit scorecard. That should make the sales executive the corporate hero. It rarely does.

The point is made by those who reverse the traditional pyramid hierarchy to put the sales force at the top (see figure 22.1). In this perspective, the role of marketing and other specialist functions is to support sales. Marketers, naturally, believe sales are there to support them, or at least their brands. Therein lies a perpetual tug of war which sales tend to win during recessions and marketing during the economic upturns. The tussle is unhelpful. A thread throughout this book is the need for partnership, for marketing by cross-functional teams including sales.

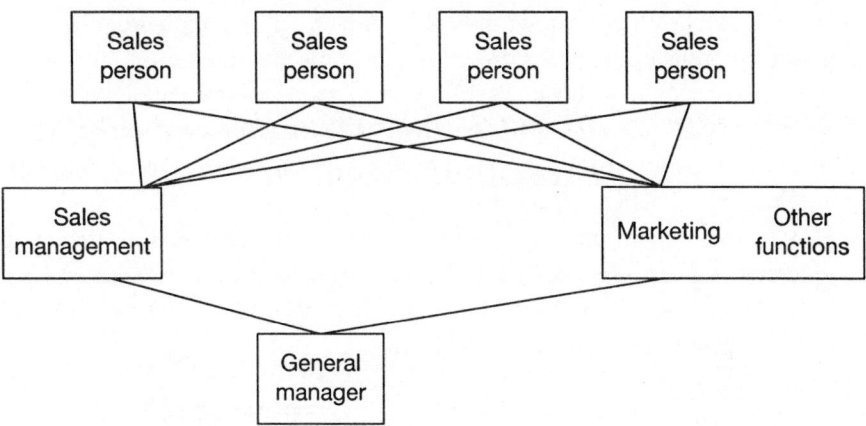

Fig 22.1   Sales force as vanguard

Figure 22.1 is an important perspective when considering the focus on sales and the immediate customer. Here marketing is indeed in support. When we are considering the final consumer or end user, however, the roles are reversed. In this chapter we consider customer relations.

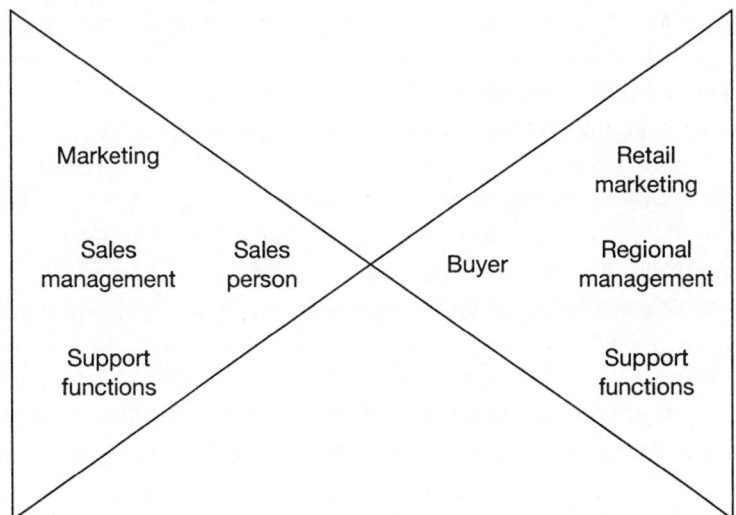

Fig 22.2   Bow tie

Figure 22.1 implies a large number of sales people in proportion to the rest of the business. Most sales forces have been shrinking in number as retailing has become more concentrated and as retailers have discouraged branch level calling. Figure 22.2 shows the single sales person as the spear point with the rest of the business supporting that role. On the opposite side, the retail buyer points the other way, supported in turn by the rest of the retail organization. For obvious reasons, this is known as the "bow tie" model. Its attraction, whether in consumer or business marketing, is the recognition of the importance of support for the sales executives. They are the flag bearers. Their commitment, enthusiasm, passion, determination translate directly into corporate success. There is no substitute.

Have you ever come across a business where someone would not draw you to one side and explain confidentially that you should ignore appearances: "this is really a people business"? Is there any other kind? The fundamental seller/buyer transaction is fueled not just by mechanistic economic factors but by personal trust and beliefs, by relationships. Where is the fulcrum of these human qualities if it is not the sales force?

> **Personal selling is an organic part of the business fuelling not only customer relationships but stimulating the marketing function with feedback from the market.**

Products move through the distribution chain both in response to consumer *pull* and to supplier *push* or personal selling. One may be more effective than the other, but both are needed for all forms of marketing. Network marketing, such as Amway, Tupperware, and, more recently, air fresheners and water purifiers, depends largely on personal selling and then word of mouth.

To the marketing manager, personal selling is more than just an element of the marketing mix to be costed against advertising or PR or promotions, it is an organic part of the business fueling not only customer relationships but stimulating the marketing function with feedback from the market.

The current "middle-age" of marketing, seems to be an identity crisis. Now that the whole business is marketing-oriented, what is the role of the marketer?[1] The performance of marketers is criticized relative to other functions. Sales too have sought to step away from their old glad-handing image. They accept that they are still relationship managers but the role has become more professional in the following ways. Retailers expect:

[1] Simon Broadbent, "Changes in the way Marketing is Managed – a Personal View" *Journal of Marketing Management*, vol. 11 (1995).

- Category management and other retail marketing analysis.
- Consumer research and other hard numbers, not marketing whimsy.
- Continuity, feedback on promotions, and long-term learning.
- Everything to be paid for.
- Not to be surprised by their retailer competitors' pricing or promotions.

And, of course,

- Tickets for the big matches, same as ever.

While sales executives have done their best to pick up these skills, they now want more focussed support from marketing, now called "trade" or "customer" marketing, and discussed below (see page 247). They have also asked for the bow tie to be reversed, (see figure 22.3).

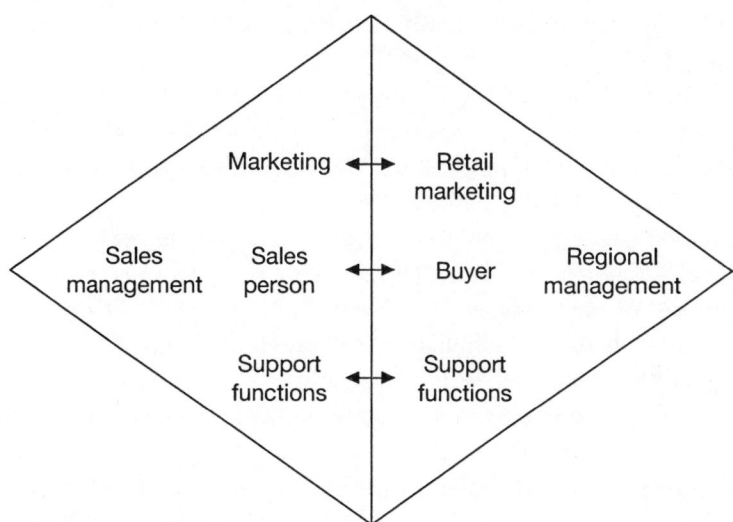

Fig 22.3   Reversed bow tie

COST EFFECTIVENESS

Attention to personal selling focusses partly on how to maximize the value from this specialist form of marketing and partly on cost. Taking salary, bonuses, car, expenses, and on-costs together a junior sales person may cost $100,000 a year. A specialist industrial sales person may cost twice that. If a junior makes 1,800 customer calls a year and a specialist 1,000, a cost per call ranges from $50 to $200. Small wonder companies have cut numbers back and looked for lower cost alternatives.

Personal selling here includes two of the most popular lower cost variants: telephone sales (now called, misleadingly, telemarketing) and brokers. The techniques for telemarketing differ from those of personal visits more than was at first thought. Information systems support, for example, is more critical. The needed database support parallels other forms of direct marketing such as mail. With about ten times the daily calling capacity and half the base cost structure, the cost per call is nearer $3 than $50. (All figures in 1995 money). Development of such databases is growing in significance. They offer substantial competitive advantages as well as contemporary values.

Brokers and telemarketing bureaux (or "call centres") offer shared sales services. If the supplier has a small portfolio, brokers and bureaux provide critical mass and cost-efficiency. They have developed specialist sales and management skills with, consequentially, greater productivity. They can be compensated on a commission basis, or at least piecework. Arrangements vary but tying selling costs tightly to sales is valuable to many businesses, especially for those just starting up.

For larger companies, these outside services are perfect for the "extras" but there is less dedication and corporate learning. For the crucial customer relationships and marketing mix elements, these services should be brought in house when it is cost-efficient to do so.

Should the brand marketer develop the same skills as brokers? Some do. The Mars group, for example, has an outstanding record for training and management of sales people. But to some the sales force is almost taken for granted. As the most traditional, in a sense, of company functions and making only rare appearance in headquarters, the sales force's greatest visibility in these companies is as an expense in the profit and loss account.

As noted above, increasing costs and retailer power together with declining margins have forced a re-examination. No longer do retailers want store visits from sales people; some will not accept them. They want lower prices, but want also to control their own supply of product and information to branches. As the big retailers increase their share of the market, so the size of the sales force diminishes, but their importance does not. The key account sales person handling that retailer might have the power to make or break the marketer.

This has led to the complex customer contact patterns symbolized by the reversed bow tie, where the marketer sells to the retailer at several different levels, e.g. regionally, and functions. The key account sales person's relationship with the buyer is thus flanked by the regional sales manager's relationship with the customer's regional management and the sales director's relationship with an opposite number. In this respect, consumer brand marketing has moved closer to industrial marketing, where these complex multi-link relationships have long been the norm.

This complexity has brought sales understanding more deeply into Head Office. Good. Sales is less likely to be seen as just a cost on the P&L account. But the perspective is still on bringing home the bacon: making the sale. Most companies underestimate the crucial roles sales can play in bringing back customer feedback on the brands and competitive **Tying selling costs tightly to sales is valuable to many businesses.** intelligence. Sales executives regularly complain that nobody listens to them. If you are going to spend this much on the sales team, and you are, then *listen* to them. Not only do they have important things to tell you, it will raise their morale and their performance.

MANAGING RELATIONSHIPS IS A PERSONAL BUSINESS

That convergence is underlined by the creation of "trade" or "customer" marketing departments. Large consumer marketing companies both in Europe and the USA have recognized that the power of large retailers, the complexity of promotions and relationships are demanding specialist attention within marketing. The product manager is ultimately concerned with the consumer, and may not be giving the customer enough attention. Furthermore, there may be as many product managers as brands. If the brands are big, there should be. That is fine from a consumer viewpoint but customers expect suppliers' activities to be coordinated across these brands, if not tailored, especially for them.

A trade marketing department has the responsibility of bringing promotions, sales presentations and information together, both brand by brand and in total, for the customers with their attitudes in mind. While it is then up to the sales person to manage the ensuing relationship, performance can be hugely increased by professional pre-packaging of the sales effort.

Improved performance can be measured not just in sales turnover, better mix and margins, but in improved control over price promotions and the contributions paid over by brand marketers.

There are good reasons for the division any company makes between the promotional funds in the marketing department budget and the discounts and allowances that come from sales or from the gross margin. From the point of view of sales people, giving money from the marketing budget will look better than giving it from their own. Product managers may also prefer this if they are getting what they want. Furthermore, the funding in the marketing budget may be split with an overseas sup-plier. Nevertheless, if the promotion is really a customer discount and is not likely to build brand equity, it should be charged to sales, not the brand budget.

> **Sales executives should be profit *and customer relationship* responsible.**

A number of computer packages now offer systems to measure account profitability and, as a byproduct, the profitability of the sales person respon-sible for those accounts. There are many ways to reduce the cost of promo-tions, but three basic steps are:

1. Sales executives should be profit *and customer relationship* responsible so that goals are consistent with those of the business as a whole. The cus-tomer relationship is part of brand equity.

2. Ensure the sales executives have all the information relevant to that account. Now that electronic point of sale (EPOS) data can match pro-motions granted to consumers with those given to retailers, the sales person has high quality information to help fine tune terms. Sales execu-tives today need facts from databases, not exhortation and stories.

3. Raise productivity by providing specialist support through trade market-ing. Measure performance of this support too.

The management of a sales force is subject to cultural norms. Brits expect to be independent, Germans to be regimented, Italians to be creative, the French to be intellectual, South Africans to think they are training for rugby. Feel free to apply your own stereotypes. A universal feature, however, is the reg-ular sales conference. Budgets may influence the frequency and extrava-gance of these events, but management should use the occasion to listen and convince the sales team that it truly loves them.

The value of a sales conference cannot be measured, nor should it be skimped. It is a high point of inspiring passion and commitment. Every day cannot be a sales conference but a lot can be done to maintain those attitudes through the year.

"Closer to the customer" is a modern cliché but the appeal is real: if you are close enough to feel how the customer feels, you are also that much closer to the customer's wallet. But the concept fails to take account of the sales person who is already close to the customer. Why not get closer to the sales force?

SELLING AS PARTNERSHIP

Understanding your business from the outside in, from the consumer's point of view and also the customer's, is basic to marketing; that is what market orientation is. The supplier is in partnership with the customer; as is increasingly recognized, their roles should not be adversarial. Together, supplier and customer market to the consumer.

A partnership relationship within a distribution channel can be shown to be more profitable for both sides than parochial maximization of profitability. The ECR movement in the US grocery business is thought to be able to release $30bn for suppliers, retailers, and consumers.

For this reason, companies should regard their sales personnel more as consultants assisting customers to realize their profit opportunities. Any marketing trend creates a counter-trend as companies look for points of difference. Moving further and further into the customer's business as consultants has benefits of involvement and understanding, but problems of cost and distraction. The counter-trend is to revert to the basics

> **Companies should regard their sales personnel more as consultants assisting customers to realize their profit opportunities.**

where the supplier is hammering away at the front door to get volume and market share.

Modern selling has wide variations from foot-in-the-door to consultative, short-term (transactional) to long-term relationships, individual to team, volume orientation to profit responsibility. The list does not stop there. The UK John Lewis organization, for example, call their sales people "partners" and treat them in exactly that way. In aggregate these characteristics make up the company's "style" of customer relationships. Even if the perfect balance can be found, style will need to change over time both to refresh and stimulate the team and to provide competitive advantage.

Review the size, balance, and composition of the sales effort every year or so, but do not stop there. The whole approach to customer relationships needs fundamental consideration every now and then. Marketing is ultimately the managing of relationships. Nowhere is this more central than in personal selling.

Memo to file

Subject: PERSONAL SELLING

- Are the sales executives the heroes of the business? Do they have the passion, commitment, recognition, and support they need? Are they listened to? They should believe they are the most important people in your business and they probably are.

- Managing relationships begins, and is sustained by, the customer relationship. What training, information, and support will improve those relationships? What is done at the centre that could be better done in the field? Would specialist trade marketing help or just add to overhead?

- Personal selling may be the most expensive component in the marketing mix. Optimize the size of the sales force and rebalance territories or responsibilities annually. Remember what brand, customer, and competitor intelligence they can bring back.

- Compromise the quantity of sales executives if you must, but not quality. Ensure profit responsibility and measure customer relationships. Then their goals synchronise with those of the business as a whole.

23

PRAGMATIC PLANNING

The agenda that brings the team together to optimize expenditure and results

Key issues

● **Why plan at all? Strategy and the illusion of control. Problems arising. Reducing planning resources while increasing quality. Rehearsing your future. How many different types of plans or planning processes?** ● **Planning as learning. Imagination vs. control. Consistency vs. innovation. The need for cross-functional teams. The dimensions of learning** ● **What should a plan contain? Impact of paradigms. How long should it be? Format** ● **Harnessing finance and systems support**

WHY PLAN AT ALL?

The conventional wisdom is that a business, or a brand, should define its long-term objectives, and define broadly how to get there, allowing for the competition. This is "strategy." By comparing the present circumstances, the environment, and the strategy a short-term, usually 1–3 years, plan can be derived to include tactics and the budget. That is simple enough? It isn't and it's wrong. Not many companies do that with any rigor and the evidence that such a process produces better results than not bothering with all that, is slim. Almost all companies bother with some of it; budgeting is almost universal.

Only a small minority of medium/large UK marketing companies produce full "plans," defined here to contain at least analysis, strategy, actions (who is going to do what and when), and a budget. This rough estimate was taken from a study by Laura Cousins.[1] On the other hand, 60 per cent have some kind of planning process. For most companies, strategy is what they discover they were doing after becoming successful. Luck forms a part. So do responses to unforecast events. Strategy is fine if it gives a consistent orientation to deal with the unexpected. The artificial cascading of plans from the unknown future to the general to the specific may be little more than *the illusion of control*. Planning, in short, can be dangerous to the health of your business.

Frank McKenna[2] investigated why average drivers think they are better than average drivers. Any comprehensive cross-section of drivers indicates that, on average, they believe that they are safer than "the average driver" and less likely to have accidents. This anomaly could have two causes: drivers are optimists and/or believe they can control their chances of accidents. The same people, as passengers, expect to have the average number of accidents which removes the optimism hypothesis. The illusion of control encourages driving too fast and without enough care. It is fostered by the removal of traditional speed cues: rushing wind, concentrated energy. The fastest humans may get up to 20m.p.h. on their own legs. In their modern cars, drawing rooms on wheels, they may be travelling five times faster with no effort and little sensation of speed.

Plans, to the accountant or bank manager, are vital to *control*. Money will not be released without a sensible looking plan which shows that their money will grow. Furthermore, they can verify each month that actual performance is in line. Consequentially, many managers have come to see plans as being just that: drudgery necessary to getting approval for expenditure. The largest reason for planning in the Cousins study was control (32 percent). Under these circumstances, plans will provide the illusion of control for managers just like drivers. The danger is that average managers will say, and believe, that their plans are better than the average plan. This cannot be true.

Resultant problems include:

● Insufficient realism, i.e. objective assessment of current situation and responses to planned initiatives.

● Failure to anticipate future market changes, i.e. moves by consumers, retailers and competitors.

[1]   London Business School PhD, 1994.
[2]   Frank McKenna "It won't happen to me: Unrealistic optimism or illusion of control?," *British Journal of Psychology* (1993), 84, 39–50.

- Insufficient creativity, and paradoxically,
- Fixing what ain't broke.
- Inflexibility. Once the plan is agreed, persevering whatever happens.
- Manager rotation. No memory of past successes and failures and no expectation of still being in post when the results come in. Brand/product managers in the UK and USA have an in-post job expectancy of about 16 months. Few get to do a second plan for the same brand.

In the light of this, it is not surprising that 60 percent of managers in the Cousins study considered that planning gave poor cost benefits and/or was irrelevant; 18 percent lacked resources for planning or found greater resistance to planning than was worth the struggle.

Underlying much of this is the rate of change in the business and/or its environment. If the rate of change is very high, planning can *reduce* profits – diversion of resources, inflexibility, impossible to forecast. At the other extreme, a very slow rate

> **A company should have a clear "vision" of its desired future which defines the strategic thrust and leaves the detail to be worked out as the business goes along.**

of change also means that planning is a waste of resources. What will happen tomorrow is much the same as happened yesterday. Crafts are learnt from experience. Crafts people do the same thing each time, but just a little bit better.

Modern strategy writers, such as Gary Hamel, have concluded that detailed planning is indeed a waste of time. A company should have a clear "vision" of its desired future which defines the strategic thrust and leaves the detail to be worked out as the business goes along. Decisions made at the last possible minute are more likely to be right. Anticipation dissipates time and resources. Planning productivity depends on knowing when to start planning and when to stop. Start later and stop sooner than you think. Narrowing the company's *planning window* reduces the resources employed and increases the quality of the plan.

Thus far we have seen that the case for planning is far from self evident. In high or no change situations, results appear to decline pro rata to planning effort. Where detailed plans are required, they tend to be extrapolations, thus driving out the very benefits they should incorporate. In a study with The Boston Consulting Group,[3] we found that the formal planning process had no

[3] *Brand Development: Towards a Process Model of Extension Decisions.* Tim Ambler and Chris Styles, unpublished working paper, London Business School, 1994.

connection with brand and line extensions, successful or unsuccessful: the figures were only brought into the plans *after* the launch decision had been made. This testifies to the way many firms conduct planning and real decision making in two separate worlds.

We must be careful to distinguish here between results from planning as it is now practiced and what *could* be achieved if planning became a learning process rather than an exercise in control.

The poor results from planning may have two roots: the plan itself or its execution. Planning is essential because we only live once but we can rehearse the future as much as we like. Very few performances cannot be improved by practice. The amount of practice, the types of practice, and how much resources should be devoted to rehearsal versus performance, however, are all questions that should be asked, but rarely are.

More often, one planning process is created. When that fails to predict precisely, another is added. Companies began with budgets. When they proved inaccurate, planning was approached more formally. The Institute of Chartered Accountants of England and Wales, amongst other learned bodies, has provided "best practice"[4] based on what a panel of accountants believed, albeit without a shred of empirical support. Control was the underlying point of view. Take this from the first paragraph of the first leaflet: "Control contributes to the achievement of success and, from the management viewpoint, it contributes *all* [my emphasis] the essentials of good management."

Engineers see the world similarly: construct the right controls and feedbacks and the machine will perform to specification. If variances develop, improve (increase?) the controls. The end product of this thinking is visioning, strategic plans, business plans, long-term plans, short-term plans, marketing, and other functional plans, quarterly forecasts ... May I stop there?

The consequences are that excessive resources are devoted to planning. Each plan has to be reconciled to the immediate past and to the other plans. Thus realism *decreases*. Top management gets *more* surprises. Heads roll. Eventually top management recognizes that the planning system itself is to blame, which everyone else knew all along.

For the rest of this chapter, let us assume the happy position of being able to design a pragmatic planning system. We need to select the good features and dispense with the bad. To summarize thus far:

● Few would deny the importance of control in business systems but it is not pre-eminent.

---

[4]　A series of *Guidance to Good Practice* leaflets (1986).

- Planning provides the illusion of control which can be dangerous. We rehearsed some of the problems.

- Planning provides the opportunity to rehearse the future and thereby improve performance.

- The resources devoted to planning should be critically reviewed to achieve the fewest number of separate processes, the shortest elapsed time, and the latest possible planning period prior to decisions being needed. An after dinner speech is more helpfully rehearsed before the dinner than the month before.

PLANNING AS LEARNING

Arie de Geus is usually credited with the simple, but far reaching, idea that planning is learning.[5] Napoleon and other generals recognised that plans are not important; planning is. The point of planning is to change minds. Before planning, a set of individuals, if they have thought about future actions at all, will have different, mostly suboptimal, ideas of what action should be taken. The *result* of planning should be:

- Consensus on what actions should be taken.
- Those actions should be the best imaginable.

The concept that Process > Plan explains why so many fine performers have such lousy plans. The changing of minds and the agreement between the key players may not be influenced by what goes onto paper or electronic records. If the money managers are satisfied by any old plan, and from high performers they often are, then those high performers may not be too troubled by an accurate record of their intentions. Should this let them off the hook? If they intend to stay, perhaps it should. If they may leave, capture their learning before they go.

> **A plan is merely a toy which, if well designed, should help managers learn.**

De Geus makes the point that we all learn by playing. We use toys as models of real objects. A plan is a model of the future; it is merely a toy which, if well designed, should help managers learn, *all* the managers. Four consequences:

1. The people who need to learn are those who will have to act. Plans should never be prepared by one group of people for another.

[5] A. P. de Geus, "Planning as Learning," *Harvard Business Review* Mar–Apr 1988.

2. Production has largely been mastered, and, with the aid of computers, rapidly. Any product success can be quickly imitated. The speed with which an organization learns and adapts to the environment dictates how well it will do. Slow learners will die, moderate learners will survive and fast learners will thrive.

3. In a single unit (SBU) business, the commitment of plans to writing is unlikely to be critical. In a multi-unit business, however, recorded plans are necessary so that each "toy" can be shared with interdependent units.

4. Planning, including brand plans, should be multifunctional. Marketers are fond of pointing out that marketing is a whole company orientation, not just a functional department. Marketing is too important to be left to marketers. Accordingly, all functions should contribute to the thinking, and especially those who have to carry it out such as sales and production.

An advantage of team planning is that paradox gets full rein. The planning toy is there primarily to stretch the imagination but it should also help realism. As noted above, plans should be innovative and yet consistency is important. Promotions may be seen to be essential for the short-term and disastrous in the long. Necessary advertising may not be affordable. Doomsters should not get the upper hand but the negatives have to be faced. Different team members will, usually, argue opposing points. Learning should develop from that very argument. Quantification which, naturally, accountants see as essential (that old control bogey), is really only necessary to resolve which is better. This is how the toy works. The managers playing with the plan agree how to translate action alternatives into forecast outcomes and match those against previously agreed objectives.

Team planning is more likely to bring all those into question. A primary reason for marketing failures, notably advertising, is that the objectives were never agreed between those responsible in the first place, still less the likely outcomes of actions. Realism was missing. Each individual submitted forecast outcomes and, if they reconciled and were acceptable, that was it.

Marketers soon figured that the way to get a plan accepted was to start with an acceptable bottom line and work up. Sales would be forecast to be whatever was necessary to produce that bottom line. The probability of those sales actually happening was only greater than the brand manager still being in the job at the time of reckoning. This is the very antithesis of marketing: it should work from the market to the bottom line, not the other way about.

Where this happens, *top management is to blame*. They have allowed the *plan* to become important rather than the *process*, i.e. learning.

We need to analyse organizational learning, the subject of numerous books,[6] just a little more before setting out a typical marketing plan format. There are just four *dimensions* of organizational learning:

1. **Across time**. One of the principal benefits of written plans is that they can be compared with what happened, before the next plan is prepared. Generally speaking, what works should be retained, with whatever is needed to keep it fresh, but the failures are instructive.

2. **Horizontally**. The multifunctional team approach to learning should automatically produce cross-functional learning, assuming all members are represented and speak up for their interests. The horizontal dimension goes much wider: what can be learned from competitors and affiliates in your own market and overseas? Some companies formalize this into benchmarking though that is rarely applied to marketing decisions.

3. **Depth**. Craftspeople, which is all we marketers are, usually know *how* to deploy the tools of our trade but not *why* that should be so. In other words, we are practitioners, not theoreticians. Moreover, we have learned to distrust theoreticians; in marketing, they have a pretty dodgy record. Level 1 learning concerns the "how": managers learn to do that by copying one another or by being told what to do. The "how" is programmed into corporate cultures: "this is how we do things around here." In successful businesses, the "how" gets passed on; those who do not get it, get out. Scientists are distinguished from craftspeople because they know *why*: this is level 2. If you know the cause, knowledge is transferred more easily and can be developed. If you know why bridges stand up or fall down, you can build bigger, cheaper, and stronger bridges. Level 3, and we are not going any lower today thank you, concerns the "way we think." Just as not knowing *why* limits the ability to develop the *how*, so the habits of thought we have developed limit our ability to have new thoughts. Level 3 concerns paradigms. In marketing there are largely three: neo-classical, conflict, and relational. These paradigms affect the type of plans companies write. A manager who has just joined from a business whose thinking is neo-classical will have difficulty in producing an acceptable plan in a conflict-driven organization. Scientists working on the same topic, e.g. human memory, but from different paradigms, e.g. biology and computer sciences, may have similar difficulty in respecting each other's work.

4. **Hierarchy** (height). Top-down planning is often compared with bottom up. Neither work. Nobody ever said learning was easy; learning from

[6] C. Argyris, *On Organizational Learning*, Cambridge, Blackwell Business, 1993.

your bosses and subordinates seems especially difficult. Revisiting the past may be a chore, horizontal (peer level) learning may be shot through with NIH (not invented here), and discovering theory is best left to academics. Any organization too big to allow managers to conduct planning in one group has the hierarchy problem. Some favor top-down planning in which the top echelon calculate what is needed and feasible and pass those targets down to the next lower echelon as targets they must meet. And so on. This model can be found in North America, paradoxically the home of marketing. It causes marketers to forget the market and work from the required profit up to the sales and share needed to deliver it. In hard times, the lower units typically doubt their own plans as a result. Europeans are more likely to work bottom up. If the top echelon like the numbers when they add them up, everyone can go home happy. In hard times, the totals are usually unsatisfactory; either they switch to top down mode with stated objectives or the cycle restarts. Debates about whether top down or bottom up is preferable are sterile: you need both.

With peer and hierarchical processes, it is easy enough to get each side to make a presentation to the other; learning is more difficult. The senior level believes it can teach the lower; the lower knows that those old fogeys upstairs are out of date and out of touch. The market today is both different and more difficult. Today, they

> **Mutual learning is essential for consensus and consensus is essential for effective implementation.**

fondly believe, life is far more competitive. Some things do change, technology especially, but marketing fundamentals hardly ever do. Marketing textbooks were as concerned with own label (UK) or private label (USA) in the 1960s as they are in the 1990s. When was pricing not an issue? Worse still, both sides may see the interaction as a competition for control: "this is my patch" versus "approving the plan, or not, is my decision."

Mutual learning is essential for consensus and consensus is essential for effective implementation. If everyone who has to execute the plan agrees with it, believes in it and is committed to it, they are a great deal more likely to carry it out. And make whatever fine tuning turns out to be needed.

No company will get all the pieces in place, though Japanese companies are notably better at all four dimensions than Westerners. In Japan there may be signs that the appetite for learning is diminishing. If so the opportunities for others will increase. The appetite for learning, which could be called vitality, distinguishes thriving organizations from the rest. When learning stops, death will surely follow.

PLAN HEADLINES

Written plans are necessary in multi-unit businesses but they should be short and tightly focussed. A plan is two things:

1. The toy that the planners have played with. Revealing the toy indicates how it has been used.
2. Minutes of the agreement between the planners.

As such, the plan should be short and focussed, probably between 20 and 40 pages. More than 40 lacks focus, less than 20 will omit vital learning. Extra material can be appendixed.

Should there be any fixed format? Creativity may be driven out by a planning process that requires boxes to be filled in. Format writers impose their thinking on the planning team. Every brand and every year is different. Filling boxes will cause irrelevant detail to be included. Piffle! Planning is learning. Format-free planning makes as much sense as leaving education to ten-year-olds to figure out for themselves. The format of a marketing plan derives directly from the governing paradigm (neo-classical, conflict, or relational). That should certainly be open to challenge and review. Any particular business will have a blend of the three, not one in pure form. Debating the format and debating the paradigm are one and the same but, at the end of the day, senior management have an obligation to determine the shared language

One format allows comparisons, and thus learning, to take place across all dimensions.

and structures for the organization so that inter-unit understanding, peer level learning, can thrive.

As a result, no one format fits all companies. They should give very serious thought to what suits them. In a diversified organization, like Ladbrokes with hotels, high class gaming and betting shops, multiple formats may prove to be needed, but try just one first. One format, much though it will be resisted, allows comparisons, and thus learning, to take place across all dimensions. The same format as last year, the same as affiliates in other markets, the same as the parent company, all mean that extensive translation does not have to be done before understanding can take place.

A marketing plan format mirrors the way a unit thinks about marketing. If you want them satisfactorily to share their thinking, they should share their format.

In reality, plans have many uses. Most frequently, their purpose is to gain approval for spending, from more senior management, from financial controllers, from the bank. As such they may be as much directed to winning favor from those with the money as they are concerned with what the unit will actually do. As a result, many marketing plans are too financially oriented.

Then again, a plan may be a political campaign document. Rallying others in the company behind one particular brand campaign is more likely to be good than bad, but, again, the content of the plan will be influenced by that purpose – likewise plans prepared for suppliers and those which are shown to major customers.

Here we deal with one of many typical working document formats that the marketing team should prepare. This is the "toy." There are very few ingredients that should be in *every* plan. Thereafter we will review the impact of the different paradigms.

- **Brand positioning statement** (see chapter 16). This sets out what the brand is, how it is differentiated, and why it is better. Target consumers, competitors, and immediate customers are defined. If you are invited to review a marketing plan without this, reject it out of hand. The positioning statement is the cornerstone of any plan.

- **Key lessons.** What has been learned from implementing last year's plan, from competitors, from affiliates in other markets.

- **Assumptions**, especially any that have changed. Get your excuses in first. These should include relevant changes in consumer values and the economic and social environment, inflation for example. Brevity is vital: bullet points only.

- **Market forecasts** derive from the assumptions and may be part of them. Key is to show several years back and the forecasts, perhaps graphically, *on the same page.* You would never believe this but some marketers conceal the J curve by putting history at the beginning, and the future 20 pages or so later. Seeing trends at a glance is crucial to *all the numbers presented.*

- **Costed actions**. What will be done during the plan period and what each action will cost. This is the heart of the plan.

- **Profit and brand equity outcomes**. Trends here again are crucial: comparative figures should at least show last year's actual figures, current year's estimates, and the planned results. If each set of these three numbers, when shown graphically, is not a straight line, explanations are needed. Minimum P&L numbers are usually: sales volume and turnover, gross margins before marketing expenditure, and profit contribution after all attributable expenditure. Brand equity numbers are at least market share and relative price (see chapter 2 for a selection).

After that, format headlines become a matter of taste and particular business circumstances. Some organizations like executive summaries, others believe that they reinforce top management's predisposition

> **The positioning statement is the cornerstone of any plan.**

to judge a plan by the bottom line. Listing a few popular headlines under the relevant paradigm may be helpful:

Neo-classical

The advantage of the traditional textbook approach is in forcing the team to consider all aspects of the marketing mix. Distribution, for example, is often overlooked unless the format prompts its review. Most of these headings should be separated for consumers and immediate customers.

- **Product, packaging, quality**.
- **Costs and pricing**.
- **Advertising and PR**.
- **Promotions and merchandising activity**.
- **Distribution**.
- **Selling and other direct customer communications**.

Conflict

Here the focus is on the competitors. Typical headlines include:

- **Economic and social environment**. Strategists love this environmental stuff but it is often a waste of time. Few environmental changes directly impact marketing actions. Include those that do in "assumptions," as above. If you cannot resist the urge to get into this more fully, a separate document is one way to prevent too much carbohydrate in each brand plan.
- **Strategies**. Given the brand's overall objectives, usually listed, these set out the main lines of attack.
- **Competitor reviews**. How strong are they? What are they likely to do? Strengths and weaknesses (SWOT) analysis. Some practitioners love them; others include such analysis only where appropriate.

- **Tactics**. Focus here on the timetable of activities and the geography of the market place. In such a huge market as the USA, for example, even large brands tend to be strong in some states but not others. You would expect to see CDIs and BDIs for each state or market. A CDI ("Category Development Index") shows the consumption of products in that category, relative to the USA as a whole. If, for example, the US per capita consumption of all popcorn is 8 lbs p.a., but consumption in Iowa is 12 lbs, then the Iowa CDI for popcorn is 150 (150 percent). Similarly if the brand Momma's Popcorn has a national consumption of 2 lbs but is 2.4 lbs in Oklahoma, then the Oklahoma BDI ("Brand Development Index") would be 120. This is a useful concept as it forces discussion of whether you wish to build on strengths or repair weaknesses. Few can afford to do both.

Relational

This way of seeing the marketing process is more one of emphasis than format. The particular emphases you would expect to see mostly relate to brand equity and include:

- Brand relationship with consumer. What would you like it to be (positioning), what is it and how can the gap be closed?
- Brand relationship with retailer. Ditto.
- Other brand/customer relationships, e.g. importers, wholesalers.
- Other brand relationships with those who could influence sales and reputation, e.g. journalists, but are outside the distribution channels.
- Retailer/consumer relationships, i.e. how the retailer and your brands could help each other. Distribution, display and service, pre- and post-sale, considerations.
- Other in-channel relationships.
- A drawn network summarizing the key relationships and showing where the most attention is needed.

HARNESSING FINANCE AND SYSTEMS SUPPORT

Serious planners may find this unprofessional, but a short cut is to keep an electronic copy of last year's plan. Just alter it up to this year's, highlighting the changes. Anything that takes the drudgery out of planning and releases energy for learning is fine. That is the catch. Just using last year's format, or last year's plan, may get through the approval process (they bought it last time) but misses the point. Taking the drudgery out is only meaningful if creativity comes in.

Planning. It should be a lively interchange between all those involved in building the brand and the profits of the company.

The reconciliation of the numbers within the plan, i.e. internal consistency, is also simple if the plan is short and incremental. What is not simple, in a large organization, is the reconciliation of the differing forecasts and plans from the other business functions. Furthermore, the outcome of the planning process needs to be spread across accounting periods and budget centres so that the plan numbers can be compared with the actual results as they come through.

If the marketing manager is left with this role, as many are, demotivation will follow. The planning process will lose value as the business of producing a physical document takes over from analysis and innovation.

The relationship between marketing and finance can too often be seen as that between poachers and gamekeepers. Control again. Bringing finance into planning teams will also bring their financial modelling skills. Better than last year's plan on disk is a full system that will keep the numbers whole while the team try options out. A well-built model is fun to play with.

Companies should demystify. Teach marketing to accountants and accounting to marketers. Bring information systems specialists and accountants into the marketing processes. The marketer will be delighted provided the numerical chores of number crunching and data entry can be uplifted by those functions. Companies that have made this transition have noted the change of attitudes that results.

Planning processes acquire redundant routines over time the way a ship attracts barnacles. Perhaps a one-off question has been made permanent or research is routinely revisited. Is the timing of the planning cycle still right? Streamlining the planning process needs to take place before bringing new technology to bear. A plan is simply the synthesis of management's intentions. Those intentions need to be brought together as close to the moment for action as possible. A plan that is too early or too late is a waste of effort.

The ideal planning cycle should be dictated by the seasonality of the business. Working backwards, the timing of actions should dictate the date of the plan, which determines the timing of the prior analysis, and back to when measurement is needed. The planning cycle should be determined by the market not the financial year of the corporation. If they are out of sync, change the corporate year or find some way to buffer marketing expenditure so that it is driven by the market, not financial analysts.

Planning should not be a dry rendition of words and numbers on paper. It should be a lively interchange between all those involved in building the brand and the profits of the company. Planning should be fun.

Memo to file

Subject: PRAGMATIC PLANNING

- Planning provides the illusion of control. That can be dangerous. Control is important but subsidiary. More planning may mean less control. Balance the resources allocated to the future with the likely benefits.

- Planning is the opportunity to rehearse the future and rehearsal improves performance. Measure twice; saw once.

- Planning is learning and we learn by playing. Plans are toys.

- Learn across four dimensions: from the past; horizontally from peers, competitors, and affiliates; from understanding *why* things work; hierarchically from bosses and subordinates.

- Plan formats reflect the paradigm, or way of thinking, of those that prepared it. Organizational learning is enhanced by a shared format.

- Different organizations need different formats but all should include brand positioning, key lessons, assumptions, market forecasts, costed actions, and planned profit and brand equity outcomes.

- Bring finance into the planning team and use systems to keep numbers consistent both internally in the plan and with all other planning and control systems in the company. Product managers should not be used as number crunchers nor keyboard operators.

- Revisit the planning timetable. How narrow can you make the planning window? Plan less but better.

24

QUANTITY ERGO SUMO

Size, volume and market share, however impressive, are not everything

Key issue
● **Do you really want to be bigger?**

This title may put Descartes before the stable door but how important is volume? Early work from the PIMS organization in Cambridge Mass. supported the long held view that market share drives profit. To become more profitable, it seemed, the priority was to drive volume in order to gain share in order to lower costs and dominate the category. Good macho stuff. The bigger get bigger and the weaklings go to the wall. Sumo is the paradigm.

This view was not obvious to the accountants. Below a certain level you do not achieve critical mass but beyond a certain point diseconomies of scale also set in. Why trouble to sell ten widgets for $1 each when you can sell one for $10? The perfume industry limits distribution, and thus sales volume, in order to prop up the price; even more impressively, it has persuaded the EU to bless these arrangements even if others dislike them.

> Below a certain level you do not achieve critical mass but beyond a certain point diseconomies of scale also set in.

We have considered in chapter 19 the effect price has on the perception of quality: it is possible to increase both price *and* volume but not often. But what the classic price/quantity trade-off implied by the curve really fails to account for is the longer-term effect: a higher price today, if it is positive in terms of brand image, will be beneficial for sales tomorrow.

Similarly, while higher sales today can be beneficial for future volumes, there are many cases where the reverse is true. For example:

- **Supply or demand is limited**. A widget sold is a widget less to sell. For durables one would maintain high prices on innovation, were it not for competition, and only reduce them slowly as demand at each price level was satisfied. On the basis that a family buys only once, the aim has to be to maximize the profit on that single sale.

- **Scarcity marketing is** the delicate business of creating shortages in order to stimulate demand. Some take credit for this technique to cover up forecasting errors. The launch of Wilkinson Sword stainless steel razor blades in the sixties was an example of this technique; whether deliberate or accidental, the publicity surrounding the initial shortages fueled both reputation and future sales. Scarcity marketing has to be credible. The launch of Tanqueray Sterling Vodka in the USA in 1989 included publicity for the thousands of cases that had to be air-freighted from the UK to meet unprecedented demand. Sceptics predominated over the convinced, and the brand failed.

- **Money-off promotions**. As discussed in chapter 21, controversy surrounds the net benefits of these techniques. If consumers simply match their purchase timing to promotion dates, as many in the USA now do, total volumes are unaffected. Brand loyalists are likely to be in this category, while brand switchers will move to the promoted brand. If all brands promote equally, the net volume effect may still be neutral and profits reduced all around. The main area of controversy surrounds the impact of promotions on brand image: by devaluing the brand, longer-term sales will decrease.

- **Vulgarization**. A French term applied to the Pierre Cardin brand, among others. Once it commanded a great premium in the haute couture business. Progressively the brand was extended from one category to another. As it extended, the quality of the products declined. The name was thought to be enough. Volume increased but brand equity reduced.

PIMS later discovered that the market share/profitability linkage was flawed. The correlation undoubtedly exists but both result from the perceived quality of the products. Perceived quality permits *both* higher price *and* higher volume.

Memo to file

Subject: QUANTITY ERGO SUMO

● Chase volume only in so far as it strengthens brand equity.

● Excess weight may provide the same illusion of strength as category domination. It is not what you have but how you handle it.

● Determine optimal size based on brand equity and profitability; work to that.

25

RELATIONSHIP MARKETING

Brand equity lies in the strength and quality of the brand's relationships with its customers

---

Key issues
● **Relationship marketing has become increasingly important in recent years** ● **Marketing is the building of brand relationships or the management of a network of long-term, value added, cooperative relationships** ● **The relational paradigm** ● **Measuring brand relationships**

THE MARKETPLACE TODAY

A between-wars advertisement for a whisky brand would include a fine picture of the bottle, a reason to buy ("Scotland's finest"), maybe a couple of glasses, and the price. They were trying to sell you a bottle of the stuff.

Today, there may be no picture of the bottle, no overt reason to buy, and certainly no price. They would like you to feel good about the brand, to believe that the lifestyle the brand seems to carry would mesh beneficially with your own lifestyle.

Japanese domestic advertising carries this concept much further. Westerners may find it difficult to make any direct connection between the brand and the content of its Japanese TV commercial. However, the marketing intention is the same: if consumers enjoy the sensations of the advertisement, then their relationship with the brand that paid for those sensations will be improved.

These two examples from the consumer goods business are just the tip of a major sea change that has swept across all varieties of marketing. Ted Levitt observed back in 1983[1] "In a great and increasing proportion of transactions, the relationship actually intensifies subsequent to the sale." In other words, the end of the process is not the transaction. The sale marks the beginning of the brand's relationship with its user.

The thread is consistent. The brand is a personality. Just like us, it is not that easy to determine exactly how personal contact can be established in the first instance. The world provides more potential relationships than we can handle. Once contact has been established, however, managing the relationship lies very much in how we behave. So it is with the brand and its relationship with its customers.

This first became obvious in industrial marketing. The small number of potential customers, in many cases, makes it critical to keep every one. Firms recognized that it is harder, and more expensive, to find new customers than to retain existing ones. It is the lifetime profitability of a customer that should be considered, not the profit on any particular transaction. This thinking permeated to retail marketing. A popular, and perhaps apocryphal, example is Nordstrom, the US premium department store group which originated in the North-west. Complete lifetime customer satisfaction is their creed. One customer returned a car tyre purchased some years previously with a complaint. Despite the time lag, he was refunded in full and without question. What is so unusual? Nordstrom had never sold car tyres.

Industrial marketers seek to be so close to their main customers that the join is invisible. Just-in-time supply treats the customer's workshop as if it was the supplier's. Efficient Consumer Response does the same for packaged goods. What were once adversarial supplier/customer relationships have been replaced by maximum cooperation. Cooperation can be more profitable for both sides than conflict, and more profitable for competitors too. In order to realize the benefits of such arrangements, *all* parties need to cooperate, e.g. setting bar code standards.

Clearly relationship marketing is not appropriate for all situations. It began with complex relationships where switching costs are commensurately high. In these circumstances, one purchase from a competitor may mean the customer is lost for good. Lowest cost transactions may well not justify the relationship effort. Nevertheless the feasibility threshold is being constantly lowered by technology.

Databases hold more and more information about us all. Direct mail has

[1] Theodore Levitt, "After the sale is over," *Harvard Business Review* (Sept–Oct 1983).

evolved from junk to highly targeted missives of interest only to the recipient, or so they say. Maybe that will happen one day. Maybe also Internet, and the other network suppliers, and interactive television will provide all our marketing contact and shopping needs. Meanwhile the telephone is increasingly the carrier of relationship activity in all marketing sectors from industrial to grocery products.

> **The telephone is increasingly the carrier of relationship activity in all marketing sectors from industrial to grocery products.**

"Customer care" telephone lines are now a major marketing activity. In the USA, Pillsbury and a few other leading fast-moving brand companies developed streamlined complaints procedures into powerful two-way consumer communications. Consumers are unwilling to write and, for food products, the rare production failures need to be discovered at once. If food is contaminated, urgent recall is needed. Packaging now includes an 800 number for consumers to call with any problems.

Actual complaints dropped from 100 percent towards 20 percent of the calls as people became accustomed to the facility. They phoned for advice on product use, to make suggestions, to say thank you, or just for a chat. Marketers recognized that rather than wait for cumbersome market research or consumer information so consolidated it had lost all value, there was a rich bank of consumer data phoning itself in daily. Relationships could be assessed and nourished right on line. Independent research has since confirmed that information obtained from those consumers who trouble to phone is representative of the brand's consumers as a whole.

In the UK, consumers still average few 0800, much of which is customer care calls but they are expected to increase from eight in 1995 to 43 p.a. by the year 2000.[2]

When Sony launched its "PlayStation" computer games machine in 1995, they developed care lines to handle queries. The machine cost about £300 plus software on CDs, but declining service at retail level meant that customers needed new facilities for problem resolution. Direct contact was necessary to maintain customer relationships. Manufacturers of personal computers do the same. For Sony, the UK phones were actually answered by the "Decisions Group" company who specialize in call centre services. The staff, already trained on care usage, experienced PlayStations for themselves

[2]   Henley Centre, *Teleculture 2000* (1995).

and, with on-line information available on their screens, were able to deal with queries of all types. The customers believed they were talking to Sony and that goodwill added to the Sony–customer relationship.

In this section we have ranged across some current manifestations of relationship marketing in the consumer sector. We have seen that marketers are now not so much concerned with making the individual sales as maintaining long-term customer contact. Managing these relationships has become the business of marketers.

THE RELATIONAL PARADIGM

To recap more formally, the recognition that the market should be seen as a network of commercial relationships came together in the 1980s from a variety of sources:

- Industrial purchasing behavior was shown by Scandinavian[3] writers to be networks of long-term relationships.

- In the USA,[4] marketing academics increasingly recognized that the transactional view of marketing, based on microeconomics and now dubbed "neo-classical," was not enough. A special edition (Fall 1983) of the *Journal of Marketing* was devoted to alternatives.[5]

- Marketers of services increasingly understood that it is cheaper and easier to retain an existing customer than find a new one. The vast majority of the business of large professional firms, such as Coopers and Lybrand, comes

[3] Christian Gronroos, "Relationship Approach to Marketing in Service Contexts: The Marketing and Organizational Behaviour Interface," *Journal of Business Research* 20 (1990), pp. 3–11.
Evert Gummesson, "The New Marketing – Developing Long–term Interactive Relationships," *Long Range Planning* 20 (1987), pp. 4, 10–20.
Evert Gummesson, "Relationship Marketing – A New Way of Doing Business," *European Business Report* 3Q, (Autumn 1993), pp. 52–56.
H. Hakansson, *Interactional Marketing and Purchasing of Industrial Goods: An Interaction Approach* (New York: Wiley, 1982).

[4] Leonard L. Berry, Relationship Marketing, in *Emerging Perspectives on Services Marketing*, L.L. Berry et al. eds (Chicago, American Marketing Association, 1983), pp. 25–28.
Hans B. Thorelli, "Political Science and Marketing" in *Theory in Marketing*, R. Cox, W. Alderson, and S.J. Shapiro eds (Homewood, IL, Richard D. Irwin, Inc., 1964), pp. 125–36.
Hans B. Thorelli, "Networks: Between Markets and Hierarchies," *Strategic Management Journal*, vol. 7 (1986), pp. 37–51.

[5] Johan Arndt, "The Political Economy Paradigm: Foundation for Theory Building in Marketing," *Journal of Marketing* (Fall 1983), pp. 44–54.

from their existing clients. Emphasis switched from getting new clients to keeping existing clients for life. Firms of accountants started inviting their alumni to drinks parties.

- Study of distribution channels illustrated the importance of cooperative over hostile seller/buyer relationships.[6]

- Economists[7] sought to explain why firms did not use the supposed efficiency of free markets but traded regularly with the same partners, even at higher prices. Sometimes firms vertically integrated and functions were "internalized." Williamson showed that the "transaction costs" of dealing ad hoc were greater than the efficiencies that could be had from regular dealings between the same people. If these transaction costs were added to market prices, the apparently higher prices of relational dealings became justified.

- These theories have since been manifested in the USA with ECR (efficient consumer response) under which firms seek to cooperate through linked distribution, ordering and computer systems to smooth the flow of goods to the consumer and reduce inventory. The original report[8] showed a potential saving in the USA grocery business of $30bn.

- Database marketing identified consumer and brand common interests on a segmented, if not individual, basis. General Motors introduced credit cards as much to gain access to details of their (potential) customers as to provide credit. Ford has launched *Ford Magazine* with an initial circulation of 650,000. Both intend to build brand relationships with existing and potential car owners.

- The Chinese, both at home and overseas, have always traded on relationships. The word "guanxi" (business connections) has only been in use for the last few years but the idea that business should grow from friendship is far older. In the West, we do business first and make friends, perhaps, second. Thus whereas Westerners may be rather uncomfortable when

---

6 James C. Anderson and James A. Narus, "Partnering as a Focused Market Strategy." *California Management Review* 33 (Spring 1991), pp. 95–113.
7 R. H. Coase, "The Nature of the Firm," *Economica* NS4 (1937), pp. 386–405.
   Oliver Williamson, *The Economic Institutions of Capitalism* (New York and London, The Free Press, 1985).
   Oliver Williamson, Discussion of 'Breach of Trust in Hostile Takeovers' in *Corporate Takeovers: Causes and Consequences*, Alan Auerbach, ed. (Chicago, University of Chicago Press, 1988).
8 Kurt Salmon Associates Inc., *Efficient Consumer Response: Enhancing Consumer Value in the Grocery Industry* (Washington, Food Marketing Institute, 1993).

giving business preference to friends, their Chinese equivalents are uncomfortable when they are *not* doing so.

These strands were brought together to form what is widely known as "relationship marketing."[9] The terminology is pervasive. The clerk who looks after your account at the bank or the telephone utility is now likely to be called your "relationship manager." Universalization may trivialize the concept. That would be a pity; it is a revolution in marketing thinking.

The term "relational paradigm"[10] is more precise and emphasizes just how fundamental is this view of marketing, or of business. The traditional microeconomic paradigm[11] is no more "wrong" than early astronomers were "wrong." Paradigms are just different ways of understanding. The challenge of the reformers is that the microeconomic paradigm is too mechanistic, too transactional, too internally focussed on the company's actions, too rational, and too financially oriented:

● **Too mechanistic** because sales are seen as a function of the marketing mix. Traditional marketing thinking is more sophisticated than this but the equations above illustrate the *type* of thinking that is implicit.

● **Too transactional** because the focus is on the sales, or other results, from the period under examination rather than the accumulation of effects over the long term.

● **Too internally focussed** because the paradigm concentrates on the alternative marketing mix levers, i.e. what the company will do, rather than competitor actions. Outcomes may well be expressed in relative terms such as market share or share of voice but planned actions tend not to be influenced greatly by competitive advantage.

[9] Martin Christopher, Adrian Payne and David Ballantyne, *Relationship Marketing. Bringing quality, customer service and marketing together*, (Oxford, Butterworth–Heinemann Ltd., 1991).
Jagdish N. Sheth and Atul Parvatiyar (eds), *Research Conference Proceedings, Relationship Marketing: Theory, Methods and Applications*, June 11–13 (Atlanta, Centre for Relationship Marketing, Emory University, 1994).

[10] Tim Ambler, "The Relational Paradigm: A Synthesis," in Jagdish N. Sheth and Atul Parvatiyar (eds), *Research Conference Proceedings, Relationship Marketing: Theory, Methods and Applications*, June 11–13, (Atlanta; Centre for Relationship Marketing, Emory University, 1994).
David T. Wilson and Kristan K.E. Moller, "Buyer–Seller Relationships. Alternative Conceptualizations." *New Perspectives on International Marketing*, Stanley J. Paliwoda (ed.) (London, Routledge, 1991) chapter 5, p. 87.

[11] The best known textbook, taught universally to MBA students, which enshrines this approach is: Philip Kotler, *Marketing Management: Analysis, Planning, Implementation and Control*, 8th edition (Englewood Cliffs, NJ, Prentice-Hall, 1993).

- **Too rational** because, like the economics on which it is based, the underlying assumption is that people make rational choices based on analyzed information. In practice the marketer has to address the emotional and experiential components of decision making and these are not separable.

- **Too financially oriented** because money is assumed to be the scarce resource. More often, managerial time is.

Recognition of these weaknesses led, in the 1970s, to the emergence of marketing *strategy* and "sustainable competitive advantage."[12] This generated the second marketing paradigm which may be termed "conflict." The dominant concept here is of competition. Market share is the key indicator of success.

> **The market is a network of "value laden relationships" connecting the brand, customers at all levels, and other influence**

By comparison, the central concepts of the relational paradigm are:

- Marketing is rooted in exchanges from which both parties benefit as a result of cooperation, not competition. This is not the zero sum game which the conflict paradigm implies for the marketers, e.g. total market share always equals 100 percent.

- Competition is thus important but secondary. It is, of course, essential to ensure choice, fairness, and innovation.

- The market is a network of "value laden relationships"[13] connecting the brand, customers at all levels in the distribution channels, including end consumers, and other influence groups such as advertising agencies. Some systems include networks internal to the marketing organization.

- Long-term relationships reduce risk as well as transaction costs and are thus beneficial for both sides.

- Money is a key variable but so is managerial time. Relationships depend not so much on what is spent on them, though it helps, as the care and attention (both time issues) that they receive.

[12] Henry Mintzberg, "The Fall and Rise of Strategic Planning" *Harvard Business Review* (Jan–Feb 1994).
Henry Mintzberg and James B. Quinn, *The Strategy Process*, (Englewoood Cliffs, NJ, Prentice-Hall International, 1991).
Michael E. Porter, *Competition in Global Industries* (Harvard Business School Press, 1986).
Michael E. Porter, *Competitive Strategy* (New York Free Press, 1980).

[13] Philip Kotler, "From Transactions to Relationships," address to the trustees of the Marketing Science Institute reported in *MSI Review* (Spring 1991).

The marketing process is therefore the managerial activity to improve the relationships in the network from the perspective of the brand in order to improve brand equity, some of which may be distributed as short-term profits.

In this section, we reviewed the origins of the relational perspective, namely that the market should be seen as a network of long-term, value added, cooperative relationships. We contrasted that with the traditional, neo-classical paradigm, largely based on microeconomics, and the conflict paradigm which describes the market in terms of competition. None of these paradigms is wrong; they supplement each other.

MEASUREMENT ISSUES

There are two approaches to measuring relationships, direct and indirect:

1. Directly seeking to measure the state of relationships requires the marketer to establish what is in the minds of customers. The main variables are awareness and, depending on the category, attitudes such as perceived quality, perceived value, saliency (relevance), differentiation, esteem, familiarity, liking, and fashionability. Some of these overlap.

2. Indirectly, customers' behavior, whether they buy or not and under what circumstances, indicates the state of their brand relationships. Consumer behavioral variables include market share, relative price (share by value divided by share by volume), penetration (the percentage of the target market that have bought the brand in last year), and loyalty (there are about four ways of measuring this variable including share of category requirements). Retailer behavioral variables include availability or distribution, share of and position on shelf, and pipeline (number of days' inventory).

Neither approach is ideal and most businesses that seek to measure brand equity use some combination. The main problems with the indirect approach are:

● **Not indicators of what is in store**. Market share and relative price are key indirect indicators but neither necessarily reflect the current status. They may reflect what has just been taken *out* of the brand, rather than what has been put *in*. For example, market share may be increased by bringing future sales into the current period. Loading the pipeline is common practice for sales forces bonussed on volume sales. In this example, market share goes up when brand equity actually goes down, i.e. the indicator moves the wrong way.

- **Market share is subjective** in the sense that the category chosen as the denominator is arbitrary. Smirnoff, for example, can be portrayed as a dominant force in the vodka category or a weak force in the white spirits sector. It can be gaining market share in one sector and losing market share in another. Since we have defined brand equity as an asset, a definition which leads to the conclusion that the asset is getting bigger and more valuable, at the same time that it is getting smaller and less valuable, is not very helpful.

  > **Perceived quality may prove the single most important measure of brand equity.**

- **Behavioral measures look back**. The marketer wants to know what the customers *now* think because that is a better guide to what now needs to be fixed.

The main problems with the direct approach are:

- **Cognitive bias**. Human decision making is based on a complex web of emotional, experiential, and cognitive (rational thought) processes which cannot be separated. A consumer reaches out for one brand or another as the trolley passes through the aisle with barely a thought. When confronted by a surveyor with a clip board, the consumer feels impelled to make sense of this jumble to explain behavior in terms of awareness and attitudes. This rationalizing, and thereby inaccurate, process is known as "cognitive bias."

- **Variation by occasion**. A brand suitable for one occasion will not be chosen for another. In human terms you might have immense respect for your boss but not seek your boss's company at weekends.

- **Family**. "Consumers" do not always buy for their own use. In some ways this is akin to business-to-business marketing where buyers meet the organization's specifications rather than their own. The consumer is buying for the family, including household pets. What the family member buying cat food thinks may not be important; cats will express their own opinion and that tends to be definitive.

- **Hypothetical questions**. Consumers are reliable respondents for factual and behavioral questions, e.g. what price *did* they pay, so long as they can remember. They are not reliable when it shifts to the hypothetical, e.g. what price *would* they pay. "Would you pay $5 for this product?" tends to get the answer "yes" even when, in reality, they refuse to pay anything more than \$4.

While neither direct nor indirect measures provide certain information on the dynamics of market change, i.e. what attitudinal shifts lead to what changes in market share, perceived quality has been shown[14] to give some indication of future profitability, and thus current brand equity. As such, it may prove the single most important measure of brand equity.

The selection of measures is less important than tracking them consistently over time. Many measures correlate, e.g. market share and brand loyalty, so that the direction of change over time is more significant than instantaneous variation between measures.

[14] Bradley T. Gale, *Managing Customer Value* (New York, The Free Press, 1994).
Robert Jacobson and David A. Aaker, "The Strategic Role of Product Quality," *Journal of Marketing* 51 (October 1987), pp. 31–44.
Ram Narasimhan, Soumen Gosh and David Mendez, "A Dynamic Model of Product Quality and Pricing Decisions on Sales Response." *Decision Sciences* 24(5) (1993), pp. 893–908.
Lynn Phillips, Dae R. Chunget and Robert D. Buzzell, "Product Quality, Cost Position and Business Performance: A Test of Some Hypotheses." *Journal of Marketing* 47 (Spring 1983), pp. 26–43.

Memo to File

Subject: RELATIONSHIP MARKETING

- Relationship marketing, in various forms, has emerged from the 1980s as a key concept, fundamental to all forms of marketing which shifts attention from short-term transactions and immediate profits toward a process of creating value through building and managing a network of value added, long-term relationships.

- Marketing is the function of building brand relationships.

- Identify the brand's relationships network. Resources (money, energies, and time) should be focussed on those relationships which are more important and/or more capable of beneficial change.

- Then track them, directly and indirectly, in a consistent fashion over time.

- Live as if you will die tomorrow but manage the brand as if you will be managing that same brand forever.

26

RESEARCH IS ALWAYS INCOMPLETE

Tempting as it is, you cannot do marketing by numbers. Some pitfalls.

Key issues
- **Understanding the market is so totally crucial that any new CEO should get out the broom for a thorough sweep**
- **Sweep 1: Clearing away special interests. Research as a political weapon** ● **Sweep 2: Reviewing what is available. Technology is changing the game** ● **Sweep 3: Eliminating the nice to know. Decisions should drive research;** *not* **research drive decisions** ● **Sweep 4: Putting research in its place. Integrating external research with internal information. Competitive issues**

UNDERSTANDING THE MARKET

Professional marketers accumulate research like badges on a boy scout. The more they have the more proficient they seem to be. Research is always incomplete: the more about the market you know, the more you recognize the unknown. Tracking down a subject in a library reveals sidetracks which are always more attractive. Books pile up faster than you can read them.

The great marketing companies have so much information that some researchers have not been seen for years. Before a multi-million dollar decision, the marginal cost of just a little more data is minimal. That analysis can

Research is Always Incomplete 281

lead to paralysis has been known for a hundred years. Most firms today take active steps to curtail it. Speed to market is critical.

Market research is supposed to supply the diagnostics needed for marketing decisions. A thorough understanding of the market is vital for all the top team and especially the Chief Executive. This is not something to be delegated to third parties. The irony is that this mass of research information on paper and disk may actually be hindering market understanding. What do you do? As Chief Executive, make a clean sweep.

SWEEP 1: CLEAR AWAY SPECIAL INTERESTS

If you have internal market research professionals, sack them. As major marketing companies will not take this advice and small firms did not have any on the payroll anyway, is this suggestion a bit theoretic? Let us review the arguments for in-house market researchers:

- **Continuity**. Researchers are likely to have been around longer than the marketers and can supply lessons from the past and ensure comparative figures are truly comparative. Fair comment but you should do this anyway.

- **Interpretation**. External researchers will use jargon and/or not understand the client business. The in-house team can use their wider knowledge to explain the findings more reliably. This may be true but the greater truths will come from the two experts, the marketer and the researcher doing the work, challenging each other. The in-house facilitator is as likely to add prejudice as light.

- **Costs.** Much of the external cost lies in data manipulation as distinct from gathering the raw figures. Manipulation can be brought in-house and save money. The externals have the programs to do this full time. Don't buy it.

- **It takes one to know one**. In other words, distinguishing top professionals from rogues needs an insider. Any specialist could say that. Professional researchers will better know what is available, just as librarians know what is on the shelves. But, like librarians, they are interested in the information, not what can be done with the information. Most often, not a lot.

- **Enforcement of common standards across different research suppliers and business units**. Probably the best argument and one that many multinationals find convincing. The work certainly needs doing, though not necessarily in house.

Good researchers make a vast contribution to understanding customers and consumers. That is not the concern. The danger is that they begin to frame managerial understanding within their own paradigm. Every researcher has been brought up in an academic discipline. Some are statisticians, some psychologists, some steeped in economic models, and they see the world in their terms. Price elasticities should fit the model. These models make useful toys but they are no more than that. You should be able to take them or leave them. If they are toys offered by outsiders, they are less likely to become addictive than those evangelized daily by the internal team.

The research paradigm assumes consumers can supply the answers. Boiled down it goes a bit like this: "marketing is the business of supplying consumers with what they most want in a way that is profitable for the marketer. So let us ask consumers what they want and then supply it. Of course, asking the consumer needs the sophisticated techniques which I just happen to have. Leave it to me and I will be back in a few months with the

> **The need to outsource research is part of the wider problem that research is used as a political weapon.**

answers." Plausible – yes; realistic – no. Consumers generally do not know what they *will* want and could not express it even if they did. The research business is vital to marketing but cognitively biassed. Keep them at a safe distance.

Find your researchers nice berths by all means. Provide them or their new employers with contracts to smooth the transition. But say goodbye.

The need to outsource research is part of the wider problem that research is used as a political weapon. The old joke compares it to the way a drunk uses a lamp post: for support or to urinate against but not for illumination. A multinational in the food business, identity necessarily concealed, witnessed a boardroom struggle between the international marketing Vice President and his opposite number responsible for Europe. The former had research to prove that his new advertising campaign should run. The Europe VP has incontrovertible research to prove that it should not. The Group Chief Executive was infuriated that two separate research projects should have been commissioned for the same issue. In fact it was the same, single, research study. Their two assistants had just picked out the pieces they liked. Both, on this occasion, were using it for support.

Any research agency can regale you with examples of the alternative lamp post usage, meticulous work being rejected because the clients did not believe the findings. Maybe the clients were right.

Those who paid for the lamp post thought they were buying illumination, not of the world, but of the immediate vicinity. If sweep 1 has cleared away politics and special interests, the ground is clear to review what research suits what decisions.

SWEEP 2: WHAT IS AVAILABLE

Understanding market research does not involve technicalities. The glossary at the end of this book has some jargon for the bold to surprise the experts but, like trying your three words of Dutch in Amsterdam, the response may bewilder. Games apart, the clearer researchers are, the better they are. They should want to explain what techniques they are employing and why.

Businesses are not as different as they think they are. Though too polite to say so, researchers are likely to have seen the problems before. Otherwise, you have the wrong professionals. If they are too quick to open up the toolkit before they have really understood the problem, they are certainly the wrong lot. Some travel with only one or two tools they hope will fit everything.

Convention divides research into two types: qualitative and quantitative. Qualitative uses few respondents but gets to greater depth. Quantitative uses samples large enough to be representative of the whole target market. Expenditure in the UK has been roughly 10 percent and 90 percent respectively though qualitative work, partly due to budget pressures, has been gaining ground. Qualitative is supposed to find the right questions and quantitative to answer them. Qualitative is thus thought to be the unreliable precursor to real research. In this paradigm, everything important can be counted and, if it cannot be counted, it cannot therefore be important. If you believe that, you are reading the wrong book. At the same time, qualitative research is, by definition, not representative of the market and should be treated with care.

Qualitative research

The most popular qualitative format is the focus group. About six to eight members of roughly the same demographic group (i.e. age, sex, socioeconomic group) are recruited for an hour or two of gentle conversation. They are nicely rewarded and it helps if the surroundings are good too. The need to relax is paramount. Do not mix groups and get rid of disruptive elements at once. Groups need to be harmonious. Professional facilities include taping (video and/or audio) the proceedings and a one way mirror to conceal non-participants. These facilities are always explained to the respondents. Quite quickly they are forgotten. Sitting one side of the glass is disconcerting when people are admiring themselves in the other. First impressions are that they are looking so lovingly at you.

Discussion is led, usually, by a trained psychologist from the general to the specific. At this point opinions diverge on how focus groups should be used.

One theory is to run many different groups until some consensus emerges and then quantitative research. The scientific method identifies all the variables, pins some down, and ruthlessly analyses the rest. The resulting certainty may be as accurate and expensive as the racing tip you were given in the pub last night.

The other theory is that focus groups provide rare shafts of illumination. These cannot be counted but you recognize them when they strike. Consumers talking about your brands and marketing ideas will put into a single sentence, occasionally, the critical insight you seek. Just one statement by one consumer might be the revelation that unlocks millions. So be there. Psychologists will miss the nuances. They do not know your business. Several weeks later a 20 page report, which the onlooker barely recognizes, will drop through the letter box. Do not blame the psychologists. They report the way they hear it, and most do so thoroughly. They filter their observations through their own experience; they cannot do it through yours. Be there.

> **Just one statement by one consumer might be the revelation that unlocks millions.**

Some marketers are so enthusiastic about discussion groups that they train to become group leaders. In third world situations, that is not just the best solution, it is the only solution. Nevertheless the roles are better separate.

We have lingered on discussion groups as the primary building block of market research. They are used for new brands and changes to existing ones: positioning, products, packaging, advertising concepts, promotional ideas. Beware that word "concept" though. Few consumers can give reliable responses to anything except tangible reality they have experienced or can see in front of them. Future possibilities are opaque. Show a real advertisement, not a sketch, even if production costs serious money. David Gluckman, the London focus group facilitator without equal, conjures up mythical press releases to give reality to new products.

There is much to be said for hiding two new concepts amongst real but little known products. Compare like only with like, i.e. the two new ones, not new and old. Expect only the simplest of responses. Sophisticated exercises such as rank ordering decreases reliability.

Other forms of qualitative research include depth interviews and projection techniques (see Appendix). Depth interviews lack the interactive stimulus of focus groups but do allow the interviewer to pursue specific interests. Conjoint analysis, for example, requires the interview to identify the key dimensions that distinguish one brand from another and then make choices on each dimension. For a cognitively driven decision, such as a washing machine, that works fine. If emotions play a role, think again.

Quantitative research

Given the balance of spending, the wider range of quantitative services comes as no surprise. Traditionally they split between bespoke and syndicated, though technology is reducing the difference. Make sure it is reducing the bill too.

Some bespoke classics, albeit not comprehensive:

- **Placement tests** leave products, or whatever, for consumers to try in their regular consumption pattern.

- **Personal interviews** track brand usage, awareness, attitudes, what product attributes contribute what to quality, both for you and the competition. They may be pre-arranged or "mall intercepts" in shopping areas. Traditionally the interviewer or the respondents themselves will complete a formatted questionnaire. A newer technique is to capture answers electronically.

> Now that electronic point of sale data gives your competitors the same test market data you have, simulation has become attractive.

- **Observation studies** note consumer behavior without questioning. Eliminates rationalizing, up to a point, by the consumer but has obvious limitations.

- **Telephone interviews** allow questioning in less depth but at greater speed and less expense. These are now computer assisted with the data being encoded as it is collected.

- **Simulated stores or test markets** are amongst various high tech options. In the virtual reality store, consumers "buy" using VR helmets thus allowing packaging, prices, and market shares to be tested. Simulated test markets model buying behavior and allow small amounts of data to be expanded on the basis of prior test markets to give the equivalent data.

Now that electronic point of sale data gives your competitors the same test market data you have, simulation has become attractive.

- **Campaign pre-testing**. There are always new fads here, usually turning out to be old fads. In the 1960s, eye cameras tracked what consumers watched in ads and dials showed interest levels. In the 1990s, they were rediscovered. It is well worth discussing with the agency what is new in campaign pre-testing, what they like, and what they hate. Pre-testing should not, naturally, be used to decide campaigns but they do help get bugs out. Agree with the agency what makes sense but do not let them do it. See the bugs for yourself.

All the above are tailor made to your needs and aim to reproduce the marketplace as closely as possible.

Many other facilities are available on a wholly or partly syndicated basis. Questions can be added to general "omnibus" surveys, so named because anyone can climb aboard the questionnaire, e.g. Gallup. If you can restrain your curiosity, great value.

Shared or syndicated services include:

- **Target Group Index (USA: Simmons, Media mark. UK: TGI):** huge annual survey of consumer usage patterns by media, product category, and brand.

- **Retail distribution, sales, and consumer databases.** Nielsen is the best known but IRI are catching up. Originally a way to track retail level sales by adjusting purchases with changes in inventory. Electronic point of sale tills now make far richer data available. Better still, consumer panels log all their purchases using wands or encoded cards. No more checking consumer cupboards and garbage bins as used to be the case. Marketers may now, if they wish, monitor the results of advertising or promotion directly on their targets' shopping baskets.

  Nielsen numbers were traditionally too aggregated and too late to be much help to total market understanding but the regional analysis provided the heavy metal marketers used to beat up the sales force. This six times a year ritual was much enjoyed. It would be a pity if it disappeared now that data is continuous and on-line.

- **Media expenditure:** LNA, Leading National Advertisers and Arbitron (US), MEAL (UK press and TV); OSCAR (UK roadside posters); RBL (UK bus posters); TRAC (London Underground).

- **Media readership/circulation:** ABC (US and UK), JICNARS (UK press); BARB (UK TV); JICRARS (UK radio).

- **Demographics:** the census in most countries collects information about us all. These, and most other government statistics, are available for sale. IRI and Neilsen are in USA and Europe. In the other cases, similar services are available in most developed countries.

In short, the UK has more marketing data around than anyone is likely to need for decisions and this is being compounded by technology. Once somebody somewhere encodes data, it is not long before they wonder who they can sell it to. Some UK supermarket groups, ASDA for example, will now part with their EPOS data, at a price.

SWEEP 3: ELIMINATING THE NICE TO KNOW

At face value, there is merit in using research to keep tabs on the big expenditures. Large advertising expenditures should be tracked at least for awareness and attitude shifts. True, but you are starting at the wrong end. *Brand equity must be tracked and, after that, what else is there?*

Big marketing expenditures should not have the pro rata research budgets that some control theorists demand. That is just piling cost on cost. Brand equity apart, research should be decision driven: what are the options, what is the most ingenious (i.e. cost/beneficial) way of assessing the options, how credible will the research be when it arrives?

The type of answers you will get depend on the category. Where experimentation is cheap, it will often be quicker and less expensive to try it than research it.

Textbooks begin the marketing planning process with a blank page. Real businesses have years of experience on which to draw and they do not go looking for trouble. Plans are usually incremental unless there is a crisis. The Rule of Chi provides warnings about accepting this process but that is how it is. A crisis is a crisis because the awful facts are staring you in the face. If the ship is at 45° and going down, those who research will go **Marketers have great difficulty in defining the key choices they face but no difficulty identifying the research they need.** down with it. If your ship is proceeding well enough, then list the incremental changes you could make, i.e. the team might agree. There are unlikely to be many. Incrementalism has the huge advantage that both decisions and the relevant information can be kept to human proportions.

Marketers have great difficulty in defining the key choices they face but no difficulty identifying the research they need. This would be strange if it did not appear that the research needs are from the textbook while the choices have to come, newly minted, from life. Chuck the textbook.

Hang tough on determining those choices. Then:

- What do you need to know to decide each one?
- Is the data already around or freely available? If not, can it be found? At what cost?
- How long will it take?
- Will everyone accept it when it arrives?
- Is it easier/quicker/cheaper to experiment?

Not much will get through those hurdles but what does is worth doing. What about the rest?

Much exists because it was once commissioned and no one said it should stop. Other research just provides comparatives. No decision is expected to need the research but it might be needed one day. Other research continues because comparative figures may later be needed. There is no challenge to brand equity tracking studies. These are essential and are likely to include periodic (about three yearly would be normal) "usage and attitude" studies to investigate consumer behavior and opinions in more depth.

Environmental scanning is a popular form of research in some companies but the benefits are far from obvious. Naturally marketers should keep up to date, even ahead – plenty of media review trends and the changing consumer. Applying this broad picture to the daily decision is difficult though it can be relevant to, say, new brand introduction. Does it need paid research? Read the Sunday papers instead.

Sweep 3 has been concerned with clearing away the dead paper. The more research some organizations have, the more they seem to need. New questions are different to the old questions. Many organizations would be better off with fewer reports; more trees would live and the wood become a lot clearer.

SWEEP 4: PUTTING RESEARCH IN ITS PLACE

The thrust of this chapter has been to recognize the importance of research to marketing but not allow it to become too close to the decision making process. This is partly because the paradigm of research is different to the paradigm of marketing but also because of the dangers of selective and political use.

Keeping the paradigms apart is not the same as keeping the information apart. Technology is finally allowing external research to be consolidated across different sources but also integrated with internal information such as sales and pricing. Hallelujah! The deluge of data now available seriously threatens to drown the marketer. Turn the problem of decision support systems over to your IT people (see chapter 9, "Information Systems Survival Kit"). Integrating external and internal information is a key step towards full market understanding. It is also why both sets of data need to be pruned to the essential before they are brought together.

> **Integrating external and internal information is a key step towards full market understanding. It is also why both sets of data need to be pruned to the essential before they are brought together.**

Decisions are about the *future*; research can only tell you about *now*. Research provides driving mirrors, and side windows if you are lucky, but not headlights. It is especially dangerous in the fashion area.

A manufacturer of teenage radios, radios for teenagers that is, discovered that pink was the color the radios should be. By the time the pink radios hit Main Street, pink was out and purple was in. Worse still, the competitors had done similar research and had also flooded the market with pink.

The second, competitive, moral from this true story can be useful. Few companies think hard enough about competitive intentions. If you are lucky enough to have a research-driven competitor, then your competitor's marketing moves can be predicted by your research. And vice versa if you fall into that category. The logical consequence, unpalatable as it may seem, is that, if your competitor is research driven, you should do the research and then do the opposite of what it advises.

Memo to file

Subject: RESEARCH IS ALWAYS INCOMPLETE

- Seek illumination, not support. At best, research can only reveal the present, not the future: mirrors not headlights.

- Separate the research and management paradigms by using external top professionals. Research is rational; managers and consumers are not.

- Sweep away all but the essential: brand equity tracking and what will really influence decisions. The nice to know is always incomplete.

- Integrate what remains with internal information for full market understanding.

- Focus groups are not representative but can be insightful. Be there.

- Are your competitors doing the same research? Use that to change your decision.

27

SURGICAL SEGMENTATION

Tailoring the offer to fit each consumer group

Key issues
- **Focussing on multiple targets** ● **Defining segments**
- **Demassifying marketing through more precise information**
- **Complexity versus benefit**

FOCUSSING ON MULTIPLE TARGETS

Segmentation, in theory, divides a market into groups of similar consumers so that the marketer can target different appeals which precisely match the needs of each group. The manufacturer of hair colorant, for example, can promote the fashionability of hair tinting to the young and restorative coloring to the middle aged. This is different from the positioning concept which focusses a single appeal to a single target group; segmentation implies multiple warheads each precisely aimed at its own target. This is not easy.

The most common form of segmentation is by country. Coca-Cola varies its global campaign to meet the needs of each national identity. As a general rule, if *within group* differences are less than those *between groups*, segmentation may be worthwhile because appeals can be separated and personalized, to some extent, to that group. The theory is that specialist concentration on limited markets marshals resources.

Segmentation takes many forms: language, ethnic groups, sex, locality, and age group are but five ways of grouping consumers. More sophisticated segmentation involves psychographic measures of life styles, loyalty factors, and whether consumers are trendsetters, followers, or laggards. Price, size of packaging, flavors and product characteristics are brand attributes that can be used to partition markets. Occasions of use may define still other segments.

In all cases, marketers are recognizing that consumers differ. Even if they could market directly to all the world in one go, it would not be economic to do so.

An airline fills a plane through price discrimination. Those prepared to pay, or have their employers pay, first class fares do so. Those who need to book ahead pay more than those ready to chance standby. A single plane may carry customers who have paid a dozen or more different prices for their seats. Comfort and service differ but they all fly from A to B. The airline maximizes its profit by maximizing each higher fare paying group before opening its doors to the next cheaper. So long as no one pays less than the marginal cost of the seat (minimal), the airline wants to fill every seat.

British Airways designated First, Club Class and Economy as separate "brands" ("Club World" and "World Traveller" for inter-continental routes) with separate management. To achieve segmentation, an airline erects "walls of discrimination" in order that the price differences are legitimate. A ticket that requires the customer to return after the weekend, for example, will be attractive to holiday-makers but not to business travellers. The sophistication of computer systems in allocating seats to the different fare categories and helping airline sales people juggle the remaining vacancies can distinguish the profitable airline from the loss-maker. Brand equity and profit are both improved by upgrading loyal customers, identified by cards or the computer, where there are vacancies in the more expensive seats and excess demand for cheaper. British Airways Executive Club cards themselves provide at least three segments according to airline usage and preparedness to pay for the privilege.

Segmentation theory divides consumers into like clusters so that marketing can be neatly and relevantly focussed. Virginia Slims were the first cigarette to be successfully targeted to women. Global marketing takes segmentation across national boundaries. The entertainment industry, for example, will target by age group for music or films worldwide. Perfume brands target the international traveller.

A narrow initial target is usually essential for a new brand to gain a beachhead. Otherwise it needs to be a revolutionary product and/or be backed by a massive budget. Defining a narrow section of the population simplifies positioning, distribution and the marketing mix. As the brand grows in popularity within the initial target group, the marketer is faced by a choice of continuing to increase share there or include other segments or go for the whole market. Premature expansion to too wide a target can be as deathly as lingering in the first segment while others take over the expansion. Segmentation opens up the middle ground between the niche and the mass market.

One of the most successful US airlines, Delta, owes its profitability to its historical dominance of the Atlanta traffic. In 1988, Delta had 11 percent of the US airline market defined by passenger miles. If that had been spread evenly across the USA its position would have been relatively weak. With about half the Atlanta traffic, however, it was able to exert considerable leverage on consumers within that segment as well as achieving economies through localized services.

> **Manufacturers are abandoning mass production in order to add value by tailoring products, to segments.**

This illustrates the dangers of using market share as a forecaster of profitability. Which market applies? Atlanta or the USA? A larger share of a smaller market is likely to be more profitable than a smaller share of a larger market. This strategy plus the benefits of price discrimination cause today's marketers to look more closely at segmentation.

Manufacturers are abandoning mass production in order to add value by tailoring products, if not to individual customers, then to segments. In some categories this has already led to the "segment of one." I can now order a car engine, body shell, coloring, trim, and upholstery covering to my own specification, albeit from a short list of each variable.

The earliest example of this as a countertrend was the development of General Motors. Ford, through the universality of the Model T, dominated the post-World War I market. General Motors was put together from a hotch-potch of independent companies but rapidly became a family of brands each positioned for one segment of the market. By outflanking Ford, Alfred Sloan took over market leadership.

More recently, Ernest Saunders faced the same problem when Guinness acquired the Distillers Company. Their whisky brands were undifferentiated and competed largely with each other. The marketing task was to give them separate targets, positioning, and segments.

Some researchers argue that there is no such thing as a niche brand; there are only big brands and small brands. The niche brand concept implies that a small number of users are unusually loyal to that brand which can therefore, for example, afford to raise prices above its larger competitors. All Bran is a cereal with special properties and a following which will not switch to more popular brands. The evidence of buyer panel data is that smaller brands have fewer customers who also buy the brand less often. This is known as "Double Jeopardy." A niche brand, according to the sceptics, should certainly have fewer customers but they should be more loyal and buy at the usual rate.

Those who believe in niche brands may be shocked by the finding but the issue is largely semantic. The term "niche brand" comes from the concept of hiding away from more powerful competitors. Charles Darwin used the term for those species who survived predators and/or winter by storing fat when food was available and going into hiding when conditions were adverse. This is a pretty sensible strategy for weak brands. Through careful differentiation and segmentation of its drinker targets, a brand such as Pilsner Urquell, the Czech lager, is in a "niche," or shelter, compared to Carling Black Label in the UK or Budweiser in the USA.

Double Jeopardy research indicates less loyalty to specialist brands than their owners would like. On the other hand, achieving high shares in small segments is still a better strategy than a small share spread across the market.

DEFINING SEGMENTS

A mature brand may have its strength with an aging consumer group. Should you reposition the brand to appeal to younger and more affluent consumers? If so, how can you avoid alienating those now providing the cash flow? One answer may be to market separately to these two segments. But how should they be described?

The traditional consumer description was in demographic terms: age, sex, family size; and socioeconomic class. The UK tended to simplify "class" to occupation or spending power: A and B for higher and middle, C1 for white collar office workers, C2 for blue collar, D for minimum waged and E for the rest. With A only representing 2 percent of the population it was lumped with B. As blue collar working is progressively taken by mechanization, the coarse grain of this analysis is of diminishing value: it really was just there to make the lot of the media buyers easier. As the media expressed their readers or viewers in that way, they knew what to look for. In terms of significant disposable income, there are mostly only two groups now, AB and C, too coarse an analysis for sensitive segmentation.

The USA uses rather more specific breaks of earning levels, education, ethnic and occupation groups. Such groups are easy to identify with and to research but the format says little about the behavior characteristics of the target.

In the 1970s, attempts were made to supplement these demographic classifications with psychographics, i.e. personality and behavior characteristics. The marketer was glad to deal with portraits of real, or more real, people. Measurement became more expensive and less reliable. Does measurement matter? Empathy is the most important benefit of a clearer picture of the consumer and this does not need quantification. On the other hand, the size of the segment, how much they spend on the category, competitor shares all feed into the planning process.

Early psychographic measurement suffered from subjectivity and variation. Each researcher created different segment definitions. When we describe our own personalities and ways of life on questionnaires, how accurate and truthful are we? In the 1980s, researchers codified their practices and tested them from country to country. What they did was to compute huge volumes of psychographic data to produce clusters of consumer groups that would behave consistently, from time to time, country to country, product group to product group.

> **What they did was to compute huge volumes of psychographic data to produce clusters of consumer groups that would behave consistently, from time to time, country to country, product group to product group.**

These methodologies are branded in different ways. Sometimes the same product is used with different names by different advertising agencies. A classic "VALS" (Value And Life Styles) was invented by SRI International to distinguish nine psychographic clusters of consumers. Young & Rubicam used it during the 1987 UK general election. Y&R had been tracking the ratings of the political parties and concluded that the election outcome could be shifted by a late change in strategy based on a VALS view of consumer preferences that differed from those of Conservative Central Office. The greater sensitivity of the VALS psychographic information reinforced the Prime Minister's concerns with the direction of the campaign and enabled her to make the necessary changes to win.

USING MORE PRECISE INFORMATION

Just as computer systems link point of sale through to production lines, direct marketing uses databases to select appropriate customers for quite low volume brands. Some services work the other way round: consumers can search product and supplier databases both for the brands they want and also the best terms.

The niche marketer can specify the target and the computer can prepare mail to go to those consumers that match the specification, or produce a list of numbers to be telephoned. In 1995, Seagrams targeted the 15 percent of malt whisky drinkers believed to account for two-thirds of UK consumption.

Drinks mailings rose from 47 in 1992 to 127 in 1994.[1] One day even the call may be automated so that the consumer can interact with the computer direct. As the pattern of consumer orders builds up it becomes easier to forecast the type of purchase the consumer may make. Those who order often, spend a great deal, and have done so recently are prioritized by the computer system.

Some consider this new world with horror. The database marketers, however, claim that consumers far prefer the tailoring of offers to their likely needs to the junk mailings of the past. Where the process is consumer initiated there can be little doubt that it can offer substantial advantages to trailing around shops filled with the product in the wrong colour or the wrong trim.

> **Those who order often, spend a great deal, and have done so recently are prioritized by the computer system.**

Mail order services have been available for a century. Telemarketing develops the principle using better information more personally and, ultimately, interactively. For banking and insurance, this is a reality. In the United States special kiosks are made available for those without home computer or suitable hardware.

Marketing matches consumers with brands. What was done in the mass can now be done, with electronic help more precisely to get riches from niches.

COMPLEXITY

Segmentation is a key part of the trend to demassifying marketing. The marketer with a portfolio of brands in the same category can target each at a different segment though that is not segmentation in the full sense. In toothpaste, one brand may appeal to the health conscious, another to those seeking the whitest teeth, another to healthy gums, and another who want a deal on price. Through the use of factor and cluster analysis, each market can be separately identified and quantified. The effects of specific marketing programs on specific clusters can, up to a point, be measured. Perhaps more importantly, marketers can identify with the particular segment they are addressing. The more precisely you can "see" the consumer in the mind's eye, the better the presentation of benefits can be.

The identification of a particular brand, and especially a new brand, with its specific target was ever vital. Segmentation in the full sense, however,

---

[1] *Marketing*, (August 3, 1995), p. 30.

means targeting a single brand at multiple segments, as does British Airways. This requires the marketing team, the sales force, and the agencies to remember which is which and distinguish the activities accordingly.

> **Segmentation in the full sense, however, means targeting a single brand at multiple segments.**

For this reason, few brands truly practice segmentation within a single market. Those large enough to make it worthwhile should bite the bullet and divide the roles. In effect, segmentation is dividing the market. Focus can be achieved by having each market separately managed. For the toothpaste example, one manager and agency might deal with the "value" segment and message while another team looks after the "health" message.

Dividing activities loses economies of scale and can confuse consumers unless the segments are truly distinct. Mass media are rarely efficient if used in a niche way.

Nevertheless, segmentation is a powerful weapon in the battle to get more from less marketing spending. Choosing between segments in terms of their response rates to marketing programs can achieve higher profits by concentrating growth in areas of strength and then using that increased strength progressively as a springboard for wider segments.

Memo to file

Subject: SURGICAL SEGMENTATION

● Segmentation provides the brand with multiple precision targets. In theory, this allows more efficient use of resources than a single niche or the entire mass market.

● Appeals should be uniquely relevant to each segment.

● Segmentation is made possible through improved information and direct marketing.

● The disadvantage of segmentation is the complexity of differing programs for the same brand. The theoretical benefits have to be balanced against the planning, execution, and control on-costs. Separate marketing teams will probably prove necessary.

28

TRAINING THE PROFESSIONALS

Big money rides on marketing decisions. Are your marketers fit enough?

Key issues
- Top professionals in other areas train continuously to keep up to the mark. Why do marketers resist it? ● Why train? Rehearsing the future ● Marketers love to teach. Encourage that by cross-fertilizing best practice

---

THE RESISTANCE TO TRAINING

The most important assets of many companies are their brands. Many others without major brands still depend on marketing for their existence and prosperity. Increasing the value of those brands, outwitting the competition, dominating the marketplace, all these critical functions are led by the company's marketing professionals. These people spend huge sums on advertising, merchandising, and promotion. Even huger profits should result. The connection is not a matter of science but craft. The inputs and outputs cannot be precisely linked. Companies have to depend on the finely honed instincts and experience of their marketing people.

Professional footballers similarly depend on their skills and instincts, rather than science. These are built from years of practice. A match is rehearsed for many more hours than it is played. R&D people, the accountants, the human resource managers, the junior assistant company secretary have all had more formal training than most marketers.

None of these people put the business at the same degree of risk. None have as much opportunity to realize great profits or destroy brand equity.

With luck your marketing people will have had some or all of the following:

- A year or so as a sales merchandiser or the equivalent – a good start; there is no substitute for the marketplace itself.
- Formal marketing courses teaching the Four Ps usually lasting a week at a time.
- Time in an advertising agency gaining a wonderfully cynical view of their clients' strengths and weaknesses. A fine opportunity to study advertising may also distort the importance of advertising. Advertisers understanding marketing is more vital than the reverse, though both would be nice.
- Study of trade books and magazines and especially their gossip columns.
- Experience with a leading marketing company. Serving an apprenticeship with a good marketer has equipped most of today's top marketers with all they needed to know.
- An MBA and/or some formal education in marketing. A mixed blessing since it will probably have overweighted the neo-classical paradigm.

Marketing people are bright. They learn fast. A reasonable mix of the above is fine as starters. So far (up to about the age of 27 years), so good. Unfortunately, at that point the training then largely stops. Hunter-Miller (a London based executive search agency specializing in senior marketing appointments) researched the leading UK fast moving consumer goods companies ("fmcg") and the largest retailers in 1991. Within the fmcg companies, Hunter-Miller found a high level of dissatisfaction leading to movement amongst marketers in the 28–30 year age group. The marketers themselves were not able to associate cause and effect, but in all cases training had plateaued. These marketing professionals saw themselves as having had all the training they were likely to get. They felt that the company ceased to be interested in them. Unless promotion was imminent, they looked outside.

That is not to say that they would have accepted additional training had it been offered. By that stage busy, preoccupied, and feeling that they have "arrived," expectations had built up that could not be fulfilled. Disaffiliation resulted.

The loss to the fmcg companies was a gain to the retail grocery sector, who provide little or no marketing training, but used to rely on the outflow from fmcg. This is less true now.

The lesson has less to do with the motivation of marketers than with why age 27 marks such a barrier to further development. Marketing is the business of managing innovation, and change is constant. Yesterday's sales promotion was fine but it will not work tomorrow.

Here are some of the reasons why, paradoxically, marketers are reluctant to go after further training and yet are disaffected when they do not get it:

- Marketers tend to be self confident, if not cocky. Be glad of that for otherwise they would not attempt the impossible and make it happen. Once they feel they have mastered the craft, however, appetite for formal learning declines. Their enthusiasm for staying up to date does not.

- Marketers change jobs faster than other disciplines. This accelerated experience itself provides training. True up to a point – it provides width but not depth. It actually reduces learning on the time dimension, i.e. staying around long enough to learn from your own mistakes.

  Once they feel they have mastered the craft, appetite for formal learning declines.

- Marketing departments have delayered and downsized. The work is the same and as the central liaison, if not decision, point for brands, their time is much in demand. Most marketers are busier than they used to be and this is interfering with their time to think.

- Marketers think they are supposed to be original and creative. Being steeped in the thinking of others will undermine the unique contribution each can make. There is something in this but it easily turns into NIH (not invented here) and the repetition of the mistakes of the past.

- Absurd as it may seem: money. Training budgets are amongst the first casualties of austerity. Few can show any immediate profit benefits. The HR department, if faced by a choice of cutting outside training or depopulating itself, will prefer self-preservation. It is easy to get agreement to cut the course the marketer had no time to go on. The marketer would rather have the money for the brand. In austerity, the one department that can still afford outside courses is finance. Why is that?

WHY TRAIN?

The old riposte is to consider the cost of not training. Do you really want your most important assets in the hands of a team with deteriorating skills? If the world is changing should not your marketers be keeping up to date? How many have horizons limited to their own country? The UK domestic market now has 320 million consumers speaking ten languages. The USA is now NAFTA, a similar number with the Spanish language becoming as widespread as English.

Brave new frontiers such as sophisticated information systems or global marketing make attractive topics for learning. Less welcome are those old basics we all know but few practice. Back in the 1960s, every brand manager had a brand bible with all the salient points about his (yes, it was always "his" in those days) brand. He lugged it around and referred to it constantly. Any marketer doing such a thing today would be considered mad. Yet the concept is on the way back. New computer packages, such as AIM 21, bring together all the brand visuals and facts: advertising, packaging, promotional materials and performance figures. Show this to mature marketers in the 1990s and they whoop with delight. They recognize the importance of having a repository of brand learning.

> **Training benefits cannot be quantified but the waste resulting from inadequate training can.**

Training benefits cannot be quantified but the waste resulting from inadequate training can, up to a point. About half the advertising budget is wasted and anything up to 90 percent of promotions. That is no reason to stop; the evidence is that results would be still worse if you did. On the other hand it *is* an indicator of the scope for improvement if the marketers could do their jobs even better. Make no mistake: your marketing team is great. They must be. You have only just hired them. What we are considering now is a virtuous circle:

- Even better performance, leading to
- More job satisfaction, leading to
- Better retention, leading to even better performance.

REHEARSING THE FUTURE

Planning and training are both about learning, i.e. changed behavior leading to better performance. That recognition should allow companies to free up resources for training at a stroke. Call training "planning." The accountants will never cut that budget. There is really no need to distinguish the two concepts and it might be better if you did not. Both are concerned with preparing for the future. How much resource you should take out of today to invest in the future is open to question. Frittering those future resources away in multiple ways, however, is daft.

Here are some of the ways we do it:

- Up to five different sets of planning from long-term visions to quarterly forecasts.
- Outside courses.
- Internal retreats and away days.
- Internal training, including on the job.
- Succession and human resources planning.
- Consultants. They have to be briefed, then they ask our people our questions and then they report our people's answers to ourselves. Most companies could do that for themselves, if they got organized; yet the consultancy process yields huge benefits to clients, despite the cost in time and money. Fees would not have grown so much faster than inflation otherwise. Part of the benefit comes from the disciplines of taking time out, of focussed thinking, and then the pressure to implement the expensive suggestions.

None of these are under challenge. Were it not for outside courses, my employer would cease to exist. What *is* under challenge is their separation. They are all forms of rehearsing the future and should be seen as a whole.

By integrating many of the rehearsals into a single program, marketers will find time for the training they need.

Our football team cannot fully distinguish between training, studying the competition, planning, and coaching. To have these as totally separate activities run by different people would hardly prepare them for the game on Saturday.

By integrating many of the rehearsals into a single program, which we will call planning in order to protect the resource, marketers will find time for the training they need.

CROSS FERTILIZING BEST PRACTICE

Marketers, after their late 20s, may not be too keen on being trained but they are usually generous in their enthusiasm for passing on their skills and insights. Training is not the same as education. (If in doubt on this point, reflect on whether you would prefer sex education or sex training.) The word "training" itself is part of the problem. Replacing it with "planning" may secure the resource but marketers like that even less.

One solution to the problem, which is purely one of internal marketing, is to reposition the product as "cross-fertilizing best practice." Marketers will not dispute that they should be continuously curious about markets, marketing, and what others are doing. They also believe that the best sources of such wisdom are practitioners, not academics. Building a climate that encourages mutual learning is not easy but of great importance.

> **Building a climate that encourages mutual learning is not easy but of great importance.**

Some US companies have introduced marketing audits. Worried by practice being less than professional, visiting consultants, academics, peers or seniors assess local marketing processes, standards, whether positioning statements are realistic, and so on. The motivation of top management is clear enough but it reeks of control, of Big Brother. A fun thing, an opportunity for marketers to share experiences, insights, and skills with peers, would reinforce the motivation of the marketers. Can the word "audit" convey that? Or does it imply controllers arriving in their green eyeshades?

At the very least, marketers should be encouraged to learn more from one another. Every company has its share of mavericks who have succeeded and pedants who have added value. Every experienced marketer has something to contribute. Failures are perhaps the best. If marketing is accepted as a craft rather than a science, how can those craft skills be shared across internal, or national, boundaries?

If marketing is too important to leave to marketers and if brand plans should be created by multifunctional teams, marketing skills need to be shared with non-marketers. Use marketers as teachers and marketing training will take care of itself. Textbooks will be dusted off, fundamentals will be rediscovered, marketers will enjoy and improve each other's teaching. Experiences and skills will be relayed in the gaps left between theory and reality. Failures are the best training but, as responsibilities grow, failures are becoming more expensive. Teaching marketing to non-marketers and then preparing brand plans with them is next best. Then the failures can become case studies and show a return.

Memo to file

Subject: TRAINING THE PROFESSIONALS

- Go for the virtuous circle: training reduces waste in marketing expenditure → improves performance → improves job satisfaction → improves retention → improves learning = training which reduces waste ...

- Cross-fertilize best practice with peers and non-marketing colleagues. Teaching is fine training. See how many books appear on their shelves.

- Cross-fertilize failures too. Promulgation provides valuable lessons and, with any luck, wards off repetition.

- Training, learning, planning are just some of the ways organizations rehearse their future. Integrate them to use less resource and get better results.

29

Ugly Duckling

Great new brands become swans but seem ugly ducklings at first. So do ugly ducks. Getting innovative brands through the organization.

> *Key issues*
> ● **Truly major breakthroughs can be unrecognized initially**
> ● **How to create pathways for their development** ● **The need for champions** ● **Get the ducklings out of research and into the water**

RECOGNIZING THE BREAKTHROUGHS

Great brands rarely seem so great at their beginnings. In television, Star Trek and Minder performed dismally in their early days. They only just survived. Baileys Irish Cream, today the world's leading liqueur, researched badly and began hesitantly. Early cars were the cause of hilarity. In 1962, the Decca record company rejected the Beatles on the grounds that boys with guitars were outmoded.

It may be going too far to claim that initial failure is a requirement for greatness but successful research should be taken as a warning. Why so is explored later in this chapter. Unfortunately disasters also research badly. This is the ugly duckling problem: swans begin as ugly ducklings but so do ugly ducks.

The true parentage of great brands can be obscure. Most companies will only talk about success after the event, ostensibly for commercial security reasons but often because they were just as surprised as the rest of us. In reality, this lack of recognition of future winners is a boon to security. It is not necessary to conceal the pearl of the orient if everyone thinks it is a marble. Just put it in with other marbles. For the great innovation companies, such as 3M, or those, such as Unilever and Procter and Gamble, with horns locked in competition, trying to appear foolish lacks conviction. The rest are quite happy to consider other people's innovation daft.

For the moment, the veil of discretion can stay over the moment of our ugly duckling's conception and how it got into the wrong pond. There lies the deception. We can all forecast that an ugly duckling swimming around with a Unilever swan is likely to become another Unilever swan. Competitive factors will do their best

> **Many great brands owe their existence to a series of mistakes**

to knock it out of the water as best they can. The most frequent move is instant imitation. When P&G launched Vizir in Germany after six years' preparation, Henkel, the main competitor, had Liz on the market within days.

Is a noisy launch really to impress the trade or just proud parenthood? Is making a splash the equivalent of passing round cigars? Or is it to frighten off the competition?

Companies cannot camouflage their new brands in alien ponds. New brands need constant nurture and attention. They need the physical and moral warmth of management and siblings. There is some commercial logic in putting new brands out on their own just as Spartans put their babies on the hillsides. The survivors may have been tough but they lost a lot of Spartans.

In the fairy tale, the ugly duckling got into the wrong pond by happenstance. Many great brands owe their existence to a series of mistakes but then, don't we all. Looking down on this marketplace, or pond, what distinguishes the ugly duckling?

An ugly duckling:

- Paddles like hell to get anywhere.
- Makes the below the line activity all too visible.
- Is awkward and, somehow, doesn't quite fit in. People notice it. Perhaps they laugh at it. Remember how the English mocked the French for drinking bottled water?
- Is unsure about direction or where the next meal is coming from.
- Is grateful that the pond is too small for serious threats.
- Tries to fly but cannot.

Hans Andersen was not a Professor of Marketing (he and Arthur were accountants) but he had the basics right there. Compare that with the final swan which:

- Sails serenely along, the object of admiration.
- Maintains momentum without visible below the line activity.
- Is graceful, elegant, and always in fashion.
- Seems to know where it is going and that you will be casting your bread on the water.
- Has no fear of predators. Lesser fowl make way.
- Flies majestically.

The business of new brands is serious and so is the analogy with procreation. Companies that do not propagate the species die out.

Glaxo became the leading UK pharmaceutical company on the back of Zantac. Ski yoghurt revitalized Express Dairies. International Distillers and Vintners grew under the GrandMet umbrella from a marginal company in 1974 to the world's largest wine and spirit company largely through acquisitions, but those acquisitions were made possible by the high profits from new brands such as Croft Original, Baileys Irish Cream, Malibu, and Piat d'Or. Dunhill became a world brand from a small pipe maker by stumbling into luxury goods for Japan. These are four examples of old companies finding new life from new brands.

Accidental meetings, good luck, people prepared to take risks, and groping in the dark play their part in the conception of ugly ducklings just as in other forms of life. New brand development can also be a whole heap of fun. There must be something of the unexpected in a great new brand, something requiring randomness which any formula will eliminate.

The main reason for new brand development is to maintain the lifeblood of the company. This is not just a matter of profits from the brands themselves. Introducing new brands is invigorating for the company as a whole. It boosts morale and sales force enthusiasm. It wrong foots competition. It is enjoyable. No one in business just for the money understands it.

PATHWAYS FOR NEW BRAND DEVELOPMENT

Whatever the reasons in your company, let us assume that a strategy meeting has taken place. It was agreed that you (being out of the room at the time) would lead the first new brand initiative the company has had in ten years. Giddy with this tribute to your creativity, you reel back to your office and call for coffee. Now what?

The brainstorming concept was invented in the fifties. Variants have appeared ever since under other names. The idea is to liberate creativity by positive reinforcement. Ideas spark from one member of the group to another. Each goes one leap of imagination further. Someone writes all the ideas down. The only rule is that no criticism or negative comment is allowed. Every idea must be applauded so that the group can progressively think the unthinkable. The immediate effect can be intoxicating, and so can the morning after. There are more disciplined methodologies which shift from individual to group to individual ("IGI") brainstorming raising the quality of ideas at each stage. Team building is good. Even so, brainstorming is usually a reliable means of producing a heap of junk.

In addition to commissioning you to create a new brand, the strategy meeting concluded that you were a marketing-oriented company or a market-oriented company or something like that. Strategy is about direction, not precision. The meeting discussed being best not biggest, what "best" meant, and getting closer to customers. Before getting closer to the bar, the meeting agreed that every member would ride with sales people for three days a month. If they can spare the time. The sales force, a fine team it was agreed, would benefit from more contact with top management. Ideas straight from the marketplace will refresh corporate direction. An extremely good note on which to go to lunch. The Chairman had every right to be well pleased.

Your colleagues tell you how lucky you are to have the time to follow up this decision. If only they too could get away from their desks. Three field days later they are proved right. You have had an interesting and refreshing time. It has been very worthwhile and you have learnt a lot. Each of the sales people agreed that a new brand was essential and knew exactly what was needed. It had an uncanny resemblance to the brand the competition launched last week. Another door closes.

Field visits are exhausting. It is time for a spot of hedonism. The Client Service (hah!) Director of your advertising agency is taking you to lunch. You agree that it is wrong to expect sales people to be creative. Leave that to creative people. Why not turn the new brand problem over to the agency? Why not? Money and core competence. The likelihood is that your agency is good at advertising but not new brands. The certainty is that they will be expensive.

Advertising is ephemeral; new brands are supposed to be eternal. Agencies are preoccupied with image whereas the thrust needs to be on consumer value, beginning with the product itself. Agencies are not really in love with the client's brands, still less the client. They are in love with advertising. Brands are just mannequins: not interesting in themselves but for the way they show off the advertising. Involving the agency in the new brand creation process makes sense but think twice about turning it over to them.

Lunch was fun but maybe a professional new brand development agency is the answer. Interviewing the shortlist is impressive. So many seemingly long-established brands are new to the world in the last fifteen years. Put the best of their professionals on your team.

From here on the process will be influenced by the process agreed with the professionals as well as by a host of category and competitive factors. How long will everything take? How much R&D is involved and what will it cost? What are the costs and leadtime of getting a prototype to market? How can activity be camouflaged from competition?

If the cost of R&D and new prototypes is low, then the competition can be confused by sheer number. Scatter ducklings everywhere and competitors have a problem. Expensive? Not necessarily. Confusing also to sales force and customers? Not if the trial markets are kept small and they understand the game. The critical factor is the cost of prototyping.

Stop. What about looking for a market gap? If you had not been out with the sales force, not to mention long agency lunches, the market research manager would have got through to you. In fact, you have been avoiding the market research manager's calls. Statisticians are not for you. The means and standard deviations are but not that unwavering look of certainty.

How long is it since your last U&A (usage and attitude) study? Two years. Eyebrows raise. U&A studies are one of the great earners for market research people.

Market gaps are an attractive idea. Hindsight is on their side. Any new brand fits in somewhere between those that existed before. At the same time, there is something odd about the idea that the consumer is waiting for something new to turn up. Ask in any focus group what they want that is not already available and mystification sets in. There are no market gaps out there waiting to be filled. Ships do not fill gaps in the water. New brands just barge their way into the market, creating gaps for themselves.

By this time your next board meeting is coming up. You have been conspicuously out of the office, have put new brand professionals on a retainer, and have alienated the market research manager. The progress report may be brief. Could this be the moment for just-in-time delegation? A brand manager has joined with impressive skills and a CV that includes new brand development. Innovation requires new blood, new thinking, new ways of looking at things. How lucky to have someone closer in age and lifestyle to the target market. Problem solved.

You are right to put the newcomer on the team. Liaison, progress chasing, tracking the money are going to need more time than you have. Unfortunately, you cannot turn the problem over to the novice however keen the newcomer and the HR department are that you should. Surely this is an opportunity to provide experience. The project has little or no budget and carries no risk to the mainstream business. Sit by Nelly graduate training programs are long gone. Put the newcomer in charge, they say. Many companies do this. Brand managers do rank themselves by spending

> **Involving the agency in the new brand creation process makes sense but think twice about turning it over to them.**

budget and the political importance of their brands. There is as much sentimental charm in giving new products to junior marketers as providing four-year-olds with puppies. Pretty – yes; smart – no. Experienced parents know a) there is going to be a mess, and b) who will have to clear it up. The current Seagrams whisky new brand developer, Tom Jago, is aged 70, has been practicing the art for 40 years and claims now to be getting the hang of it.

To summarize the pathway established so far: sales force suggestions and market research have been discounted. The advertising agency, new brand professional and junior marketing manager are on the team but not in charge. Something, or rather someone, is missing.

THE NEED FOR CHAMPIONS

The champion concept is usually ascribed to 3M. It is a manager, probably senior but not from that part of the business, who has made a personal commitment to the idea and is prepared to crash through the barriers and inertia that exist in all large companies to make the idea happen. A new brand champion is just one example. Few marketing departments welcome this intrusion on their turf until the champion culture becomes accepted.

The champion system recognizes that great brands in the past have come about through human qualities of vision, belief, enthusiasm, and determination far more than mechanistic analysis. A champion needs experience and understanding of the product category and its marketplace. Great brands have some real product advantage to offer the consumer but it may be so subtle and unexpected that it only becomes apparent after the event. Luck perhaps plays the greatest part. The best any system can do is to give luck a sporting chance. The champion system is part of that.

Complete the team with senior representatives from R&D, finance, or planning, and production all of whom will have seen so many marketers come and go that they have become marketing experts themselves. The need for product advantage is the reason why senior R&D involvement in the team is critical. Whatever else, the team must be able to complete the sentence: this is the best brand in its category because …

In no time (you think, and aeons everyone else thinks) the champion has the new brand concept fleshed out. Just one? Surely you need a battery of concepts from which the consumer will select the best? Brainstormers like the hopper approach: throw all the ideas in the top and see what comes out the bottom. Others refer to it as the scattergun or the shot gun. With enough pellets, something is bound to hit.

> **The champion system recognizes that great brands in the past have come about through human qualities of vision, belief, enthusiasm, and determination far more than mechanistic analysis.**

The concept is fallacious for three reasons. All the ideas are unformed and unfinished at this stage. How can you tell which foetus is Beethoven and which the village idiot. The second problem is that it spreads the development effort required to get the ideas to judgement stage over too many candidates. Thirdly, no one cares passionately about any one of them. Brands are like people. They need hand rearing. Crafting a brand takes enormous time, care, patience, and conviction. Money too. Quantity will damage quality.

This is not a contradiction: one champion should bring just one brand to market. The corporation has to remember that new brand development is a game of chance. However much the odds are stacked in favour of the fledgling, success is still unlikely. The answer lies in developing a culture with many champions but few brands. Strong champions make strong brands.

With one, or maybe two solutions, we can go to focus groups. "Concept boards" (written descriptions of the brands) are popular practice but no substitute for the real thing. Short cuts of this type introduce the very unreality to research that invalidates it. Is it practical in your business to dummy up some form of prototype? If not, do the best you can. Spoof advertisements can be realistic and enable the presentation of the benefits to be checked at the same time.

Focus groups are an opportunity to see the ugly duckling through consumer eyes. Blemishes, missed internally, may become obvious. The language used by consumers can be useful. Focus groups are an opportunity for the team to gain insights, albeit no more than that. Chapter 26, "Research is always Incomplete," develops this topic.

GET THE DUCKLING OUT OF RESEARCH AND INTO THE WATER

Most likely the focus group has persuaded even the proud parents that the duckling really is ugly. Back to R&D it goes. Several prototypes and groups later, the duckling now must hit the cold water. No research is as good as giving customers and consumers the opportunity to part with real money. Speed to market is ever more important; it is cheaper and better to be right enough than to wait for perfection.

It is cheaper and better to be right enough than to wait for perfection.

Using the market for trialing has one major drawback: once it is on the water, competitors can see it too. Initially it may not be taken seriously but as the results start ringing tills, their market research may start ringing bells. Modern electronic information systems provide fast information to your competitors. Can you handle retaliatory action and/or imitation, in time? What is their lead time?

For this reason, computer test market simulations are available in developed countries. Draught Guinness in a can was an early UK user. The attraction is that they use small samples of consumer response, hidden from competitors, which the computer extrapolates to forecast what would happen in a real test market. As data builds up, first in research and then in test, the forecasting becomes more reliable. The purpose is to gain competitive time.

Maybe the duckling swims first time and maybe it needs more nurture first. It is tough to know when to let it survive and when it needs to recuperate back in R&D. If everyone beats up on it, it may look dead when it is not. With some oxygen, it still may be a winner. Or it may really be dead. If so, the chances for the next bird are greatly improved. The duckling rearers have learned something.

The Ugly Duckling story is a fantasy? Sure. That is what marketing is made of.

Memo to file

Subject: UGLY DUCKLING

- Establish the new brand development team. If you cannot find a better candidate, you are the champion. If no one believes in the concept enough to be champion, find a new concept.

- R&D deserves a top role to provide a product which is the best because ...

- Use research for insights but do not allow the process to be driven by it.

- Build corporate learning through frequent small trials and therefore failures.

30

VALUE MARKETING

The word "value" too often means cheap.
It should mean satisfaction

Key issues
- **Every decade redraws the maps of consumer values. It could be time for an update**
- **Value =** $\dfrac{\text{Perceived quality} \times \text{Quantity}}{\text{Price}}$

Value is a word full of ambiguity. "Value for money" is cheap but "added value" is expensive. The early 1990s recession coined the term "value marketing" to mean price cutting, low margins, giving extra quantity, and low budgets. To 1980s marketers, talking cheap was worse than talking dirty. Higher price meant higher quality. These things are cyclical.

When inflation marches hand in hand with rapid increases in living standards, price hikes are tolerated. If a price increase proves too high, a few months will correct the differential. Meanwhile the competition will have been encouraged to increase prices too.

The need for value never changes but the perception of value does. The arithmetic is simple:

$$\text{Value} = \frac{\text{Perceived quality} \times \text{Quantity}}{\text{Price}}$$

Value is relative to competition. If they, thanks to recession or whatever, are carving price, then your relative value is diminishing even if quality and price remain the same. As the marketing budget and the price premium are two sides of the same coin, a reduction in prices may well demand a reduction in budget as well as the reverse. "Value marketing" is almost a contradiction in terms; it is a regression. In place of adding values (that word again), marketing expenditure is shifted to price promotions, i.e. discounts, and/or more quantity for the same money.

The regressions are necessary from time to time, albeit disagreeable. Like dieting. And just like dieting, it becomes a cult for a while. Trendy brand managers compete in value marketing, i.e. passing out the very discounts they would have considered deplorable the year before.

Presentation (packaging) should reflect these changing consumer values. The continuous packaging updates recommended in chapter 18 need to move in sync with the materiality of the age. Less flashy in the 1990s relative to the 1980s. Are we right to speak in decades? Perhaps not, but it is convenient. The 1960s may have seemed to swing compared to the 1950s yet permissiveness grew again in the 1970s. The oil price shock created a brief recession at half time. Inflation ripped. The Thatcher 1980s poured more money into more pockets than any decade in history. Aids heralded a new morality (or hypocrisy?). Materialism flourished.

Perhaps it was inevitable that the 1990s would bring an economic hangover. People had to take stock eventually of balances of payments, health, education, empty promises, and empty bottles. Marketing recognized that the mood had changed. Increased international competition make the market wider but tougher, the EU in particular.

The twin realities are that consumer values will continue to change, and that marketing will have to be more skillful to produce better results from slimmer margins and budgets. Is either of these new? Of course not but earnest marketers will tell you that it is.

In the paradoxical way of marketing, countertrends co-exist. As the mass market squeezes margins, specialists will find ways to provide more service and use that differentiation to price up. Niches offer warm hiding places to those that can make them their own. Some call this narrow manufacturer-to-consumer channel "vertical marketing" to distinguish it from diffusing products through the ever widening layers of distribution in the conventional model.

None of this alters the basics of marketing: differentiation, adding value, and the marketing mix remain critical, perhaps more so. Only the magnification increases; more has to be done with less. To do that, *brand* values have to be re-engineered in the light of the new *consumer* values.

Shifting attitudes may require strategic repositioning. Pray that it will not, for more than incremental repositioning is expensive and uncertain. Revisit also the cherished experience of what works in all elements of the marketing mix. Value chain analysis, or engineering, takes each item of cost in the product and its marketing against the value it adds for the consumer. MBA students love the rationality of that process though the reality of that form of analysis is open to doubt. Its usefulness lies in providing an agenda of challenge. Over time features are added, each intended to provide more value for the end user.

Japanese cars are an example. Any time Detroit added a feature, Toyota went one better. Consumers are asked at each stage "would you like Z as an extra, at no extra charge." End users like each one. In aggregate, however, they are confused by all the buttons and would gladly pay someone to take them away. In the 1990s, they did.

> **The twin realities are that consumer values will continue to change, and that marketing will have to be more skillful to produce better results from slimmer margins and budgets.**

A decade is a good interval to measure basic consumer value shifts. To challenge the whole set of "givens" once in a decade is as sensible as doing so every year is daft. Depending on the circumstances, some other interval may be better. Increasing the research budget when marketing headcount, budgets, and costs are being cut will not be easy, yet the return from improved focus can be substantial. Value marketing may be new packaging for old ideas, but it should also be a spur for a major review of each brand and the way it is marketed.

Memo to file

Subject: VALUE MARKETING

- When did you last conduct a strategic review of the brand positioning against current consumer values? Is it overdue?
- Use value chain analysis as an agenda, not a science.
- Agree what research is needed and ensure it will be available in good time.
- Withstand the pressure to cut prices and budgets to conform to the times. It may be necessary but the marketing fundamentals do not change.

31

WHICH AGENCY?

How to select an advertising, or other creative, agency

Key issues
- **The agency mix. How many marketing agencies should you employ? And what types?** ● **Should you change agencies? Prophylactic appraisals** ● **Account conflicts** ● **Methods for shortlisting creative agencies** ● **The final selection. Defining the deal**

THE AGENCY MIX

Very few organizations have no marketing agencies but quite a few wish they could start again with a clean slate. Reality is that the room for maneuver is limited: marketing agencies and their clients have both invested mightily in their existing relationships and learning how to address the marketing problems. The pace of client management turnover is such that the agencies provide the continuity. Not unusually, the agency's account planners are the true guardians of the brands.

The conventional conclusion, and indeed the reality, is to review the agency roster very infrequently – usually when exasperation has set in. A mistake. Appraise your agencies, and have them appraise you, every year. Some agencies, Bartle Bogle Hegarty in the UK for example, now undertake this mutual annual audit as routine. Few agency relationships cannot be made more productive. By the time serious trouble erupts, it is probably too late.

Some reasons for the annual appraisal:

- The variety of marketing agencies is huge. Ad agencies now come in separable segments: media buying, creative, consultancy. There are new products, package design, and direct marketing. Specialist sponsorship agencies offer their services alongside PR that once handled the role. Promotions agencies offer a variety of activities. Different research agencies have different skills. The separation between above the line (advertising) and below the line (promotions) is breached by "through the line" agencies offering "integrated marketing communications." Thus there is both consolidation and dissipation of specialities. What else would you expect? The only good news is that the idea of bringing diverse agencies under the same holding company and pretending that (financial) group could provide an integrated (marketing) service has now died. Saatchi and Saatchi were the last to try that before they discovered that separation is sweeter. Given this diversity, the mix any company needs will evolve over time.

- Inherent in those consolidation and dissipation eddies is the trade-off between administrative simplicity and specialization. Each of these agencies take up considerable management resource (time) but those with broader skills will interpose at least one layer of "account managers" (or whatever) between the client and the true specialists.

- Likewise there is a superficial trade-off between outsourcing marketing activities and doing them in house. As client marketing departments decrease in size, more work has to be outsourced to more agencies? Probably not. Downsizing means that the client should handle *fewer* agencies, though it depends on how many they started with. And how they use consultants in quasi-managerial roles. Many clients today try to work with more creative agencies than they can really handle, thereby exacerbating tailspin.

- How well does the mix of agencies match the marketing mix? If media advertising is a small part of the budget and not critical, then a variety of agencies is inappropriate.

- More clients are now including performance payments or bonuses in the remuneration packages. The importance in this concept lies less in focussing agency staff on commercial measures than on ensuring conversations will take place on objectives and whether they have been met. Agency directors are well used to refuting the client view that agencies are more interested in their own creativity than brand performance. The debate is sterile as both are essential.

- The agency/client relationship is legally different from employee/

employer and PAYE is not deducted from payments but for practical purposes they can be seen as similar. Motivation, understanding, development, achievement, and continuity are all important. If appraisals are standard practice for employees, the same should apply to marketing agencies. To keep life simple, why not use the same

> **How well does the mix of agencies match the marketing mix?**

appraisal formats and bonus systems? The more the agency is a regular member of the team, the better.

An annual appraisal of the agency roster should, therefore, be more dedicated to getting the best out of the relationships than sacking some and hiring others. Changing agencies (or clients) is disagreeable, after the first virtuous glow from "doing the right thing," and time consuming. Changes are minimized by regular maintenance.

The annual appraisal is essentially prophylactic in nature. Serious deterioration of relationships can be caught in time. Changing agencies without dealing with the roots of the problems makes their repetition highly likely. Many in advertising believe that clients get the advertising they deserve. At the least, clients are intimately involved. Blaming the agency for poor advertising and taking the credit for good is symptomatic of difficulties ahead. A formal appraisal of brand equity results against objectives is more meaningful if money rides on it. A full audit of factors contributing to successful advertising, positive and negative behaviors, is worthwhile. For example, too many layers of decision making within the client is a frequent complaint in one direction and lack of agency responsiveness in the other.

Collecting the complaints, by itself, may do more harm than good. Some employ third parties to ensure impartiality and a positive attitude. The benefit comes from their review and shared problem solving.

Nevertheless, the marketing mix does change; and the agency mix needs to change to match. Advertising may give way to PR or to direct marketing. Each needs its own specialists. Larger competitors switch their accounts causing a knock on effect. Agencies buy and sell each other. Key agency executives move on.

However reluctantly, we have to consider "which agency?." How can the ideal partner be found with the least effort? And how can the new agency hit the business running?

ACCOUNT CONFLICTS

Time was when account conflicts allowed clients to prevent their competitors from muscling in. An agency would not pitch for business in the same category and, if approached, they would ask, in order to be polite to the approacher, but expect the answer "no." Today, the client is most likely to suffer when agencies merge or when international factors come into play. The two are connected. There are also some dirty rats, but very few, who will readily accept any larger account and wave goodbye to the incumbent. Easy come, easy go it may prove to be but that is poor consolation.

With the onset of global marketing, international marketers have increasingly appointed the same agency worldwide and asked them to resign competitive accounts.

With the onset of global marketing, international marketers have increasingly appointed the same agency worldwide and asked them to resign competitive accounts. The local agency may be delighted with the win but less happy to resign a favored account and the client reciprocally. Faced by this, medium sized agencies have merged to become stronger in their local market and/or form international alliances to participate in the global game. The only real alternative for dealing with global clients is to be so strong and creative in your local market that the client is prepared to put their other national agencies into an adaptation and media role.

Then there is the sensitive relationship with the megaclient in, say, Chicago who requires the agency to resign potential conflicts in other offices worldwide.

Whether from knock-on effects from globalization or mergers or over-sensitivity, there is always a risk the client will get fired by its favourite agency. Nothing personal, you understand. There is not a great deal to be done about it. The risk can be assessed during the annual appraisal and prompt the client to start preparations if it is real. Shortlisted new agencies can be dropped if a future conflict with a larger account seems likely.

More rarely:

- Counsel the agency, if you are close enough, to form better, from your viewpoint, mergers. Derail prospective deals you find threatening your interests. Is that not what "partnership" is about?

- Persuade your international colleagues and the agency to fall in love with each other. This is rare because the political situation usually forces the agency to support the local team *against* the internationals. You will have to figure out the courtship for yourself but one clue is to use market research as the political weapon it usually is in multinationals. Any international marketer would be dumbstruck to be shown positive research in the local market of the international marketer's advertising elsewhere, especially by the local agency. You don't have to run it, dummy, just show the research.

METHODS FOR SHORTLISTING AGENCIES

The world is not short of agency selection advice.[1] The principles are broadly the same for any form of creative marketing agency be it advertising, PR, design, promotions, direct marketing, or new products. We will focus on *advertising*, only because that makes the issues clearer. The remainder of this chapter is intended to apply to all *creative* marketing agencies, including direct marketing, new products, design, PR, and promotions, where similar principles apply.

The main methods for short listing agencies are:

- **Formal.** A long list is created from all sources, reference books, recommendations, friends, admired advertising. The long listed agencies are then sent details of the client, specification of need, and a questionnaire about the agency. A panel of clients' managers sifts through the responses.

- **Active Broker.** A professional go-between interviews the client management to establish needs and compatibilities. The broker knows the agency market and has built up an understanding of compatibilities. By interviewing the client, needs can be established and matched with agency available talent.

- **Neutral broker.** Here go-betweens offer no active role but make knowledge and expertise conveniently available at one location. If pressed, they may make suggestions but that is not their role. One example is the Advertising Agency Register set up by Lindy Payne in the UK and a number of other countries. The client here reviews selected show reels from the stock provided by agencies. Top agencies have reservations about this service but most supply show reels anyway.

---

[1] e.g. William M. Weilbacher, *Choosing & Working with your Advertising Agency* (Lincolnwood, Illinois, NTC Business Books, 1991) .

- **We are available.** The announcement that a major account is becoming available produces a flood of speculative approaches. Clients have a range of attitudes to this from "we would never hire an agency that had to resort to speculative approaches" to "we are not interested in any agency which cannot be bothered to make a speculative approach." Having to respond to unsuitable but persistent agencies is a problem which drives some clients to abandon their natural courtesy.

The problem with mating games of all sorts is that every relationship differs. Neither side really knows ahead of time what they want. The most unlikely bedfellows turn out just fine. The success rate of dating agencies is probably similar to the formal profiling concept. The questionnaire in both cases is a great turn-off. The more intrusive the questionnaire, the more the turn-off.

Others dislike the active broker concept as much as Westerners would hardly choose their spouses on Auntie's recommendation. The idea of using one consultant to hire another seems extravagant. Furthermore, the broker will have all kinds of vested interests and prior obligations. Brokers are often from whatever type of agency world is being searched. There is the suspicion that an old friend or colleague will get the nod. How can the broker express the special needs of the client as well as the client does?

Apart from the flood of new friends an available client suddenly discovers, early announcement lengthens the hiatus between working with the old and getting the new one up to speed. Existing agencies may well have secured agreement to pitch alongside newcomers. This is fair, softens the blow, and may well rejuvenate the relationship. The problem is that the regular business goes into limbo while the preoccupation becomes agency selection.

The choice of methods may be helped by recognizing that an agency is not an inert lump being located in a wilderness but a sentient, creative organism that would much prefer to make the choices. In other words, flip the process: how can you help the right agency find you?

This question changes the process. Under no circumstance send out long questionnaires which agencies will hate to complete. Even if they are hungry enough to do so, they will not love you for it. Make your account attractive. This may require a hard look at some present practices which caused the existing relationship to turn sour. Make sure the right sort of agency knows you are available. Few can resist a letter telling them that their advertising is wonderful.

Of course, some clients like to find the new agency before they have told the old one that it is fired. This limits their ability to flaunt availability but not much. Many marketers like to keep in touch with the agency whirl as part of keeping up to date. If formal or active broker processes are employed, the word will get out. Agencies have even been approached to pitch for their own accounts. Frankly, I do not care for that. The agency should be told where it stands before the search begins. If you agree that they can be included in the short list, often a sensible benchmark, so be it.

In other words, the normal marketing perspective applies here too: outside in. Treat the agency as the consumer and as you would wish to be treated. The agency/client relationship is little different from any other dyad of relationship marketing:

> **How can you help the right agency find you?**

- Long-term, not transactional.

- Mutual commercial benefit and, preferably, enjoyment.

- The quality of *service* needs to be considered alongside the *functional* quality. In theory results matter, not the manner of their achievement, but in practice both sides will only get satisfaction if the relationship feels good as well as being productive.

Thus, shortlisting should be achieved by multiple methods:

- List admired advertising, and thus agencies, from related categories.

- Get recommendations from professionals in the business, including agencies who for some reason cannot pitch, advertisers, and others involved in the business.

- Consider the use of an active broker to help get the word around and sift recommendations, note plural, with the help of a neutral broker.

- Make your account desirable and encourage publicity of your availability. Exaggerating the ad budget rebounds later but being fun to work with is a fixable objective. If your other agencies are not prepared to publicize that, you really do have a problem.

- Conversely, make your account undesirable to those you would rather did not apply. This may be difficult or next to impossible, but the question should help identify the criteria for selection.

THE FINAL SELECTION

By now, all the best available agencies have applied and your panel has somehow whittled them down to a shortlist. Intrusive questionnaires are tiresome but assembly of comparative data is helpful. A series of quick visits to twice the number of agencies you want to shortlist may be helpful. Receptions speak volumes – as most agencies know. Big agencies spared no expense in the palmy days when 15 percent was 15 percent. Today agency receptions are more functional. In the UK and USA, the big accountancy firms have the really ritzy receptions.

Interesting that. Is it money only wishing to speak to money or just that the accountants sign the checks?

Every five minutes sitting in an agency's reception will be roughly twice as informative as each five minutes with the prospective agency's management. As you can hardly sit in the agency's reception and *not* see the management, it is worth remembering that the main point of the interview is to raise their salivation levels. The more they drool over your account, the better.

These visits, immensely time consuming as they are, can be spread around the selection panel. The process of shortlisting can be democratic; the final selection should not be.

Competitive pitches are much debated. Even the most high handed agency is happy to show its work, walk prospective clients around and talk about the processes they use. Investing in speculative work is another matter. Tough minded clients believe that is the only way the relationship can be tested. Some are prepared to pay at least 50 percent of the costs to do so. On the face of it, handing the creative brief (brand positioning statement) to three or four of the best agencies in town, adopting the best advertising that results and then running it, is a neat idea. All the decisions are packed into one. The agency is being selected on the basis of a winning campaign.

That is the theory. In practice the winning campaign rarely runs. However good the idea, the agency has had inadequate time to interrogate the brand until it confesses its essence to paraphrase David Ogilvy. Nor has the agency client relationship matured to handle that rough passage.

The observer may conclude that the outcome of the debate over competitive pitching will determine the ensuing agency/client relationship. Clients determined to be dominant will tend to show their hand in enforcing their rules. Agencies determined to be dominant will insist on their position. The combination of unalikes, assertive with cooperative, either way around, may be more likely to produce great advertising than paired thugs or wimps. Shared values and interests may be more likely to sustain a relationship than different languages. But I would not put money on these generalities in any particular case. Flying crockery can be compatible with great relationships; mutual sensitivities can be productive; mutual incomprehension can lead to a lifetime's happy discoveries.

Hiring a marketing services creative agency is little different from hiring a senior executive:

- Check out each other's track records and credentials.

- Probe references early and in depth. If this is left late, the decision, and maybe the wrong one, has already been made.

- Have the people who will do the work, on both sides, get to know each other. Some agencies have specialist account getters. You may never see them again. Some client managements insist on choosing the agency but do not have to work with them.

- Spend enough time together to establish whether the chemistry seems to work. An essential agenda for these discussions includes a review of the agency's and the client's advertising successes and failures, why they happened, views on the best process for producing great advertising, what the advertising can realistically achieve in the light of the client's budgets and how the agency will be rewarded.

> **Hiring a marketing services creative agency is little different from hiring a senior executive.**

- The US is more contract-oriented than Europe but these conversations with the different agencies provide the basis for your new contract. Some written understanding is important even though you would be right to keep lawyers out of these discussions. Back in 1963, 109 US advertising contracts showed no less than 448 different types of clause, in aggregate. By now, the proliferation will be immense. Most agencies will say they have their own contract form, hallowed by time and success, and that no other format will do. Similarly, large clients, especially multinationals, have their own format. The format issue is not worth fighting over but four issues are:

  1. Specify what the agency will achieve. It is too soon to specify brand equity objectives as the briefing will not have gone that far. Nevertheless, the path to setting those objectives and the general principles can be specified.
  2. Who owns the copyright of creative material? Some agencies, though fewer in the 1990s, try to hold onto copyright. What you pay for should be yours. Some clients insist that everything presented becomes their copyright whether it runs or not.
  3. Remuneration. One of the great benefits of discussions with short-listed agencies is achieving a good understanding of the market rate

for your business. Agencies are both right and wrong to be lofty about cash: "the truth is that remuneration is a detail you sort out once you have decided to work with someone." (Robert Bean of Bean MC) and "remuneration is not central" (M T Rainey of Rainey Kelly Campbell Roalfe).[2] They are right that remuneration is a secondary matter. Finding the right relationship is far more important than its cost. On the other hand, if the client does not use the selection process to establish market rates and to make the remuneration part of the deal, then the client can expect trouble later. Would you hire an executive without agreeing salary and the likely bonus? Flat fees have rather gone out of fashion, prompted by clients *understating* their budgets at pitch time. The rate of commission, and fee if any, will depend on the size and complexity of the account. Agency and executive recruitment should follow the same guideline: carrots not peanuts. You do not want monkeys and you should motivate performance against brand equity targets.

4. Termination. Not usually a sticking point (this is romance time) but the deal the agency expects from its predecessor is, generally, a good yardstick for the deal it should get on the way out. What happens with conflicts? To what extent can you keep others out and what happens when you cannot? International ramifications?

● Some form of competitive pitch may be mutually interesting, if it is remunerated in its own right. Valuable learning can result for both sides. Time may be saved through introducing a new campaign that much sooner, a wish likely to be unfulfilled. It is an artificial test of a future relationship. Few prospective executives are asked to show how they would perform in a board meeting. More realistic, and it does apply to prospective employees, is to request an analysis of the marketing situation and what variation should be made to the brand positioning statement. This makes far fewer demands on agency resources and they should be assessing that anyway.

At the time, the hiring process seems endless and yet enough time has probably still not been given to it. Time taken has to be saved somewhere. In this case, the "somewhere" is at the end. If the right agency is chosen, briefed and motivated, the creative result should not even need client approval. It will be right first time.

---

[2] *Marketing* (Aug 3, 1995). p. 19.

Memo to file

Subject: WHICH AGENCY?

- How many agencies do you need? Match them with your marketing mix priorities and then settle for fewer. Maintaining productive agency relationships is time consuming.

- Maintain each agency relationship with a formal annual appraisal – in both directions. Compare brand equity objectives with outcomes. Better still, bonus success.

- Incremental agency changes may be necessary, wasteful as they are. Most of your marketing learning may be in your agencies.

- Determine your policy on conflicts. Even so, your international colleagues or agency mergers may still push you out of your favourite agency. You may be able to anticipate conflicts and get your retaliation in first.

- Why should the right agency want your account? Make it attractive for them to find you.

- Competitive creative pitches may be worthwhile for both sides but are probably not. Engage an agency the way you would engage a senior executive. Will the candidate get the results? Will the candidate fit in?

- Use the round of selection interviews to establish the market rates for the new contract. Especially: what the agency should achieve, basic remuneration and bonus against brand equity results, copyright of creative material, and termination arrangements. Agree the menu while the agency is still hungry.

32

THE RULE OF Χ

Look for the inverse of whatever marketing news you are brought

Key issues
● **Looking for the downside of the upside or the upside of the down** ● **Examples of Chi** ● **Chi in marketing**

THE ANCIENT HISTORY OF CHI

The ancients recognized that every silver lining drags along a cloud. When Oedipus came into work one day and enthused about his new woman, Jocasta, his colleagues asked him what the Chi was. For the Greeks the letter Chi, more or less the Roman X (see figure 32.1), told them that things that were getting better meant that reciprocal bad news was around the corner. The optimists can be happy with the silver lining.

Fig 32.1   The letter Chi

The ancients knew to watch out for it. Dating his mother was bound to lead to trouble. Newton came close with his third law: to every action there is an equal and opposite reaction. It is curious that progress requires this to be true.

Everyman's book of clichés is full of Chi-derivations. When one door closes, another opens. Good news ... bad news. Taoists hold that there is a similar duality to nature; Yang needs to be balanced with Yin. Some scientists believe in anti-matter. Maybe there is a whole Universe surrounding us made up of the equal and opposite of us.

Chi is familiar to us all. It is in our genes. Women have twice as many chi-chromosomes as men. Maybe nature is trying to tell us something?

Do you believe all that? Never mind. Marketing, as we have observed before, is the making of myths, shared and pleasurable suspension of disbelief. Disney knew more about that, perhaps, than anyone this century. Disneyland, Disney World and now Euro-Disney, even chain stores, are all based on a cartoon fantasy. The Disney characters and the name itself are now brands; they can command premium prices for any products to which they are applied. The Disney organization is now powerful enough to buy major media channels such as Capital Cities/ABC.

Myths are themselves examples of the Rule of Chi. When does the creation of a myth become a lie? Nobody over the age of seven believes Disney characters to be real, yet the more you know them to be fiction the more you wish to believe. On the other hand a falsehood only carries conviction until it is exposed (see figure 32.2).

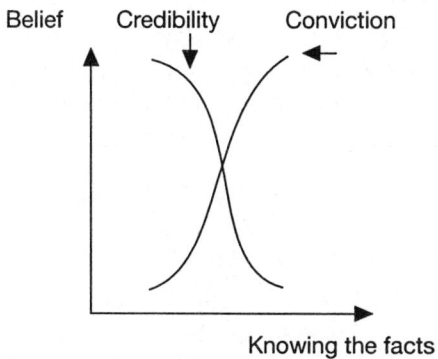

Fig 32.2 The Chi of certainty

A myth therefore can be decreasing in credibility as the "real" facts become known while at the same time building conviction. Psychologists have shown that propaganda has no persuasive effect in the short term because our rational brains discount the information according to its source. When rationality is distracted, we absorb some of the message. Thus the same propaganda that has no effect initially may well change attitudes in the long term. Perhaps advertising is similar. The Chi effects may not be immediate.

The role of marketing is therefore to create myths whilst simultaneously telling the truth. It is a recognition that the mind works at many different levels. If consumers know the facts, they are not deceived. If, at the same time, they wish to believe, and probably enjoy believing, some fantasy associated with that product, that is their choice. But it is a risky business; think how often actors are confused with the parts they play.

Consumerists seem sometimes to have difficulties with this distinction between myth and truth. Somehow a dimension has been lost. The rationalist holds that something is either true or false; myths, supposedly, were left behind with our primitive past. Anyone who thinks this should try Trafalgar Square on New Year's Eve.

> **The role of marketing is therefore to create myths while simultaneously telling the truth.**

Those who wish to buy on a price per kilo basis should do so and not interfere with those who prefer to buy their fiction with their groceries. Nescafé led TV commercials towards soap opera. We enjoy them but do not believe that Gold Blend will really bring romance with our neighbor to the boil as instantly as the coffee.

The marketer is, in a sense, in dialogue with the consumer – the successor, in a small way, to Homer. Overstatement? Yes, but reflective of a deep seated human wish for participative story telling. The ancient myths were not written down and disseminated through mass media but shared and developed with the listeners. Yes, interactive! Consumers today bring their own values to brands and invest them with their own projections of personality.

EXAMPLES OF CHI

Perhaps even the Rule of Chi itself is a projection of ourselves. Anyone over thirty will recognize the example in figure 32.3.

This is not universal, of course, but the proportion of those younger or the same age found to be attractive by the opposite sex tends to be greater than those older. Simple arithmetic and a few whiskies will demonstrate that, in effect, the older one is, the younger everyone else gets. Of course there are other factors. Never mind the depth of this research, feel the width.

Molière – who else but a Frenchman – pointed out that money can reverse the above theorem. In Florida, with the right rings flashing, the nearer you are to heaven, the greater your drawing power. The Rule of Chi still works: just flip it over.

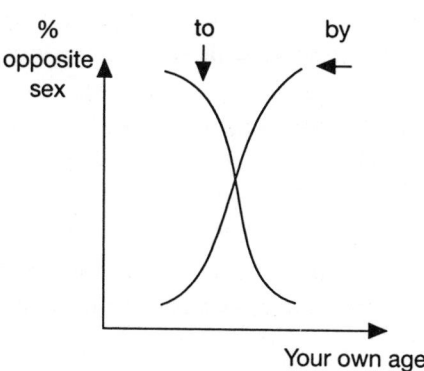

Attractiveness

Fig 32.3   Attractiveness

CHI IN MARKETING

Keep Chi at your elbow whenever anyone is selling you something.

Marketing proposals come in two formats: shining bright and only just rescuable. In both cases, the brand manager is cast as the hero.

- **Format 1:** Everything is just great. Doubts are banished lest they put awkward questions into the minds of top management. The presenter is breathless with enthusiasm and excitement. The proposals and their supports all point in the same, positive, direction. Certainty and conviction sweep the board along. The only question is how soon the brand manager can get going.

- **Format 2:** The brand is in a desperate situation. All is almost lost. Our hero will be able to salvage something only if full support and commitment is provided. "This is not a question of money" means this is a question of money. Things will get even worse before they get better. The presenter stops just short of suggesting that the board itself was asleep at the wheel. The Dunkirk spirit is summoned.

Paul Curtis, marketing supremo at International Distillers and Vintners, refers to this as the three envelope rule of employment. Manager receives three envelopes from the predecessor with the following advice: if things get difficult, open the first envelope, do what it says, and you will be alright. If things get difficult again, open the second and so on. The new manager starts work and after the honeymoon, things do indeed get difficult. Threatening noises are heard on all sides. It is time for the first envelope which reads: "blame your predecessor." Magically, everyone agrees. The clouds lift. Business even picks up. For a while. In what seems but a moment the manager is back in the mire. The second envelope reads: "tell them to have patience, things are just about to get better." People are kind. Of course things will get better; they must; they cannot get worse. But they do. The third envelope reads: "write three envelopes."

Rescuing brands in distress is tough. Not many recover. Brand manager turnover is both a symptom and a cause. To paraphrase Saki: she was a good brand manager as brand managers go, but, as brand managers go, she went.

You have received format 1 with smiles or format 2 with due concern and sympathy. Never mock the young; they'll be funding your pension sooner than you think. How can reality be brought to bear without tearing the plan apart?

We all have different ways out of this box but most add up to a way to balance the perspective. Under the Rule of Chi, every up curve has a down. Where are the reciprocal images?

Promotions are a good place to start. They are popular with the sales force. Extra cases can be loaded into the trade. Merchandising benefits. Customers are happy. Research (Ehrenberg 1991) indicates what advertising people have long suspected: promotions only have a transient effect. There is little evidence of net benefit to brand loyalty. There may well be an erosion of the brand's reputation with the consumer. A price discount communicates insecurity and confusion. Promotions may therefore lose over the longer period, i.e. brand equity, what they gain in the shorter (see figure 32.4).

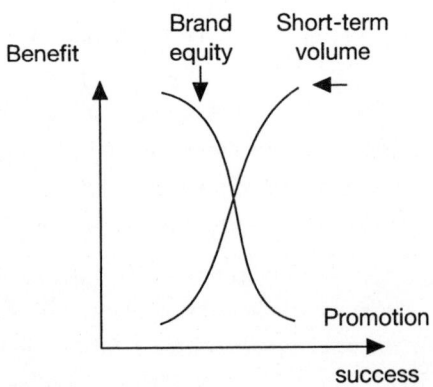

Fig 32.4   The Chi test for promotions

Both formats 1 and 2 are unrealistic. Chi tells us that life is not like that. Here are some things to look for in the format 1 presentation:

- Incrementalism. What has been ratcheted up (price) or down (quality) which may leave the brand hanging over the precipice.

- If whatever is recommended is so good, why not double it? This usually exposes that it is not as good as all that.

Under the Rule of Chi, every up curve has a down.

- The "Single Variable Scam" works on the basis that boards like to see nice two-dimensional graphs, sales versus advertising, for example. Sophisticated marketers can show a positive link between sales and advertising, and between sales and promotions, and between sales and merchandising/displays. They show only one of these charts to get support for whatever is under consideration (see figure 32.5).

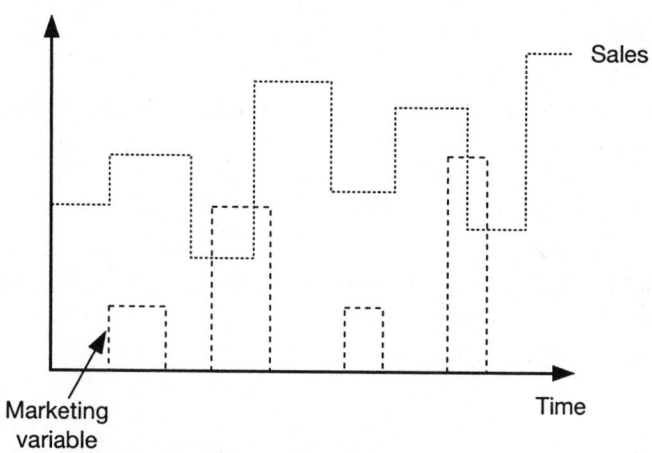

Fig 32.5   All-purpose justification chart

What this presentation conveniently ignores is that sales responded to the combination of a price cut *and* advertising *and* promotion *and* merchandising display. As is good marketing practice, these were all timed to be simultaneous because marketing mix is synergistic. The Single Variable Scam just gets support for the one variable under discussion without showing the rest. The advertising may have been completely ineffective but that is not the impression left.

Faced by a format 2 presentation:

- Which is the least bad area, product, type of retailer? Why is that?
- Invite the previous brand manager to return and tell some horror stories. You will hear some successes too.
- What small scale experiments are worth running before trying to turn the whole brand around?

Marketing follows the basic rule: no gain without pain. The Rule of Chi implies that there should be no pain without gain. Whichever way round it may be, the obverse of the expectation is worth checking out before commitments are made.

Oedipus wished he had.

Memo to file

Subject: THE RULE OF CHI

- Enthusiasm and conviction are great and necessary virtues. The team needs a contrarian too.
- There must be good news somewhere amongst the bad. Do not rebuild and hope but search for the secure foundations first. If none can be found, start testing with small experiments to find firm footings.
- Watch out for the Single Variable Scam and the three-envelope trick.

33

"Yes" is no decision

Similarly, superficial agreement is really dangerous

Key issue
- **Sins of omission are more sapping than mistakes from conscious decisions** ● **Establishing a challenge culture**

SINS OF OMISSION

Alan Mitchell[1] reviewed famous marketing failures and concluded "Mistakes do happen, and marketers can learn to live with them, and manage them. But mistakes are not the problem. It is the *malaise* of mediocre marketing that we really have to worry about." The necessity for mistakes as intrinsic to marketing innovation is widely accepted. Coca-Cola now claim that the disastrous launch of new Coke was "the best mistake the company ever made." I have suggested elsewhere (chapter 6) that it is smarter to grow big successes out of small failures than the other way about.

Mistakes from deliberate decisions, the wrong advertising, the price increase too many, the failed launch, are the visible tip of the iceberg. We have no means of knowing how many errors have never been noticed. These are the opportunities missed, possible decisions which never became conscious. Failures from conscious decision are integral to organizational learning, or should be. Failures by omission, however, pass unnoticed. How do you raise the consciousness of a business?

Zen (next chapter) supplies some of the answer. You must abstract thinking from the daily mundane. At the same time you must also immerse the

[1] *The Marketing Society Review*, (Summer 1995).

thinking in the market. Either an ivory tower or the marketplace is a good place for the mind to be. The only good reason to go to the office is to make decisions with the rest of the team. Reality is the reverse: aeons of time in the office with occasional forays to the market and away days.

> **Failures by omission, pass unnoticed.**

That the scarcest resource is management time, not money, is recognized by 21st century marketing. Some ascribe the financial instability of the millennium years to loose billions slurping from country to country in search of safe investment. Be that as it may, the banks are not short of cash for *believable* marketing plans. Any reviewer worries less about the plan's explicit intentions than factors the planners have omitted. Driving down the road at 30 m.p.h. is fine unless you have omitted to notice the 40-ton truck thundering towards you – on your side.

Until Jimmy Gulliver, of Argyll, bid for the Distillers Company, owner of Gordon's Gin and most of the brand leading scotches, in the 1980s, no one thought it was buyable. By the time Guinness successfully intervened it was too late for GrandMet or Allied Lyons, now Allied Domecq. The Scottish lobby had defended Highland Distillers against Hiram Walker and Scottish and Newcastle Breweries against Fosters. Competition rulings are quirky things.

Less spectacularly, packaging is not updated, new distribution channels are not opened, prices are not winkled up, sales forces are not remodelled because no one seriously suggests they should be. Time is limited. We concentrate on key actions and try not to fix what ain't broke. The cognac brand leaders allowed Camus to grab the duty free channel because they were not paying attention at the time. They certainly have since.

Uncritical acceptance lies at the root of "the *malaise* of mediocre marketing" that Mitchell was writing about. In other words, "yes" is no decision; it is a cop out.

ESTABLISHING A CHALLENGE CULTURE

Time does not allow everything to be challenged. Thank goodness. The very thought is exhausting. On the other hand, a plan presentation that gets ready acceptance is, after the initial rosy glow, disheartening for the presenters. They had been gearing up for a robust defence of their ideas.

Company cultures range from the excessively challenging to the passive. There are various devices for moving towards the happy mean but the chief executive usually sets the tone. Some companies deliberately set up devil's advocates to challenge plans on a peer basis. Artificial it may be, but the "no knocking" (I will not point out the flaws in your plan if you are nice about mine) alternative is worse.

Challenge may be a necessary but not sufficient condition. "Inquisitiveness" is more accurate. Perhaps imagination. The objective is not to deny the validity of whatever the plan says but to identify factors it has omitted. Challenging forecasts based on agreed assumptions is akin to head butting: it does nothing for wisdom and leaves both sore. Spotting valid alternative scenarios ("what if") is another matter.

Planning is simply a rehearsal for reality. No team has a monopoly of knowledge of what the future will bring or what competitors will do.

"No" is a better answer to a plan presentation than "yes." Without some explanation beyond "not good enough," the planners will retire pretty angry. But they will still return with a better plan.

Alternatives:

- Detect the areas of complacency and challenge those.
- Test the anticipated competitor moves. Have they really been thought through?
- Likewise for retailers.
- Is the plan format complete? What action areas, e.g. the four Ps, are missing?
- How thorough is the analysis of lessons learned from last year's plan, competitors and other market players over the current year?
- Where a particular action is to continue as before, is that because it is proving successful or because the planners have not got around to it?
- Test the assumptions.
- Test the planning process.
- (For the really dedicated challengers) compare the plan with the notes you previously made of what you would do.

This whole area of plans and challenges is a quagmire. Some of the world's great marketers write lousy plans and react badly to having them challenged. In that event, the game becomes more sophisticated. "Yes" is still a poor decision but the process of making the marketing actions more robust and successful will need more imagination. For example, consider how the proposed marketing approach would work in a different market.

The role of the challenger is not to contradict the marketers' perceptions but to widen the canvas. The foresight shown by the plan is likely to be satisfactory; the process should add "insights" and "outsights." Almost everyone can look straight up the road, but insights are those significant little details that others miss. Häagen Dazs, for example, detected that eating ice cream was, or could be, sensual. Levis presented jeans as a symbol of liberation.

Outsights are those things that some just notice on the side, peripheral vision in short. General Electric had the world's largest planning system when Jack Welch took charge. That competitors beat them to the draw in every new market was not

> **The role of the challenger is not to contradict the marketers' perceptions but to widen the canvas.**

chance. The planning system *caused* tunnel vision. Welch replaced the planning system with a challenge culture which encourages executives to see things that others do not.

Marketing that just chunters down the same old street will become mediocre, however great it once was. Testing possible turnings requires outsights to notice them and a commitment to explore and experiment. "What if?" is a start but it needs to become "why not?".

Memo to file

Subject: "YES" IS NO DECISION

- Missed opportunities are more debilitating than other mistakes. No one notices.

- Challenge to plans is as good an opportunity as any to seek what planners have overlooked.

- This can be structured or, less good, just send the planners back to think again. Searching for what tunnel vision has missed will add value. Find the "insights" and "outsights."

34

ZEN AND NOW

In other words, learn to live with the paradox, so much a part of marketing

---

Key issues
- **Marketers have to handle paradox and contradiction**
- **Resist overhasty problem formulation and analysis**

ORIENTAL MIND GAMES

To suggest that marketing managers should study Zen Buddhism may be final confirmation that this book has abandoned its trolley. Suspend disbelief. They are doing so already.

Zen is the means by which oriental philosophies have long trained lateral thinkers. This book is dedicated to the development of the non-rational, creative, intuitive aspects of marketing to balance the excessive reliance on analysis and microeconomics in conventional textbooks. The left brain (rational) and right brain (creative) model may have been discredited by neurologists, but it is still useful conceptually. Analysis is important but both sides are needed for success.

Those who know Zen will have to forgive the oversimplification here. There is space only loosely to illustrate the application of Zen and other oriental thinking to marketing. In pointing to the gateway, the language here is only directional. In addition to its direct relevancy, it may help to explain the strategies of global competitors who have absorbed these traditions within their cultures.

Zen means meditation. It is a development of Buddhism and reached Japan from China where it was called Ch'an. Taoism and Confucian thinking intermingled with the concepts of Ch'an. The intention is to reconcile intellectual, or rational, analysis with affective thinking or emotional feelings – exactly the problem faced by the marketer.

Zen Buddhism works in many ways at many levels. The central training is through the use of koan or paradox. There are 1,700 of these in the lexicon of ascending levels of difficulty. Two best known examples are: what is the sound of one hand clapping and what was your name before you were born?

> **The intention is to reconcile intellectual, or rational, analysis with affective thinking or emotional feelings – exactly the problem faced by the marketer.**

The process includes meditation over very long periods. Beginners' exercises require you to clear the mind as much as possible by counting breaths. Sitting meditation (Zazen) may involve silent concentration to maximize awareness as if you were considering a dangerous competitor. At another time the trainee will intensively consider a koan. From time to time the teachers hear their pupils' responses. Zen teachers continue to reject trainees' answers to the point of reducing them to tears. If you are spending 12 hours a day sitting in silent meditation on nonsensical questions only interspersed by walking in silent meditation, that may not surprise you.

Before dismissing such practices as nonsense, take a look at brand planning. The young manager is given an impossible brief, and told to go away and figure out how to do it. Each time his solution is committed to paper, it is rejected. The process is not only to produce a good plan but to train the brand manager.

Zen works to overcome linear (left brain) dominance by frustrating it. Rationality provides no solution to irrational problems. The mind is therefore forced into other routes. Through the development of lateral thinking intuition is brought both to the fore and under control. Call it creativity if you like. Zen exponents call the moment of inspiration when a koan is satisfactorily answered "kensho," or first seeing. Language is not precise but it does not need to be. We recognize the moment of enlightenment when it arrives.

Buddhism picked up the earlier Indian philosophy of karma the way Zen subsequently picked up Taoism. Karma is the hard-nosed recognition that cause and effect are a matter of personal responsibility. Whatever happens to you is, in some mysterious way, caused by your own actions. To rationalize this (a mistake by definition) you have to bend time and accept re-incarnation. But then, brand managers testify to re-incarnation every time they move jobs.

Tao has, it is claimed, no direct English translation. Briefly it means "the way." More accurately it means the way things should happen if they are flowing smoothly. Both Zen andTaoism are concerned with getting the ego out of the way (see Isaiah principle); they encourage development of the "ego-less self." Taoism uses concepts of balance, such as Yin and Yang, running through the natural order and needing to be respected. Through the concepts of balance come the paradoxes and the Chinese sayings that mystify Westerners.

The Zen archer thinks himself into a state where the arrow basically fires itself. The archer may be unconscious of aim or release yet the arrow is on target. Absurd as it will sound to a Westerner, the Zen archer tries to become the bow.

Marketers do not create fashions or even markets. The best they can do is to ride the waves and take advantage of what will largely happen anyway. Sure they can, and should, help things along; trends can be spotted, first mover advantage can be secured. But luck and "Tao" are stronger elements. That all is inevitable and yet success depends absolutely on the active contribution of the marketer is just another paradox: the Tao and the Karma of marketing.

That all is inevitable and yet success depends absolutely on the active contribution of the marketer is just another paradox.

At around the time of Buddha, Sun Tzu (or a collection of analysts with that brand name) wrote a book now usually called, by Westerners, *The Art of War*. Many military strategists since have confirmed its value as a primer and we have referenced it in the sections dealing with the conflict, or strategy, paradigm, e.g. chapter 11, "Kamikaze and Guerrilla Marketing." Much of it is paradoxical, frustrating for a linear thinker. The language may seem general, vague, and confusing, something readers of this book will be well used to. But therein lies the point. Precise instructions for winning are pointless; if they worked the first time, everyone would use them and they would not work again. Marketing is no different. There can be no simple rules for success.

Sun Tzu's paradoxes are intended to make the reader *think afresh*. That is why the reader is directed to consider only a few words per week. They should trigger new solutions in each new environment.

No modern marketer is going to meditate on a page of a 2,500-year-old book for a week at a time. Nevertheless, the principles apply quite directly to modern marketing campaigns. International brand managers operating in the Pacific Basin or against Chinese or Japanese competition in particular could be underinformed without it.

MARKETING AS PARADOX

Marketing contains quite a few contradictions. At one time, personal selling makes a claim to be the keystone, at another positioning demands total attention. Every marketing guru has a different formula. They are inconsistent and yet each has something to offer. Marketing is constantly on the move. Time, or order of play, may reconcile some of the contradictions. Preparing actions in the right order and countertrending the competition is important, but this handles only some of the apparent conflicts.

We need to make space for ideas from another, a-rational, dimension. No case is made for acting unreasonably. Analysis, logic, order, and correct sequencing are vital but they only go so far. Furthermore, such linear thinking is likely to match the competition's. One of the main virtues of research is to predict what the logical competitor will do. Logic neither surprises competitors nor delights consumers.

To develop intuition, we can learn from Zen. The trick is deliberately to frustrate our rational instincts in order to build the others. We could compile a list of koan and retire to a mountain top. Here are some familiar starters:

- Is short- or long-term profitability more important?
- Which comes first: the consumer's need or the means of fulfilling that need?
- Who matters more, the customer or the ultimate consumer?
- Or beating the competition?
- What is now in a market gap? Or what was a market gap called before it was born?
- Nothing really worth doing can be measured but if it cannot be measured, it cannot be worth doing.
- The ultimate positioning strategy is to be without positioning (Sun Tzu).
- Total local responsiveness to the market is vital; so is global coordination.

Few marketers follow the Zen route; there are other ways of developing intuitive and creative thinking. Intense periods of concentration and frustration with intractable problems are common elements between Eastern and Western approaches. Common too is attempting to empty the mind. Such meditation is impossible for a beginner. Solitude, mental concentration, silence, and meditation are alien to modern life. The first stage might be to concentrate on your own breathing. The crowded razzmatazz of modern life is then driven out and replaced by calming rhythms, allowing concentration on other things.

In the more familiar world, many have experienced the phenomenon under which mental concentration seems at first to yield nothing. Then, a day or two later, a solution pops up unexpectedly with nothing appearing to trigger it. The idea may arrive when showering or shopping. Ideas arrive when the mind wanders randomly. Meetings thus can be valuable after all.

Marketing is full of paradox. That makes Westerners more uncomfortable than Easterners culturally attuned to such things. We resolve our discomfort by seeking to turn

> **Marketing is the taking of comprehensive, decisive, and rapid action but only after creativity has supplied innovation and surprise.**

the paradoxes into problems and then solve them with analysis. In our haste, creativity is driven out. Senior marketers recognize this factor in brand plans and send them back for rework. The frustration may, in Zen style, get the results but more often it simply compresses the time available before solutions are due.

Procrastination is no solution. Rather you should liberate time sooner in the process and treasure contradictions of the market. Various organizations, Synectics Inc for example, offer creativity training, some good and some frankly silly. Brainstorming is too often undisciplined to be of value. Childlike play and discovery may well be part of the process, having fun is great, but cudgeling the grey matter into fresh insights is tough. There is nothing easy about true Zen. The common thread of all these approaches is that rationality is banned until, finally, the ideas have to be turned into an actionable plan.

Marketing is the taking of comprehensive, decisive, and rapid action but only after creativity has supplied innovation and surprise. Once "it" is clear, do it now. The process of living with the paradoxes, of allowing insight to dawn, we call Zen. Marketing is Zen followed by now.

Memo to file

Subject: ZEN AND NOW

- Marketers should expect paradox and contradiction. It can be as wrong to believe one half of a contradiction and reject the other as to be frustrated by not being able to get at the "truth." Zen teaches that reflection, not rationality, allows solutions to surface.

- Marketers should maximize time in the hurly burly of the marketplace but make Zen time too.

- Bend time to do it then and Zen now.

POSTSCRIPT

Val,

I hope you have enjoyed this ramble through the by-ways of marketing. It is a fundamentally serious business with the accent on fun. Marketing is essentially the means by which an organization achieves its objectives. For most businesses, those concern building short-term profitability and the equity of its brands. For an association, the aims may involve growing the membership and meeting their needs. Does marketing have any limitations?

The outcome of major political elections, general elections in the UK, presidential elections in the USA, for example, now depend on the deployment of marketing skills. Marketing deals with big issues and uncertainty. That makes it exciting and fun. Marketers themselves are great people to do business with. They defy categorization precisely because they understand the need to be different. Some successful marketers have first class honours from the great universities. Others barely made it through secondary education. Some are rationalists, others grab every passing idea. If there is any connecting thread, it is that marketing people are very much alive to the world as it is today. They have learned to ride the waves of fashion; they cannot create them.

Good wishes again for your new responsibilities. Enjoy them.

Tim

APPENDIX 1

GLOSSARY

This glossary includes statistical and research jargon to inoculate the reader against pretentious experts. The list is neither complete, incontrovertible, nor warranted for mixed company. Use this language only when all else fails. The glossary makes no attempt to be comprehensive. Some excellent marketing dictionaries are available.

Bayesian statistics See *Subjective*.

BCG Grid This put The Boston Consulting Group on the map in the early 1970s and they have been trying to live it down ever since. 2x2 matrix dividing brands (products) into stars, cows, dogs and ? according to their ranking on growth and market share dimensions. Stars = high on both. Dogs = low on both. Cows = high share, low growth and ? = unknowns (high growth, not much share yet). Portfolio management requires you to support stars, cull dogs, and milk cows. Simplistic or what?

Bernoulli response variables Simply means yes or no, on/off, or any other two way choice. Nothing like statistics for complexing the simple. Try "My Bernoulli response variable is trending negative" = "No." Otherwise known as dichotomous or binary variables, which are in turn special (2) cases of polytomous (poly = many) variables. Here the outcome or dependent variable is a continuous number, as we normally use, but one choice from a selection, e.g. yes or no for poly = 2; jam, bread, or butter for poly = 3.

Brand associations Components of brand image, usually assessed by qualitative research methods: free association (what comes into your mind when ...), describe user, project onto picture or place or animal, analysis of choice. Can be assessed quantitatively too.

Chi-Square Tests One measure of how well your model fits the data, i.e. the "goodness of fit."

Cluster analysis Used for consumer segmentation and brand positioning. From a large number of responses, the computer clusters, or segments, the respondents into a few groups with common attitudes, needs, or characteristics. The differences *within* any group should be less than the differences *between* groups. Cluster analysis may be used for any groupings, e.g. products.

Conjoint analysis Respondents trade product attributes off against each other to establish product (brand) preference and the relative importance of attributes. Based on utility theory and consumer rationality. Better therefore for functional than fashionable brands.

Correlation Most statistical techniques simply demonstrate that two activities appear to be connected, e.g. if A goes up so does B and when B goes down, so does A. The most popular single error is the conclusion that A causes B or vice versa. Suppose A is sales and B is advertising. Statistics indicate they are connected and the brand manager demands more for advertising. The brand managers boss points out that the connection is simply that they always spend 8 percent of sales on advertising. *Granger causality* is what the economists use as a proxy: all it means is that if time series analysis indicates A happens *before* B, A is presumed to cause B. Correlation is no more than correlation.

Cross-elasticity See *Elasticity*.

Delphi technique Method of expert judgement without adequate hard data, e.g. long-term forecasting. Stage 1 is to poll experts, anonymously and separately. In Stage 2 the results are consolidated and fed back to the experts as a group. Stage 3 polls them individually again, in the light of peer group opinion. In theory, the process continues until consensus arrives. In practice, ennui arrives faster. Personally, I think the process should stop with clusters of opinions as the differences are more enlightening than the consensus.

Dissonance Cognitive dissonance arises after a major purchase (e.g. a car) when alternatives are recommended and/or dislikes emerge with the choice. To eliminate the discomfort of dissonance, the consumer will seek to rationalize the original choice, in other words find positive advantages and ignore the negative. Popularized by Festinger in the 1950s.

Double Jeopardy Smaller brands are bought both less frequently *and* by fewer people. An observation associated with, though not originated by, Andrew Ehrenberg who did much of the research to prove this is (as close as marketing ever gets to a) law. The mathematics were provided by Dirichlet.

Elasticity Measures the extent volume shifts in response to a shift in the variable under consideration. Usually a price concept though it generalizes to advertising and other mix components. Technically:

$$\text{Price elasticity of demand} = \frac{\% \text{ Change in volume}}{\% \text{ Change in price}}$$

The conventional expectation is that price and volume move in opposite directions, i.e. elasticity is negative, and at the same rate, i.e. the volume you lose pricing up \$1 = volume gained pricing down \$1. *Elastic* and *inelastic* are the nice intuitive part of this whole can of worms and simply indicate whether the product volume does, or does not, respond to price changes.

Cross-elasticity refers to the extent to which products are substitutes for one another, i.e. putting up the price of X causes users to switch to Y. Marketers use differentiation and quality to seek to minimize cross-elasticity and thus it could be seen as part of brand equity or marketing effectiveness. Technically:

$$\text{Cross-elasticity of X with respect to Y} = \frac{\%\ \text{Change in volume of X}}{\%\ \text{Change in price of Y}}$$

Exponential smoothing A forecasting technique for extrapolating historic data a few steps into the future. The more complex version, "time series analysis," extrapolates sales by decomposing them into the basic trend, short-term cycles/seasonality and random variations. Some fancy weightings and arithmetic apart, all ES does is to tell you that whatever happened yesterday is likely to happen tomorrow. Time series include ARMA (Auto-Regressive Moving Average) and Box-Jenkins.

Factor analysis Reducing the many rating scales used by the researcher to the minimum (probably three or four) independent dimensions supposedly forming the consumers' unconscious model. Mathematically this is fine but two questions:
- Is it predictive or just data mining?
- What do these dimensions *mean*? What do you call them?

Usually they are a ragbag of rating scales to which researchers apply their creativity.

FCB Grid One of the better pieces of "how advertising works" research done for the Foote Cone and Belding Agency. Not all ads work the same way. The FCB Grid groups them into four: the 2x2 matrix is high/low involvement and think/feel, depending on whether the product category is one the consumer gets involved with, e.g. cars, or not, e.g. self-raising flour; and whether the purchase is more driven by cognitive or emotional factors.

Fishbein Best known modeller of consumer attitudes. Pioneer of expectancy-value (EV) models which break attitudes into two components: the attributes of a brand and how much those attributes are worth to the consumer. Consumer actions are consistent with those expectations and values or some rapid post hoc shifting goes on. Though still popular with some advertising researchers, Fishbein is cognitively biased. Use with care.

Game theory The mathematics quickly become horrendous but the paradigm is useful for comparing decision alternatives in the light of probable/possible competitor reactions, e.g. price promotions. Negotiations, similarly, can be helped by specific consideration of *Nash Equilibria*, or saddle points, at which the minimum acceptable solution for the other party coincides with the maximum possible solution for oneself.

Hetero/Homoscedasticity Homo-s is one of the four "Gauss Markov" assumptions that allow linear regression analysis to be reasonably valid. (The variance across observations has to be constant.) Statisticians have ways of coping with the opposite (hetero-s), up to a point. Basically, where the variance is bigger, the data are less reliable and are downweighted.

Independent variables One key, but much abused, requirement of regression is that the variables used for prediction or explanation should be independent or completely uninfluenced by each other. If one variable is rainfall, for example, and another temperature, they are not truly independent; the temperature in summer will usually be lower when it is raining. In these circumstances the model works in the sense of producing a reasonable dependent variable. The problem is that the coefficients in the independent variables are unreliable, i.e. do not believe the answer.

Kelly Triads or Repertory Grids Used especially by advertising agencies and NPD specialists to elicit consumer language for the products in question. The technique works like a three-card trick, come to that it is a three-card trick. Products (or whatever) are written or pictured on cards which are dealt three at a time. The respondent is invited to pick the odd one out and explain why it is odd. The language and key discriminators are noted. Then the cards are shuffled and dealt again until the respondent becomes too irritable.

Likert Scale See *Semantic differential*.

Logit Model A version of regression analysis using an S-shaped curve instead of a straight line. Used when responses are binary, e.g. yes/no, rather than continuous numbers. This uses the "Logistic" curve. Attributed to Berkson, 1944.

Markov Model Sets out in matrix the probability that the user of each brand in a category will switch next time to each other brand. Mathematically sound and now measurable through scanners. Tends to follow the Dirichlet expectation – see *Double Jeopardy*.

Mean Sum of the measurements divided by the number of measurements or, when probabilities are around, the sum of each outcome weighted by its probability of occurring. What people usually intend by the word "average." Convenient that the other "averages" follow alphabetically:

Median The point which separates 50 percent of the bigger things from the 50 percent smaller, i.e. the mid-point in terms of the number of things being measured.

Mode The most frequently occurring measurement.

Model Anything from a set of equations to a simple diagram that helps a group of people represent reality is a simple way to share understanding. A model is no more than a toy to that group of people to play with. Some marketing scientists are so besotted with their toys which provide the so-called *normative* decisions, that reality, if different, must be wrong. Darwin is on the side of practitioners.

Multi-dimensional scaling Similar to factor analysis but mathematically purer. FA uses regular (ordinal arithmetic, e.g. 2+2=4) whereas MDS requires numbers just to increase monotonically, e.g. 2+2 > 2. Provides perceptual maps (see chapter 16) and works from rankings (A>B).

Normal distribution The bell-shaped curve that looks like this:

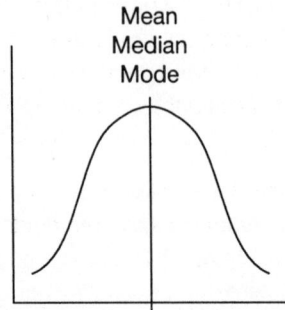

Fig App.1   Normal distribution

The word "normal" is unfortunate ("you are normal, aren't you?") as it has caused this very abnormal distribution shape to be used where it should not be. It makes the sums easier and the mean, median, and mode are all the same. Watch out for recommendations based on the assumption of this curve. If, in the real data, the mean, median, and mode are not all the same, send the statistician back to school.

Null hypothesis Acceptance of the null hypothesis (e.g. "A and B are not the same") means that you have to do nothing and is strongly recommended. Those with neuroses to encourage can worry about "Alpha errors" (rejecting the null hypothesis when it is true) or "Beta errors" (accepting it when it is false: A and B *were* the same). Also known as Type I and II errors respectively.

PIMS Profit Impact of Market Strategy, a consultancy spin off from academia and the Marketing Science Institute, in Cambridge Mass., set up to gather and analyse company data. Mainly known for suggesting that market share drove profit. Now, and more likely, the perception is that perceived quality drives long-term profit.

Probit Model Same as Logit except it uses a cumulative normal curve rather than a logistic one. Invented by Bliss/Finney, 1971.

Projection techniques Get respondents to reveal true reasons which they are unwilling or unable to admit. Can, for example, be a description of a brand of paint as a vegetable. The respondent "projects" characteristics onto another category.

Repertory Grid See *Kelly Triads* above.

Regression analysis Top of the marketing "science" pops. Totally rejected by some academics and adored by others. Full title: Multivariate, Linear Regression Model. Basic work tool of econometricians. Fits a line to a set of points so that the squares of the distances from the points to the line is minimized. In two dimensions, this can be done, roughly, with a ruler and graph paper. In more dimensions, the equations become necessary. Used for forecasting on the dubious assumption that what fitted before will fit again. Often used to forecast sales that will result from advertising. Time series analysis is a specific development designed to track what factors happen before others and to disentangle other temporal effects. The "BLUE line" (Best Linear Unbiased Estimator) is the output together with R^2 which indicates goodness of fit to the data. Powerful but dangerous in the wrong hands.

Residual error What still cannot be explained, after estimating the coefficients of the independent variables. Usually blamed on measurement or omissions as the model, naturally, cannot possibly be wrong!

Sampling Usually assumed to be random but for convenience is more likely to be pseudo-random (e.g. every tenth person) or stratified (categorized by some variable such as age group) to try to ensure the sample mirrors the total population. *Convenience sampling* is a polite expression for including just those you come across. A Director of a British fmcg company once objected to increased marketing for one of their brands on the grounds that there was no demand for it at White's, his club. His statistics were accurate but his colleagues queried his sampling methodology.

Semantic differential Typically a five point scale from a superlative (e.g. "very much") to its equal and opposite (e.g. "very much not"). Used for measuring attitudes or perceptions. One form was popularized by R. Likert in 1932 and asks the extent to which the respondent agrees or disagrees with a statement.

Semiotics Philosophy of the meaning of brand symbolism. Popular, as you might have expected, in France. The idea is that a deeper understanding of everything a brand communicates can increase harmony and strength of logos, packaging, advertising and so on. Related to the Ogilvy concept of interrogating a brand until it confesses its essence.

Sigmoid curve The S-shaped relationship that allows the dependent variable to tend to 100 percent or 0 percent rather than actually get there. More lifelike than a straight line in regression but harder mathematics. Gompertz, Urban, Logistic, and Normal curves are all near enough the same for our purposes here.

Standard Deviation Measures the dispersal of the data from the mean. It is the square root of the variance (defined below).

Standard Error Same concept. 68 percent of the results will lie within one SE and 95 percent within two SEs, for a normal curve. Thus if 10 percent of 10,000 people have red hair, we can be 68 percent confident, following data analysis that the red haired population is between 9.7 per cent and 10.3 percent. Yes, you got it: the SE was 0.3 percent. Confidence levels are one of the few vital statistical concepts for marketers when reviewing quantitative research and a key factor in deciding sample sizes.

Stochastic Fancy word for random or chance.

Subjective Until the Reverend Bayes came along, statisticians pretended decision makers knew nothing apart from the arithmetic "objective" probabilities. Subjective, or Bayesian, statisticians incorporate prior knowledge (or assumptions) into the calculations of probabilities.

Time series analysis See *Exponential smoothing*.

Variance The mean of the squares of the differences between the mean of the data and the data measurements. The square of the standard deviation (or standard error) similarly indicates the dispersion of the data.

FURTHER READING

Textbooks

Kotler's *Marketing Management. Analysis, planning, implementation and control* is the main MBA marketing text worldwide and has been for 30 years. Now in its 8th edition, its 700+ pages contain all a product manager needs to know about marketing as it is neo-classically taught. Even those on full-time learning struggle with it but as a reference work it is invaluable. Kotler brings order and discipline to every branch of marketing. Peter Doyle's *Marketing Management and Strategy*, Prentice Hall, 1994, is arguably the British equivalent.

Glen Urban's *Advanced Marketing Strategy: phenomena, analysis and decisions* is an intellectual step up for serious analysts. (Prentice Hall, 1991).

Christopher Lovelock's *Managing Services* (Prentice Hall, 1992) and Michael Hutt and Thomas Speh's *Business Marketing Management* (Dryden Press, 1985) cover services and industrial sectors.

International marketing has a host of texts including Jean-Claude Usunier's *International Marketing* which brings a refreshingly French perspective (Prentice Hall, 1993). Most of the rest are American though they have become markedly less ethnocentric in recent years.

The conflict paradigm, or strategy, is epitomized by Michael Porter's work, e.g. *Competitive Strategy*. (The Free Press, 1980).

Lighter

Hugh Davidson's *Offensive Marketing*. Most of the above are American. This is British but with a cosmopolitan tone. First published 1972 but extensively revised in 1987, it appeals to the pragmatic. As the name implies, the accent is on keeping the initiative developing from his key acronym POISE (Profitable Offensive Integrated Strategic and Effectively Executed). This is probably the marketing book to read next. (Penguin Books, 1987).

Advertising has generated plenty of literature for and against. Those against have argued that it is either unethical, manipulative or ineffective. Or all three! Vance Packard with *Hidden Persuaders* was an early challenge. Plenty have entered the sport, on both sides, since. Marketing freedoms are under constant attack in developed countries. John Philip Jones has a controversial, but quantified, contribution that should be read if not believed. (*When Ads Work*, Lexington Books, 1995).

Any book with "mega" or "wave" or "beginning" or "creating" or "trend" or "end" indicates the breadth of the reader's perspective? Of course it does. A current sample is *The Knowledge-Creating Company*, by Ikujiro Nonaka and Hirotaka Takeuchi. (Oxford University Press, 1995).

INDEX

Also available from Pitman Publishing

THE FINANCIAL TIMES
GUIDE TO
STRATEGY

The word "strategy" is often bandied about by managers, but what does it really mean?

Business strategy is now the common language of management, but as techniques and theories proliferate the subject has become increasingly divorced from the real world.

This practical and accessible guide demonstrates the basic concepts of strategy and will provide a powerful way of understanding and formulating your own strategies in a meaningful way.

£15.99   Paperback 0 273 61308 1